FUELLESS FIRE

FUELLESS FIRE

A GUIDE TO HAPPINESS

BY ANURAG JAIN

For the benefit of NEEV Trust, India

Murine press

www.bigfontbooks.com

ISBN: 978-1-950330-83-6

The cover image, courtesy of Wikipedia, depicts Agni
the Hindu God of Fire

Contents

A Word by the Editor

I am the publisher of Fuelless Fire, and Anurag ji is my teacher. I am publishing this book to raise awareness of the traditional Advaita, raise money for his nonprofit NEEV foundation in India, and finally, show a way to be truly happy to those who are open and ready.

I read many Advaita, non-duality-related books, and I even published the Course of Miracles as I found some passages profound.

Eventually, it became evident that a mishmash of Western flavored imported Eastern non-dual books might confuse and confound the reader because they do not offer a transparent methodology and offer a "path" claiming misleadingly quick Enlightenment.

In the movie Caddyshack, Bill Murray explains how he caddied for the Dalai Lama, and his Holiness gave no money but said, "on your deathbed, you will get Total Consciousness."

In Reality, we have total consciousness already. When we (aspirants) peel the onion, what do we end up there is nothing left? Nothing tangible, but Enlightenment is the same. We remove all the falsehoods of who we are, and the result is the Self (which is the same as Total Consciousness.) This book will help guide you to peel the onion.

The reader perhaps finds a portion of this book repetitive. There is a reason for that. Under a qualified teacher, detailed studying of the Vedas is not required; however, the aspirants should be familiar with the context and original terminology. Thus, the book will discuss the same or similar ideas in various chapters hereon. There is a lot to digest in this book, and many concepts are not easy to put in words. Some readers will give up on page 33, and some will read it ten times or more.

Annotations by the Editor are footnotes. Annotations by the Author are endnotes.
Namaste
AMN 2021, Woodland, California

My Journey of Self Inquiry

Self-inquiry is about understanding the nature of suffering within oneself and its ending without resorting to any belief/authority. It seeks to understand what is world, mind, body, thought, action, experience, and death are. While most people do not find the need for this, some people do: at some point in their life. Based on their Karma, self-inquiry becomes one and the only important thing in the world to uncover the Truth: the Unborn Wholeness called Self, Brahman, Tao, Awareness or Emptiness in different traditions.

Sooner or later, the amount of time one devotes to it becomes substantial. Moreover, as self-inquiry keeps exposing the falsities in which the mind is embroiled, one sees the utter futility of all organizations and institutions to solve anything psychologically. In my case, when I was 20 years old, my head went into the tiger's mouth of self-inquiry. I worked for about 22 years to create decent savings while pursuing my self-inquiry. Because of this, I was able to take early retirement at the age of 42, and in 2017 I decided to devote all my time and energy to further self-inquiry through this book and NEEV Centre for Self Inquiry.

I had been very interested in the teachings of J Krishnamurti for the last 25 years because he has gone deeply into the questions of everyday life and suffering without resorting to any belief or authority. However, I also read very widely in other fields of religion, philosophy, psychology, science, economics, sociology, history, literature, and politics to understand myself and the world. Ken Wilber was another big influence. His Integral Theory helped me create a valuable map of developmental stages of consciousness – lacking in the teachings of Krishnamurti – which I felt a great need for at that particular stage of my inquiry. All this eventually brought me to Advaita Vedanta – a Non-Dual school of Self inquiry and Self Realization – attributed to Shankaracharya. Though this is a widely held erroneous view, Shankara was a link – albeit a prominent one – in a vast tradition of Advaita that was present much before him. The technical term used by Advaita Vedanta for Self Inquiry is called Jnana Yoga.

Still, I use this term in a generic way to indicate all non-dual inquiries of different schools that help one in understanding the ultimate reality free from all subject-object duality and get released from all suffering, without resorting to any belief.

I gained direct knowledge of my true Self/Witness/Awareness through Advaita in 2012. I am indebted to Advaita teacher James Swartz, whose writings on the internet helped me get Self Knowledge. Before this, I had read the basics of Advaita Vedanta for merely a month. All my previous work with J Krishnamurti's teachings had helped me negate most of the falsity. The final nudge required by Advaita was – Tat Tvam Asi: Thou Are That. It meant I had to stop seeking Truth as an object and understand the subject: my proper Self/Witness/Awareness as the ultimate reality. This happens through an insight called the akhandakara vritti.

However, it took some time (7 years) to clear mostly philosophical doubts relating to Self/Awareness/Witness, which arose from my readings of different schools, both within and outside Vedanta, that speak of Truth in different and contradictory ways. I was immensely helped in all this by my online friend, Direct Path teacher, and philosopher, Greg Goode, who patiently had dialogue with me through all my mind-boggling questions, changes, and reversals. Not only did he help me resolve the incredibly complex issue of multiple paths. I understood that different non-dual paths are merely different vocabularies to deconstruct all perceived subject-object duality. One chooses paths according to the vocabulary one is drawn to), but he also showed me the way to Ajativada beyond Vivartavada of Shankara, with which most Advaitins are familiar.

In early 2020, I stabilized in the Self-knowledge/Witness stage, entirely beyond all doubts. My mind, body, and the universe appeared and disappeared as phenomena to the eternal Witness/Self/Awareness. Beyond this is the stage when all objects too stop appearing as entities/objects and are seen to be Awareness itself. This is when the superimposition of the Witness function on Awareness collapses, and subject-object duality ends. Everything is realized as empty Awareness. I was initiated into this stage after a series of dialogues with Greg Goode and my readings in Ajativada of Gaudpada and my readings in Direct Path (chiefly books written by Greg Goode). In Dec 2020, I realized "Everything is Awareness." After this, an individual getting enlightened does not make any sense because the very idea gets obliterated. Enlightenment is seen to be the very nature of the world, which has always been so. Individual-Creator-Creation is seen to be dream-like appearances, which have never existed objectively. Even then, from its conventional view, society would call such an appearance/person a Jivanmukta.

Therefore, the path of self-inquiry/Jnana Yoga I pursued combines J Krishnamurti, the traditional paths of Advaita called Vivartavada of Shankaracharya, followed by Ajativada of Gaudapada/Direct Path by Sri Atmananda Krishna Menon as unfolded by Greg Goode in his books.

In non-duality, paths are only spoken from a relative standpoint. Since non-duality means acknowledging that ultimate reality is always non-dual, a "path" in non-dual inquiry implies only negating dualistic conceptual errors of the mind that prevent one from resting in the always available, ever-present true nature of reality as Non-Dual Awareness.

Self-inquiry is a path requiring a highly philosophical bent of mind. For me, the guiding light for self-inquiry was the total deconstruction of subject-object duality at every level.

Talking about my journey in Advaita, in the traditional Advaita path, if one is a householder, a seeker first enters the path of Karma Yoga; after attaining sufficient mental purity, he becomes qualified to enter the path of Self Inquiry/Jnana Yoga.

However, my path has departed from traditional Advaita because I did not do any Karma Yoga. Instead, I entered Jnana Yoga through the unique teachings of J Krishnamurti. In my mind, this is a phenomenal and novel contribution of J Krishnamurti to the world of spirituality. I left his teachings at a particular stage to enter Advaita. Why I did so is a topic for a very advanced practitioner of Jnana Yoga. Suffice to say that a seeker can realize the potential of his teachings to enter Jnana Yoga of Advaita directly while being a householder and, without entering the traditional teachings of Karma Yoga, which rely on the concept of God. (Later, the concept of God is negated in Jnana Yoga of Advaita). With

Krishnamurti, one can enter deconstructive Jnana Yoga right from the word go!

There are points of divergence and contention, along with several similarities, between Jnana Yoga of Advaita and Krishnamurti's teachings. So it is unwise to conflate both the teachings and assume that they are saying the same thing in terms of methodology. One who has deconstructed the subject-object duality ultimately can see how all non-dual paths operate and quickly sift through these paths' various languages. But the different languages of different approaches are bound to confound entry-level, middle-level, and even highly advanced seekers. So it is best to have a perfect teacher to guide one through these paths.

Thus, I use Krishnamurti's teachings for the first two phases of my self-inquiry, i.e., Psychological Inquiries and Meditative Inquiries, Shankara's Advaitic Inquiry for the Witness Gaudapada's Advaita/Direct Path for the Post-Witness stage. No seeker needs to follow the same trajectory I did in my journey of self-inquiry. I just switched paths according to my changing predilections/sticking points.

Faith or Reason?

Most people believe that spirituality is a question of personal faith and belief; it does not have some universally accepted truth, which is only in empirical science. In this Chapter, through a dialogue with my friend, I reveal how Advaita Vedanta is a spiritual science that follows the same procedure as an empirical science in investigating reality: except that it goes one step higher. While empirical science demonstrates that existence is known more accurately through our mind/thought/reason rather than our senses, Advaita Vedanta shows that ultimate reality is known by an intuitive knowledge that even transcends thought. Moreover, the procedure to get this intuitive knowledge is as scientific as the discoveries made in science through the exercise of thought/reason.

Anurag: Suppose I go to a man who has not read science and tell him that it is not the sun that moves around the earth but the earth that moves around the sun. What would he say?

Friend: He will say, how do you know?

Anurag: That would be a thinking person. An average person would say that I am mad.

Friend: Yes, he would say that you are mad.

Anurag: Ok. So I can't do much with that person, right ?!

Friend: Yes

Anurag: So let's take a thinking person now? One who is ready to ask how?

Anurag: What will you tell such a person?

Friend: I will show him some satellite pictures

Anurag: Galileo did not have satellite pictures!

Friend: I was telling concerning modern times.

Anurag: No. Think about Galileo times. He wanted to show the Church the same thing. Instead, the Church showed him types of equipment for torture.

Friend: Yes, he failed

Anurag: Right. So put yourself in his place. Suppose someone is interested in listening to you. What would you do?

Friend: I will share with him the process/experiment by which I reached my conclusion that the earth goes around the sun

Anurag: Which means you will teach him science. Right?

Friend: Yes

Anurag: Right. More simply....a system of logic. Right?

Friend: Yes. Proven logic

Anurag: Because you can't show him the earth moving around the sun in any way. Now let's say you share your logic. Let's say he understands that logic. Will he see the earth moving around the sun?

Friend: Yes

Anurag: Huh ?!! Will he physically see this??!

Friend: I mean, he won't see it physically but will understand the concept

Anurag: So even after understanding the logic, he will see the sun moving around the earth. Right? I mean, don't you see the sun rising in the East and setting in the West every day.

Friend: Yes, he will still see the sun rising and setting down

Anurag: So your senses are deluding you, right?

Friend: Yes, but that's the fact for the senses because of their limited capabilities

Anurag: Right. So senses cannot perceive reality. Even after reality is perceived through thought, the senses still register the same delusion. Right?

Friend: Yes

Anurag: Ok. Next step!

Anurag: Thought is higher than senses because they show a reality that senses can't see. Right?

Friend: They understand the logic, but they cannot override thought because of a lack of proof.

Anurag: But what thought showed was the fact. Isn't it? A satellite video proves it even to the senses. Right?

Friend: Yes

Anurag: So thought has enormous scientific power. Albert Einstein's theory predicted black holes. The theory came first, then they discovered the phenomena of black holes, which proved the theory much later. Right?

Friend: But it gets completely digested only when it's certified by senses; there is a possibility of going wrong as well

Anurag: Not at all. Mathematics is thought. No sense there. That is why Plato wrote on the door of his academy of philosophy....let no one who does not know geometry enter these gates.

Anurag: Thought has the power of inference by which it can deduct the truth of phenomena.

Anurag: For example, there has to be fire if there is smoke seen at a distance.

Friend: Yes

Anurag: Right, this is a significant discovery for you, all part of Advaita.

Anurag: Now science books tell you that earth goes round the sun. Do they ask you to believe them?

Friend: No

Friend: They tell their research

Anurag: Did you believe their research?

Friend: No, I tried to understand the research by asking doubts and seeking clarifications

Anurag: Good. That means you use the system of the logic of thought. Right?

Friend: Yes

Anurag: You can get a total conviction in thought even when senses show something opposite to logic. Right?

Friend: Yes. But still, I will doubt why the senses show something different from what thought/logic is showing.

Anurag: I took a little complex case. We see the same

thing in many ordinary, daily life situations: our senses show something, but thought corrects it.

Anurag: Take the situation of a pencil dipped in a glass jar of water and appearing bent. Is it bent?

Friend: No, it's not, but my point is that the senses are not wrong, they are limited, and that thought can go above them. Senses are seeing a bent pencil because of their limitations of seeing.

Anurag: Senses are showing a bent pencil. In this case, they are entirely wrong. Right? Seeing and senses are the same. I mean, one sees through senses gross objects.

Friend: Yes, but the thought is more capable because it can see through logic, but senses can't, as they are limited.

Anurag: Good. In Advaita, the mind is the internal sense organ. Please bear this in mind. This will prove to be the most fundamental discovery for you. The whole of Advaita is based on this, which is nothing but pure science.

Friend: You mean "Thought is more capable", by this point.

Anurag: To know reality more deeply than the senses, yes. Just as we looked at the senses, we can examine thought to see its limitations in investigating reality. Right?

Friend: Yes. But I have a question

Anurag: Good. Go ahead!

Friend: When an infant is born, all it learns is through senses, then at what level thought takes over and how? Because if senses run the body, then thought should be limited to the senses.

Anurag: Infant also has thought. Even animals do. There is a difference between the brain and the mind. Thoughts are in mind. The brain is matter. Thoughts and minds are subtler than matter. No instrument can see thought. Senses don't see thought. However, senses can see the brain. Now we step into the second step of the ladder of Advaita.

Friend: I am trying to understand what could be the reason for thoughts, but this is also a thought, and in this investigation, it becomes like I am the murderer and investigator.

Anurag: Right. So don't jump ahead of the discussion. Let me lead you. You have a qualified teacher in front of you.

Friend: I didn't know that my question was jumping ahead.

Anurag: Oh! I was saying it lightly. But, on a serious note, I meant you are missing many steps in between. And without these steps, you will get caught up.

Friend: Got this theoretically, but there you showed me through the example of a bent pencil in water.

Anurag: Yes, thought knows that pencil is not bent even though senses are showing them. In the same way, there is a faculty higher than thought which shall guide us with no shadow of a doubt that view is not showing us the actual reality.

Friend: :-) (Please insert a smiley emoji)

Anurag: This faculty is called in Advaita – Buddhi (Sharpened Intellect/Intuition), which is higher than thought. Even in common life, don't we get an intuition that goes opposite to thought? But it is proved right!

Friend: Yes, but most of the time, thought wins.

Anurag: It is because we do not have a sharpened Buddhi due to our attachment to thought. It's like someone cannot solve a math problem because of the lack of sharpening of mind. Students want to see TV rather than solve math problems.

Friend: Got it.

Anurag: Right, the Buddhi is the Vigyanmaya Kosha1. Which is where the intuition of Self takes place and results in liberation. Got it!

Friend: How will I get this now? I don't have that intuition right now.

Anurag: Do you get the logic part of it? The logic of liberation in Advaita.

Friend: Yes

Anurag: Good. Now, after you know the logic of how the earth moves around the sun, do you keep bothering and checking the science book which showed you the reason, or do you forget that book as you are sure and no longer need that science book. Or do you keep your elementary maths books which showed you how $2 \times 2 = 4$

Friend: No, we no longer need the book

Anurag: Fine. In the same way, whatever the Upanishads say, you won't bother about them after seeing the truth because what you would have seen would be beyond all doubt in your own experience. Get it?

"To the knower of Brahman, the Vedas are of just as much use as to a tank of water flooded with water from all sides" – Bhagavad Gita.

Any doubts about the logic of all this?

Friend: But what if I am not able to understand the logic of the Upanishads

Anurag: That is the teacher's work and the student's effort – Shravana/listening to scriptures through the teacher, Manana/reflecting on the teachings, Nidhidhyasana/deep contemplation on the teachings. These are the tools to sharpen the intellect to get the final intuition. But I hope this removes all your doubts about whether Upanishads have truth in them or not etc. You will understand them faster and better if you go with the faith and confidence that they are leading you to the truth. Which is what I was working for in this whole dialogue. To know that the earth moves around the sun, you have first to put faith in the teachings of science. But ultimately, science, if you have studied it sincerely, will give you a surety beyond all belief. Get it?

Friend: Yes, but by faith, I understand that whatever you say, I have to follow without questioning. But that's not the way I know; I question and doubt.

Anurag: Why did you decide to read anything about science or technology in the first place?

Friend: Because I have trust in technology. Also, because I don't need to follow anyone blindly, I can question it.

Anurag: Right. Now, did I say that you must put faith in me? I am saying faith in science-in the teachings...., not me!

Friend: Yes, I got it

Anurag: Good. Regarding questioning. The whole methodology is about that only-Manan (Reflection/Dialogue), after Shravana (Reading). You have first to study the teachings and then ask questions to clarify all your doubts. As a teacher, I welcome questioning related to the science of Advaita.

Friend: That is why I got ready to get into studying Advaita

Anurag: So read confidently with the faith that Upanishads shall lead you to the truth that your own experience will ensure, not just because Upanishads are saying something. The Bhagavad Gita quote shows that Upanishads/Vedas are useless once you see the truth through your intuitive experience.

Friend: :-)_(Please insert a smiley emoji)

Anurag: This was yes or what?!

Friend: How do you get faith without reading it? If I have to cross a river, I need to know if the boat is working for me. It may have worked for others, but I have to trust the logic that only this boat can make me cross the river and not some crocodile or anything.

Anurag: So, do you have other choices available?

Friend: Nope

Anurag: When you are choiceless, you are free of all confusion. So from where does the crocodile as a source for crossing the river come into the picture.

Friend: I hat tried all ways, like Buddhism and Jainism. I got ready to study Advaita with you because you said you got to know the ultimate truth of Self after listening to your lecture on Turiya.

Anurag: Advaita takes you to a reality beyond all phenomena, space, time, and thought. Do you see anything further than this? Advaita is a totally non-dual path. Both the other reasons you have given are excellent to get into Advaita. Now take this dialogue and seal the last doubt about the teachings. This is the boat and nothing like a crocodile to take you to non-duality; there are other boats to other shores of duality like Jainism, etc.

Friend: Ok

Anurag: :-) Please insert smiley

Friend: How does faith help?

Anurag: Now forget it

Anurag: I did the work that I intended for you

Anurag: Browse through module 7 of the introductory Vedanta course I sent you.

Friend: I asked this question because I wanted to see the difference between my mother's faith in God and this faith in Advaita teachings.

Anurag: Your faith is not out of fear but out of a desire to know the truth. When you begin science, you can only start in faith. There is no other way! The difference between your mother's faith in God and your faith in Advaita is that your Mother's faith will forever keep her tied to duality and fear because it talks of a reality separate from you. Advaita will convert your faith to certainty, and the teachings will destruct themselves. The ultimate non-dual insight does not take you to any reality which you did not know, like God, instead it helps you realize what has always been YOUR ultimate nature.

Friend: thanks got it

Anurag: :-) Insert smiley

Friend: From now onwards, my complete focus will be on this (Advaita). I will pack up other books.

Anurag: Brilliant.

The Origin of Advaita

In the Hindu Epic Mahabharata, the creation of Vedas is credited to Brahma. The Vedic hymns themselves assert that they were skillfully created by Rishis (sages), after inspired creativity, just as a carpenter builds a chariot.

Despite the conventional "wisdom" that Shankara was the first to talk about Advaita, it is erroneous. The teaching of Advaita fact he belonged to a tradition of teachers called Sampradya stretching back to the time of Upanishads, which is at least a thousand years. It is noteworthy to mention that Shankara mentions 99 different predecessors of his school in his commentaries. I discussed in detail the names of some of these thinkers mentioned by Shankara in his comments and their teachings – Badarayana, Upavarsa, Sundarapandya, Kasakratsna, Brahmanandin, and Dravidacarya. Shankara counts them as teachers in his tradition/sampradaya and even reverentially calls some of them by the honorific title Bhagavan. I have yet to discuss another pre-Shankara teacher: Gaudapada, who is very significant, because unlike the other pre-Shankara teachers mentioned, his works are extant and available for our scrutiny.

However, there is a widespread notion that Shankara made some personal innovations in the philosophy of Vedanta derived from the Upanishads. Many authors have claimed that he and his teacher Gaudpada have borrowed and incorporated doctrines from Buddhism. I posit that the latter-day developments of Dvaita of Maddhvacharya and Vishishtadvaita of Ramanuja show deviations from the teachings of the Upanishads. I further assert that Shankara was only a link in a tradition, which has no human author. His teachings and methodology were grounded in the Upanishads, the revealed scriptures or srutis, whose authority was held supreme by him rather than any individual teacher.

The Uppanishads are the main source of traditional Advaita2.

Non-Human Origin of Advaita Vedanta

Abbreviations Used
B.G – Bhagavad Gita
Bg.Bh. – Bhagavad Gita Bhashya – Shankara
Bs.Bh. – Brahmasutra Bhashya – Shankara
Brhad. – Brhadaranyaka Upanishad
Br.U.B – Brhadaranyaka Upanishad Bhashya
G.K – Gaudapada Karika

Let alone Shankara; there is no human origin for Advaita Vedanta. Advaita Vedanta traces its origins to the Upanishads or shrutis, which are the concluding portion of the Vedas, dealing with philosophy rather than rituals. It is an important contention of both Advaita Vedanta and Purva-Mimamsa that the Vedas are eternal, uncreated, and authorless (apauruseya). The claim for the infallibility of these texts follows directly from this contention. If a personal author is ascribed to the Vedas, they will suffer from the limitations of authorship, defect-free sources of knowledge will be under doubt. It is well known to those who follow the Veda that the phrase 'the method of the Vedanta' refers to the method for teaching knowledge of the Absolute observed in the Upanishads. Knowledge of the Absolute first manifests at the beginning of a world period in the mind of Hiranyagarbha or Brahma, who has received the Veda from the supreme Lord. The method, carried on continuously by a succession of Teachers beginning with Brahma, has even come down to certain Teachers of modern times. And earnest seekers of release can still today achieve their goal by. Acquiring an unshakable conviction about the truths in the science of the Upanishads, taught by a true Guru. For we have the Upanishadic text, 'In search of release, I take refuge in that deity, the light of my intellect, who projects Brahma at the beginning of a world-period and delivers to him the Vedas' (Svet.VI.18). And also, Brahmā taught this knowledge of the Self to Prajāpati, and Prajāpati taught it to Manu. Manu, in his turn, taught it to all human beings [Chanogya Upanishad 8.15.1]

Shrutis as revealed Scriptures

One may wonder how anyone can access information from a non-human (apauruseya) origin. The answer lies in the word "revealed." The Shrutis (literally 'what are heard') are never referred to as records, scriptures, or compositions of any particular great personages. They are only 'heard'

and known by the disciples from the teachings of their
masters, and the truths they inculcate never depend upon
the authority of the Rishis who are sometimes mentioned
in them, Thus :

"One result, they say, is obtained with the aid of Vidya,
and another, they say, is obtained with the aid of Avidya.
So we have heard the saying of the wise ones who have
explained it to us." [Isa.10] "It is altogether other than the
known, and it is beyond the unknown. Thus, have we heard
our predecessors who explained it to us." [Ke. 1-4]

Even the Rishis are said to have received the Shrutis by
means of their good deeds and acts of discipline but not to
have themselves composed the texts:

"By the act of worship, they got the fitness to receive the
Veda, and that word they received as it had entered into the
Rishis." [Rig. 10-71-3] "The Maharshis (great seers) got the
Vedas which together with Itihas had disappeared at the end
of the last cycle, by virtue of penance, with the permission
of the Self-manifested One." [Mo. Dh.]

Even if one finds this all incredulous, it does not matter
because the final authority of the scriptures is not based on
any belief. They are a set of teachings that ultimately result in
an intuition that can be validated by anyone who subscribes
to the teachings. Finally, even the teachings are transcended.

Shrutis as the Final Authority

For those who feel that Shankara may have invented any
new set of concepts or teachings or borrowed any concepts
from other schools like Buddhism, their notions would get
dispelled when they examine how Shankara considers Shruti
to be the final authority. In all his commentaries, he has
held the word of the shrutis as the gold standard of truth
against which conflicting claims are examined, resolved, or
discarded. As a proof, I am presenting two quotes from his
Brahmasutra Bhashya.

"...for Brahman is known from the Upanishads alone" (Bs.
Bh. II.i.27)." This Supreme and sublime Brahman is to be
known from the Veda alone, but not from reasoning" (Bs.
Bh. II.i.29)

Ultimate Truth of the Shrutis – Non-Dual Brahman

Upanishadic texts proclaim non-duality: the unity of
Brahman or Atman in the most unmistakable terms. This
means that the world of plurality that we experience is not

real. What is real is non-duality, even though we seemingly see plurality.

For example, we have 'O Gargi, this the knowers of the Absolute call the Indestructible. It is not gross, not subtle, not short, not long, neither red (like fire) nor fluid (like water), neither shadow nor darkness, neither wind nor ether, not adhesive, not taste, no odor, without eyes, without ears, without voice, without mind, without brilliance, without the vital principle, without an orifice, without a measure, having nothing within and nothing without. It consumes nothing, nor does anything consume it' (Brhad.III.viii.8), "Imperceptible, inapprehensible, having no source from which it proceeds and having no colors or features, without eyes, ears, hands or feet (Mund.1.i.6), and 'Without sound, impalpable, without form, beyond decay, without taste, constant, without odor, without beginning or end, fixed, beyond Mahat (the cosmic mind)' (Katha I.iii.15).

When Shankara says that reality is non-dual Brahman, he is not creating his own fiction. As shown above, the Shrutis are declaring the attributeless, indestructible, non-dual Brahman as the Absolute reality. So we can now appreciate the following words from him, which speak of non-dual Brahman as the final reality: "There is no appropriate way of describing (It) other than this, hence 'not this, not that. (To explain:) For, indeed, there is no description of Brahman other than the negation of the phenomenal manifold." [Bs.Bh. 3-2-22]

Why Shrutis are the Final Authority?

From the above, it is clear that senses cannot perceive Brahman. Sankara refuses to accept that because Brahman is an existent entity, it can be the object of other sources of valid knowledge like other objects. 'The senses are naturally capable of grasping and revealing their appropriate objects. Brahman, however, remains unapproachable through any of them because of its uniqueness. (Bs.Bh. 1.1.2) The organs can only grasp a differentiated object within their range (Br.U.B. 3.9.26). The Upanishads speak about nature 'and the evolution of the five sense organs. Each organ evolves out of a particular element which enables it to apprehend a quality proper to it. The eyes, for example, evolve out of the subtle sattva aspect of fire and are the organs for perceiving the quality of form which is unique to fire. Therefore, it is the special relationship between sense organs and elements that empowers each one to cognize an appropriate quality. Sound, sensation, form, taste, and scent are their respective spheres of functioning. Brahman, however, has neither sound, touch, form, taste, or smell. It is without qualities (nirguna) and outside the domain of the sense organs. ("One becomes freed from the jaws of death by knowing that which is soundless, touchless, colorless, undiminishing and also tasteless, eternal, odorless, without beginning and end, distinct from Mahat, and ever-constant" (Katha. 1.3.15)) Brahman is limitless, and to become an object of sense knowledge is to be finite and delimited, to be one object among many objects. A Brahman that is sense apprehended is, therefore, a contradiction. However, perfect or magnified the capacity of a sense organ is imagined to be.

Since Shrutis are the knowledge manifested in the mind of Brahma – the Creator, at the beginning of each world cycle, which he passes down to teachers, it is the only means of knowledge (pramana) to know the reality beyond all our senses. Thus, the shrutis are also called shabda pramana. The words of the Shruti are means by which Brahman can be known. This should completely wipe off any doubts a person may hold whether Shankara invented his own system of Advaita Vedanta.

How Shrutis are the Means to Know the Unknowable Brahman

The following quotes from Shankara can help us understand how shrutis help us in knowing unobjectifiable Brahman.

Objection:- If Brahman is not an object, it cannot be consistently held to be (knowable) through the (Vedanta) Sastra as a valid means of knowledge!

Reply:- No, for the Shastra purports to wipe off the difference invented by Avidya. (To explain:) The Shastra indeed does not propose to teach Brahman as such and such an entity as its object. Still, it teaches that as one's innermost Self, it is unobjectifiable and removes all differences such as that of the knowable, knower, and knowledge." [Bs.Bh. 1-1-4]

This terse exchange needs to be fleshed out a little; in fact, quite a lot.

The Self-Luminosity/Witnesshood of Atman-Brahman

In Advaita, self-luminosity belongs to the Atman alone. For the Shruti says, "There is one Deva (the self-shining entity) hid in all creatures, all-pervading, the inmost Self of all beings, the Superintendent of all actions, residing in all beings, the Witness, the Conscious Principle, non-dual, and attributeless." [Sve.6-11].In its light, everything is illumined and known. The Self is the knower (ksetrajna), and everything else is known (kshetra) (B.G 13.1-2). As the unchanging witness of all mental modifications, it is referred to as Sakshi. (B.G – 9.18) The same awareness, reflected in mind and identified with it, becomes the jiva, who functions as the perceiver or the cognizer (pragmatic), the object cognized (prameya), and the cognition (pramiti) are all revealed by the Self as Witness (Sakshi). In any act of perception, the cognitive mode objectifies and reveals the object because it is illumined by the Self. This cognition, however, does not require another cognitive mode for its manifestation. It is revealed directly by the Self as Sakshi, as soon as it originates.

"I" or Self is Brahman

Based on the luminosity of Atman-Brahman-Witness, Sankara develops his argument about the self-evident manifestation of the Atman as the content of the "I" notion. In response to an objection that if Brahman is a completely unknown entity, it cannot become the subject of inquiry, Sankara replies "that the existence of Brahman is well known from the fact of Its being the Self of all; for everyone feels that his Self exists, and he never feels "I do not exist." Had there been no general recognition of the existence of the Self, everyone would have felt, "I do not exist. And that Self is Brahman. (Bs.Bh. 1.1.1) Earlier on, in reply to a query that an unperceived Self cannot become the locus of superimposition, he contends that the Self is well known in the world as an immediately perceived entity. It is nothing but the content of the concept "I" (Bs.Bh. Intro)

The Shrutis Do Not Posit Brahman

From the above, it should be clear that this principle of reality is called the Absolute (Brahman), since it is that which manifests in the guise of the knower, is that on which all right empirical cognition and so on depend. Its existence is therefore established logically prior to all empirical experience, including valid empirical knowledge. For, as the "I" notion and as the Self of all, it is immediately evident. Because it is a self-luminous experience, it is self-evident and does not, like pots and other objects, require anything else apart from itself to make itself known. For all these reasons, it does not require any special positive teaching. So the Upanishads do not fulfill their function as authoritative means of knowledge, in this context, through revealing a hitherto unknown object, in the manner of perception and the other means of empirical knowledge.

However, even though our real "I" being Self/Brahman, the unique nature of the Self remains unknown due to impediments. As evidence of this, Shankara cites the divergent and mutually contradictory views which different systems hold about the nature of the Self (Bs. Bh.1.1.1). The point, therefore, is that even though we are not completely debarred from all awareness of ultimate reality, we do not recognize its existence, and our understanding is incomplete. What is needed is a valid source of knowledge through which we can apprehend the unique nature of the Self accurately. The Vedas, Sankara contends, is just such a pramana(proof).

The Traditional Method of the Shrutis to Reveal Brahman/ Self/Witness: Agama (Superimposition and Retraction)

The competent authorities in this field quote the text 'But when all has become his own Self, then what could a person see and with what?': (Brhad.IV.v.15). And they say that it is only by a figure of speech that the Upanishads are spoken of as an authoritative means of knowledge. For their function is to communicate that reality in its true nature, beyond the play of the means of knowledge and their objects, merely by putting an end to the superimposition onto it of attributes it does not possess.

The Upanishads do not derive their authority as a means of knowledge solely from the fact of their being included among the texts of the Veda. They derive it from their power to lead ultimately to a direct experience of the Self, arising from the cancellation of all play of the empirical means of knowledge with their objects. This power is associated with their demonstration of the fact that the state of being an individual knowing subject, which is the prior condition for all empirical experience, is itself based on metaphysical Ignorance.

Thus, the Shrutis are using a definite method for teaching the Self, which is based on superimposition and negation. This traditional method is based on adhyAropa apavAda, by which different attributes are superimposed on Brahman, and then they are negated step-by-step till all attributes are negated, and only Brahman shines. This traditional method is called Agama.

Gaudapada taught this traditional method. For he says, 'The text denies ail that it had previously taught, by saying "He (the Self) is neither this nor that" (Brhad.II.iii.6), and by showing that the Self is beyond all perception and conception. Through this, the Unborn is able to manifest' (G.K.III.26). The meaning is that simply for purposes of instruction, the Veda first attributes to the Self, as a principle of reality, features that it does not in fact possess. And it does this even though the Self is that which alone exists, within and without (Mund.II.i.2), and is also unborn and without differentiation. Then, when the Self has been thus taught, and the work of positive instruction is complete, the Veda itself retracts whatever it had previously taught to show that none of it was the final truth.

Shankara as the Teacher of Agama: Traditional Method of Teaching about Brahman

The following quote by Shankara shows that he was a teacher following the same tradition of Agama as outlined above and not creating his own new-fangled teaching:
"The collection of specific features in the Kshetrajna due to the different conditioning associates is wholly unreal, and therefore He has been taught to be known as neither being nor non-being, by denying that (specific nature. But here) even the unreal form is presumed as though it were the property of (the Kshetrajna) the knowable just to bring home its existence (by describing it by the expression) 'It has hands and feet everywhere, etc.
Accordingly, there is (this) saying of the knowers of the traditional method, 'That which is devoid of all multiplicity

is explained by means of (deliberate) superimposition and rescission."[Bg.Bh. 13.13]

Agama and Support for Reason

Lastly, we need to understand that reason has its place in the scheme of Agama or traditional teaching of the Upanishads, but it is not any form of reasoning. It is only the reasoning supported by Agama that results in the final intuition of Brahman. Regarding this, we have from Shankara the following counsel:

"As for the other argument that the Shruti itself, enjoining reflection in addition to hearing or the study of Shruti, shows that reason also is to be respected, we reply:- Dry reasoning can find no admittance here on the strength of this plea. For, reasoning proffered by the Shruti alone is resorted to here as ancillary to intuition." [Bs.Bh. 2-1-6]

"For this reason also, one should not stand up against what is to be known exclusively by the agama (traditional teaching of the Shruti; for, reasonings which are the outcome of mere surmises without any Agama for basis, would be inconclusive; since a surmise has nothing to check it." [Bs. Bh. 2-1-10]

"We have already observed that being devoid of colour (or form) etc., this entity is no object of perception, and being devoid of the grounds, etc., it is not an object of logical inference and other valid means of knowledge." [Bs.Bh. 2-1-11]

Sruti Also Transcended After Brahman is Known

Lest it still bothers rational-minded people that everything is based on the authority of scripture, there are two things which shall quash these doubts.

"In the enquiry into the nature of Brahman, it is not merely Shrutis, etc. alone that are the valid means of knowledge, as is the case in the enquiry into the nature of Dharma (religious duty), but also shrutis and direct intuition and the like are here the valid means according to the applicability of these. For knowledge of Brahman has to culminate in intuition, and relates to an existent entity." [Bs.Bh. 1-1-2]

All commerce between the attested means of knowledge (perception, 'inference, revelation, etc.) and their objects, whether in the Vedic or secular sphere, proceeds on the basis of this same mutual superimposition of the Self and not-self

called Ignorance, as does all Vedic tradition, whether concerned with injunctions and prohibitions or with liberation.
(Bs. Bh.1-1-1, intro.)

The first point is evident. It is saying that the Shrutis are
the authority only because they lead to the direct intuition of
Brahman. So a person who has got direct intuition of Brahman only can unfold the teachings of the Shruti. The second
point says that all means of knowledge, including the Vedas/
shrutis, are functioning in Ignorance. This means once Self
is known; even the shrutis are transcended. Their authority exists only in the realm of duality and Ignorance. Their
authority exists only in the realm of duality and Ignorance.
As the Smriti too says:

"For the brahmana who knows the self, all the Vedas are
of only so much use as a small reservoir is when there is
flood everywhere." (B.G – 2.46)

Conclusion

Suppose Shankara himself was so stern and clear about
the Shrutis being the final adjudicator of truth and the
Agamas as the only method they sanctioned to know the
truth. In that case, there is no ground to believe that Shankara founded any new system or school of thought that is
based on his personal reasoning and interpretation of the
Vedas. As every paragraph in this Chapter shows, Shankara
was extremely sure that only the shrutis, when unfolded
according to Agama by a qualified teacher, can lead a seeker
to the intuition of Brahman. This Agama is a tradition that
stretches right back from Brahma to the teachers of the
present day who know this method and are not deluded by
false teachings that have intruded and corrupted the true
tradition.3 I have not gone into the details of the method
of the Agama as it would require an elaborate treatment,
which I am reserving for another Chapter.

For the Shrutis say, "A man having a teacher can know
Brahman," knowledge received from a teacher alone
(becomes perfect)," "The teacher is the pilot," Right Knowledge is called in this world a raft," etc. [Upadeshasahasri
Prose 1.3 by Shankara]

Notes

A History of Early Vedanta, Hajime Nakamura, page 89

Bhamati and Vivarna Schools of Advaita Vedanta by Pulsath Soobah Roodurmum, page 10. Several influential early Vedanta thinkers have been listed in the Siddhitraya by Yamunācārya (c. 1050), the Vedārthasamgraha by Rāmānuja (c. 1050–1157), and the Yatīndramatadīpikā by Srīnivāsa Dāsa. At least fourteen thinkers are known to have existed between the composition of the Brahma Sutras and Shankara's lifetime.

Purva Mimamsa deals with Vedic rituals and sacrifices. In contrast, the Uttara Mimamsa, also known as the Vedanta/ Upanishads, deals with the path leading to liberation from all worldly and otherworldy bondages. (about 200 B.C – 200 A.D)

There are the Vishishtadvaita and the Dvaita schools, which hold different views.

Confusion about the true Upanishadic doctrine was thus introduced by authors representing various schools of Vedanta, who made free use of quotation of texts, allied both too simple reasoning and to sophistry: Then it was that Sri Gaudapada Acarya, actuated solely by a desire to serve the people, composed his Karikas and stated the accurate traditional method in its proper form, through the medium of

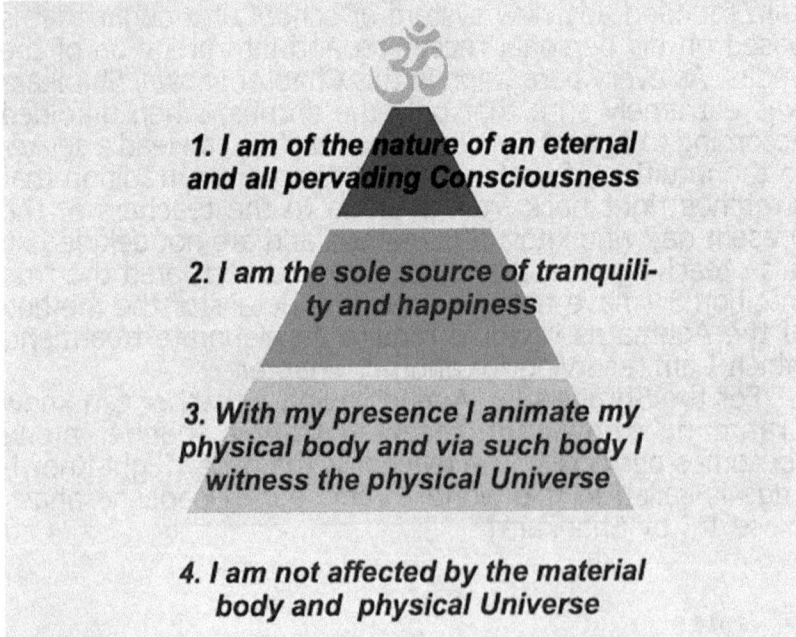

1. I am of the nature of an eternal and all pervading Consciousness

2. I am the sole source of tranquility and happiness

3. With my presence I animate my physical body and via such body I witness the physical Universe

4. I am not affected by the material body and physical Universe

an explanation of the meaning of the Mandukya Upanishad. And Sri Sankara Bhagavatpada and his pupils and followers propagated his commentaries on the three starting-points of the Vedanta (the Prasthanatraya, viz the classical Upanishads, Brahma Sutras, and Gita). It was thoroughly clarifying the accurate method and purging away the mud of all the different spurious methods of interpretation. For their conviction was that if anyone heedlessly embraced' any random way of understanding, he would be prevented from attaining the supreme good and would fall into adversity. (The Method of The Vedanta by Swami Satchidanandendra, page 10)

This method got practically lost post-Shankara after different schools started erroneously representing the teachings of Shankara. Swami Satchidanandendra discovered it. I am highly indebted to him for me getting to know the path of Shankara's Advaita, which is known only to a handful of people even today.

Confusion about the true Upanishadic doctrine is introduced by authors representing various schools of Vedanta, who make free use of quotation of texts, allied both to genuine reasoning and to sophistry.

The Vedas

Vedas Hold Authority Only in Matters That Are Supra Sensory (Beyond Perception)

Revelation, then, comes with the world, and it embodies the laws which regulate the well-being of both the world and man. It lays down first and foremost what our dharma is, our duty. This duty is more precisely defined as a set of acts which either must be done continuously (Nitya), or occasionally (naimittika), or to satisfy a specific wish (kāmya). While we would be inclined to look upon the Revelation as a more or less continuous series of historical texts, spanning close to a millennium from ca. 1400 B.C.E. till 500 B.C.E., orthodoxy looks upon it as eternal and therefore simultaneous.

Also, the Mīmāmsā (School, which considers Karma Kanda (action/rituals portion) of Vedas as primary, laid down rather rigorous criteria for its authority. Orthodox consensus recognizes three fundamental means of knowledge, each of which has its own scope of authority. Of these means (pramānas), sensory perception (pratyaksha) holds the first place, for it is through a perception that the world is evident to us. Built upon perception is inference (anumāna), in which a present perception combines with a series of past perceptions to offer us a conclusion about a fact which is not perceptibly evident. While these two means of knowledge, perceiving, and reasoning, tell us everything about the world that we wish to know, they cannot give us any wisdom about supra sensory matters. It is here that the force of Revelation comes in.

Therefore, From the Mīmāmsā point of view, for example, the Four Vedas as we call them, the Veda of the hymns (rig), the formulae (yajus), the chants (sāma), and the incantations (Atharva), are almost entirely under the rubric of "spell." The large disquisitions of the Brāhmanas are almost wholly "discussion," except for the scattered injunctions in them, and the same essentially holds for the third layer of texts, the Āranyakas. Generally speaking, Vedānta will go along with this view.

Revelation, then, comes with the world, and it embodies the laws which regulate the well-being of both the world and man. It lays down first and foremost what our dharma is, our duty. This duty is more precisely defined as a set of acts which either must be done continuously (Nitya), or occasionally (naimittika), or to satisfy a specific wish (kāmya). While we would be inclined to look upon the Revelation as a more or less continuous series of historical texts, spanning close to a millennium from ca. 1400 B.C.E. till 500 B.C.E., orthodoxy looks upon it as eternal and therefore simultaneous.

Also, the Mīmāmsā (School, which considers Karma Kanda (action/rituals portion) of Vedas as primary, laid down rather rigorous criteria for its authority. Orthodox consensus recognizes three fundamental means of knowledge, each of which has its own scope of authority. Of these means (pramānas), sensory perception (pratyaksha) holds the first place, for it is through the perception that the world is evident to us. Built upon perception is inference (anumāna), in which a present perception combines with a series of past perceptions to offer us a conclusion about a fact which is not perceptibly evident. While these two means of knowledge, perceiving, and reasoning, tell us everything about the world we wish to know, they cannot give us any wisdom about supra sensory matters. It is here that the force of Revelation comes in.

Therefore, From the Mīmāmsā point of view, for example, the Four Vedas as we call them, the Veda of the hymns (rig), the formulae (yajus), the chants (sāma), and the incantations (Atharva), are almost entirely under the rubric of "spell." The large disquisitions of the Brāhmanas are almost wholly "discussion," except for the scattered injunctions in them, and the same essentially holds for the third layer of texts, the Āranyakas. Generally speaking, Vedānta will go along with this view.

The Division of the Vedas

It is, however, with the last layer of text (the Vedānta or the Upanishads) that Mīmāmsikās and Vedāntins come to a parting of ways. For the Mīmāmsikās, the Upanishads are no exception to the rules that govern the Revelation as a whole. Nothing much is enjoined in them, nor do they embody marked spells. In fact, they are fundamental "discussion," (atharvavada), specifically the discussion of the self; and such discussion certainly has a place in the interpretive scheme of things, for this self is none other than the personal agent of the rites and this agent no doubt deserves as much discussion as, say, the sacrificial pole.

Therefore, the Mīmāmsikās find the Revelation solely and fully authoritative when it lays down the Law on what actions have to be undertaken by what persons under what circumstances for which purposes. Vedānta accepts this, but only for that portion of Revelation, which bears on ritual acts, the karmakānda. But to relegate the portion dealing with knowledge, the jñānakānda, to the same ritual context is unacceptable. It is taken for granted that karmakānda indeed defines the principle of authority in injunctions of acts to be done, but Vedānta declines on the one hand that the Upanishads embody an injunction (e.g., that Brahman or the self must be studied and known, or that the world must be de-phenomenalized) and declines on the other hand that if the Upanishads bear on no injunction they have simply the limited authoritative standing of a discussion.

Shankara's Emphasis on Jnana Kanda of Vedas or

Upanishads

The consensus of the Vedānta is that in the Upanishads significant and authoritative statements are made concerning the nature of Brahman. From the foregoing, it will have become clear that very little of the Revelation literature preceding the Upanishads were of systematic interest to the Vedāntins. For example, Śankara quotes less than twenty verses from the entire Rigveda in his commentary on the Brahmasūtras, about fourteen lines from the largest Brāhmana of them all, the Śatapatha Brāhmana, but no less than thirty-four verses from the Mundaka Upanishad, a relatively minor and short Upanishad. This is not to say that Vedānta rejects the previous literature, but that it considers all the relevant wisdom of the Veda concerning these issues to have been embedded in the Upanishads.

Upanishads are Concerned with Speaking of Ultimate Reality Beyond Mind and Reason

Upanishads Are Not A System of Philosophy

Philosophy is "the product of human thought, acting upon the data given. by the world without, or the world within, and eliciting from these data principles, laws and system." In this sense, of course, Vedanta is no philosophy, for one of the fundamental principles adopted here is 'Naisha Tarkena Matirapaneya' (This Knowledge is not attainable through speculation, Kena Up. 1-2-9).

According to another writer, 'The object matter of Philosophy', it has been observed, 'maybe distinguished as God or Nature or Man. But underlying all our enquiries into any of these departments, there is a first philosophy which seeks to ascertain the grounds or principles of knowledge and the causes of all things. Hence, philosophy has been said to be the science of causes and principles. It is the investigation of this knowledge and all being ultimately rest'

It will be noted that the Upanishads treat God, Nature, and Man – and all other creatures for that matter – and from this point of view, maybe said to cover the entire field of 'the objective matter of philosophy ' as herein described. It may not lay claim to being the 'first philosophy' as seeking to ascertain the principles of knowledge and causes of all things since it is no speculation. Still, nevertheless, in its way, it does present very definite ideas as to the nature and limitations of discursive knowledge, no less than the ultimate cause of all things. If the reader is liberal enough to bear with this slight difference, he will be willing to bring even Vedanta under the connotation of the word 'philosophy.'

However, even by this stretch, the Upanishads are not by any means a system of philosophy. 'The New Standard Dictionary' defines a system of philosophy as Orderly combination or arrangement as of particulars or elements into a whole; especially such combination according to some rational principle or organic idea giving it unity and completeness." This definition may not wholly apply to the Vedanta of the Upanishads since it is not a sensible system, as has been already admitted,

Upanishads Speak of One Grand Unifying Truth Beyond Mind and Senses: Brahman

But there is a more general description: "System is an organized body of truth or truths." Now, the meaning of this description may be taken to be wide enough to justify the view that the Vedanta philosophy is systematic inasmuch as it brings everything under one and the same idea, that of Paramartha or Reality and since all truths are comprehended by the one grand Truth Samyagjnanam that is revealed by one and the same method of ' Adhyaropa-Apavada.' For we have the following dialogue in the Mundaka Upanishad (Verses 3-6) between Shaunaka, a householder, and the sage Angiras, Saunaka, a great grihastha, having duly approached Angiras, questioned him "What is that, O Bhagavan which being was known, all this becomes known."

To him, he said, "There are two sorts of knowledge to he acquired. So those who know the Brahman say, namely, Para and Apara, i.e., the higher and the lower.

Of these, the Apara is the Rig Veda, the Yajur Veda, the Sama Veda, and the Atharva Veda, the siksha, the code of rituals, grammar, nirukta, chhandas and astrology. Then the para is that by which the immortal is known.

That which cannot be perceived, which cannot be seized,

which has no origin, which has no properties, which has neither ear nor eye, which has neither hands nor feet, which is eternal, diversely manifested, all-pervading, extremely subtle, and undecaying, which the intelligent cognized as the source of the Bhutas.

Method of Upanishads to Convey Ultimate Reality: Brahman

Here the Upanishad is clearly laying out the knowledge of Brahman as that higher knowledge or para-vidya by which all is known. This knowledge is deemed beyond all forms, perception and is immortal – that is, without decay. Now, this reality is out of the scope of perception cannot be known by senses or even thought or rationality. For we have the following

"The eye does not go there, nor speech, nor mind. We do not know That. We do not know how to instruct one about It. It is distinct from the known and above the unknown. We have heard it so stated by preceptors who taught us that." (Kena Upanishad, Verse 3)

Commenting on the Kena Upanishad verse 3 quoted above, Shankara clarifies why Brahman, the ultimate reality, cannot be known by the senses and the mind.

"Just as fire that burns and enlightens things does not either enlighten or burn itself, so the mind, which wills and determines in respect of external objects, cannot will or determine in respect of its self because its Atman is also the Brahman. A thing is cognized by the senses and the mind. We do not, therefore, know the Brahman, because it cannot be an object of perception to these"

Neti, Neti: Brahman Cannot Be Taught by Any Positive Teaching

Since the ultimate reality or Brahman cannot be an object of senses or mind, as stated above, the Upanishads cannot teach it by any positive instruction like Brahman is like this or that. Shankara says,

"We do not, therefore, know what the Brahman is like, to allow us to enlighten the disciple about the Brahman. Whatever can be perceived by the senses, it is possible to explain to others by epithets denoting its class, its attributes, and modes of activity. Still, the Brahman has no attributes of a class, etc. It, therefore, follows that it is not possible to make the disciple believe in the Brahman by [positive] instruction." (Kena Up, Verse 3, Commentary by Shankara)

Agama: Traditional Way of Teaching the Ultimate Reality Found in the Upanishads Revealed by Shankara

But it is the contention of the Upanishads that this reality can be known when taught by a teacher who knows the Brahman and the traditional way of teaching it. According to Shankara, the traditional way of teaching is called Agama, and it is a method of negation rather than a method of positing. Let's see how Shankara wields the Agama in his commentary to the above verse 3, quoted from Kena Upanishad. First, he stresses the prime importance of Agamas:

"Considering that the last portion of the text leads to the conclusion that it is impossible by any means to instruct one about the Atman, the following exceptional mode is pointed out. Indeed, one cannot be persuaded to believe in the Brahman by the evidence of the senses and other modes of proof, but it is possible to make him believe by the aid of Agamas (Scriptures). Therefore the preceptor recites Agamas for the purpose of teaching about the Brahman and says: 'It is something distinct from the known and something beyond the unknown, etc." (Kena Up, Verse 3, Commentary

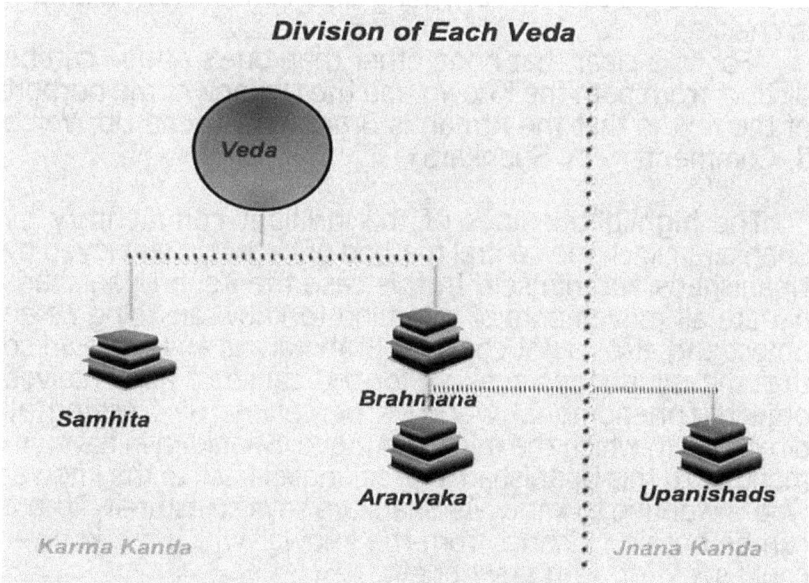

Division of Each Veda

Veda

Samhita

Brahmana

Aranyaka

Upanishads

Karma Kanda

Jnana Kanda

by Shankara)

Here he starts employing the method of Agama (method of negation):

"That is certainly distinct from the known. 'The known,' means 'whatever is the object of special knowledge; and as all such objects can be known somewhere, to some extent and by someone and so forth, the term means the whole (manifested universe) 'the known;' the drift is, that the Brahman is distinct from this. But lest the Brahman should be confounded with the unknown, the text says: 'It is beyond the Unknown.' 'Aviditat' means 'something opposed to the known;

What is known is puny, mortal, and full of misery and, therefore, fit to be abandoned. Therefore when it is said that Brahman is distinct from the Known, it is clear that it is not to be abandoned. Similarly, when the Brahman is said to be separate from the Unknown, it is in effect said that the Brahman is not fit to be taken. It is to produce an effect that one seeks for a cause. Therefore there can be nothing distinct from the knower, which the knower could seek for, with any benefit. Thus, by saying that the Brahman is distinct from both the Known and the Unknown and thus disproving its fitness to be abandoned or to be taken, the desire of the disciple to know anything distinct from Self (Atman) is checked."

"For, it is clear that none other than one's Atman can be distinct from both the Known and the Unknown; the purport of the text is that the Atman is Brahman." (Kena Up, Verse 3, Commentary by Shankara)

The highlighted lines of this brilliant commentary by Shankara clinch the central method of negation employed by Upanishads and himself. In this case the Kena Upanishads negate all movements of the mind to know anything as an object and also to not consider Brahman as an Unknown so that the mind stops seeking for the cause of all perceived objects (phenomenal world) it perceives. By freezing all directions in which the mind can move, Shankara in his commentary to this Upanishad's verse angles back to the knower who is wanting to know. As Shankara says so astutely, "there can be nothing distinct from the knower which the knower could seek for, with any benefit."

This real example shows how Shankara, in his commentary to this verse from Kena Upanishad, through negation, focuses on the knower as the primary reality of oneself as Atman. And all this can be done only by the knower of the traditional method of teaching called Agama. For as Shankara says at last in his commentary to the same passage:

"The preceptor next says how this meaning of the text that the Atman of all, marked by no distinguishing attributes, bright and intelligent, is the Brahman has been traditionally handed down from preceptor to disciple."

"And Brahman can be known only by instruction from preceptors and not by logical disquisitions, nor by expositions, intelligence, great learning, penance or sacrifices, etc. We have heard this saying of the preceptors who taught us the Brahman."

Brahman: That Which the Mind Cannot Know

In the previous verse 3 of Kena Upanishad, Shankara discusses how the primary reality is not known or the unknown but the knower or the knowing Self – Atman. However, this does not complete the matter. For further, in verse 5 of the Kena Upanishad, the mind as knower is negated too, and Atman or real Self is declared to be more interior to the mind. In fact, Atman lights up the activities of the mind.

What one cannot think with the mind, but by which they say the mind is made to think, know That alone to be the Brahman, not this which (people) here worship. (Kena Upanishad, verse 5)
(Kena Upanishad, verse 5)

Shankara's commentary on this reads:
Com.—'Manah,' 'mind.' By the word 'Manah' here, both mind and intelligence are meant. 'Mauah' means 'that by which one thinks.' The mind is equally connected with all the sensory organs because its sphere includes all external objects. The Sruti says: 'Desire, volition, deliberation, faith, negligence, boldness, timidity, shame, intelligence, fear, all these are mind.' The modes of activity of the mind are desire, etc. By that mind, none wills or determines that intelligence which enlightens the mind, because as the enlightener of the mind, that is the mind's controller, the Atman being in the interior of everything, the mind cannot go there. The

capacity of the mind to think exists because it is enlightened by the intelligence shining within, and it is by that, that the mind is capable of activity. Those who know the Brahman say that the mind is pervaded by the Brahman. Therefore know that to be the Brahman, the Atman, the interior intelligence of the mind.

Agama as Attributing False Superimposition (Adhyaropa) Followed by Negation (Apavada)

The last few paragraphs were an attempt to lead the reader gradually to the true method of teaching reality adopted by Upanishads, and known only to a teacher of the true tradition, or Agama as one can appreciate by now that the method is not just negation but what is called superimposition followed by negation or adhyaropa-apavada. In this, first, the attribute-less reality is 'falsely' provided with an attribute which it actually does not possess (superimposes/ adhyaropa), and then when a seeker grasps that subtle reality, the teacher negates this subtle reality (apavada) and leads the seeker to a further subtler reality until one comes to the subtlest and ultimate reality which cannot be negated further. In the example of the Kena Upanishad verses 3 and 5 that I took above, one can see how Shankara applies this method by

First negating the reality as something known or unknown and focusing on the reality as the knower /Knowing self as Atman

Negating even the knower or knowing self in the next step and showing that the Atman is even beyond that.

The Atman-Brahman is finally intuited by the mind in a flash when this teaching is presented to a qualified seeker. This is because the final reality is self-shining. As Shankara says in his commentary, "The capacity of the mind to think exists, because it is enlightened by the intelligence shining within, and it is by that, that the mind is capable of activity." Once all false superimpositions on this shining entity are negated, the self-shining truth reveals itself. As an analogy, one may say that when the clouds that were covering the sun drift apart, the sun reveals itself. Only the clearing of clouds is required. No effort needs to be made by anyone to show a seeker the sun as the sun is self-revealing. All that was required was to remove the clouds. In ignorance, just like the clouds hide the sun, we superimpose various notions on the Self/Reality like it is the mind or body or intellect or God, etc. The work of a teacher wielding the teachings of the Upanishads is to negate one by one all the false attributions we have imposed on our true Self, and when the last one is removed, the Self shines and reveals itself by its own accord. This is the method followed by the Upanishads and followed by Shankara to reveal the truth.

One can now see how one cannot come to the Ultimate reality/Brahman by any mental process, like logic, reasoning, or rationality, because the absolute reality is beyond the mind. In this Chapter, I just took up two verses from the Kena Upanishad along with Shankara's commentary to demonstrate how the process of Agama works to communicate reality beyond the mind to a seeker. In the actual teaching methodology or Agama, many more examples are used from various verses of the Upanishads to lead a seeker from the gross phenomenal reality he perceives as true to the Ultimate Truth, Advaita Non-dual, without any duality, partless, without phenomena.

Seeing Like Shankara

In a recent dialogue with one of my friends and a student of Advaita, we came upon a particular verse from the Brhadaranyaka Upanishad.

"This (Self) was indeed Brahman in the beginning. It knew only Itself as 'I am Brahman.' Therefore It became all. And whoever among the gods knew It became That; and the same with sages and men. The sage Vamadeva, while realizing this Self as That, knew, 'I was Manu and the sun.' And to this day, whoever in like manner knows It as 'I am Brahman,' becomes all this universe. Even the gods cannot prevail against him, for he becomes their Self. While he who worships another god thinking, 'He is one, and I am another,' does not know. He is like an animal to the gods. As many animals serve a man, so does each man serve the gods. Even if one animal is taken away, it causes anguish; what should one say of many animals? Therefore it is not liked by them that men should know this. "~ Brhad. Up. Verse 1.4.10

There cannot be a more explicit statement from the sruti about the non-dual nature of absolute reality and how worship of any God cannot take one to the realization of the whole non-dual truth of Brahman. Thus my friend was puzzled that if there is such a clear appraisal of the subordinate nature of Gods and worship, how come there is any talk of worship/Bhakti of God by any follower of Advaita?

Personally, I have always had a strong intuition of an ultimate formless reality since my childhood. So I never warmed up to worship of God or Bhakti at any point of my seeking. As I mentioned in my Chapter, Stages of Self Inquiry, I never went through the traditional Vedantic preparatory phase of Karma Yoga and Bhakti Yoga. Instead, I directly went through the path of Jnana Yoga/Knowledge Yoga, first through the teachings of J Krishnamurti and then through the teachings of Advaita of Gaudapada-Shankara. This is the path I teach in my two groups – NEEV Advaita Study Group and the NEEV Psycho-Philosophy Inquiry Group.

Yet, many others take the traditional Vedanta path of Karma Yoga (Yoga of Action) and Bhakti Yoga (Yoga of Worship) for mental purification to enter Jnana Yoga and attain final knowledge of Brahman finally. This being the case only if one has a strong predisposition for non-duality. Otherwise, one may continue with Duality/Dvaita or Qualified Non-Duality/Vishisthadvaita as the ultimate vision of life. These are schools that sprung up after Shankara. Now my friend's question and curiosity was, why does Advaita have to talk about Bhakti/Worship and God at all, if they are only conditional realities that have to be ultimately sublimated?

So I decided to write this Chapter to answer his curiosity. And also address the perplexing question of why and how Advaita Vedanta, which is ultimately not theistic but a non-dual path, accommodates the Creator God as a conditional reality to be ultimately sublated in its quest for enlightenment or knowledge of Absolute Brahman.

Bhakti Yoga in Bhagavad Gita

Bhagavad Gita, a scripture accorded the status of a smriti, which Shankara chose to comment upon, has got numerous verses detailing the path of Bhakti; it even seemingly exalts the path of Karma/Bhakti over Jnana. For instance, in this verse, Arjuna asks Krishna to give his judgment of which out of the two paths – Jnana or Bhakti is better.

"In this manner, there are devotees who, abidingly committed, meditate upon you. Some seek you as one who is not subject to decline and not available for objectification. Who among them are the greatest knowers of yoga?" (B.G. 12.1)

Krishna answers here conclusively that those who follow the path of karma/devotion to form are the greater yogis,

"Endowed with steadfast faith, their minds committed to me, being ever united with me, those who meditate upon me are considered by me as the most exalted." (B.G. 12.2)

And then he says that those who follow the path of knowledge reach liberation (gain me).

"However, those who contemplate upon that which is not subject to decline, indefinable, not available for objectification, all-pervasive, not an object of thought, abides in Maya. It does not move and is eternal-those who have complete mastery over the group of sense organs, who are equal-minded and take delight in the welfare of all beings, gain me." (B.G 12.3-12.4)

A superficial reading of the verses may seem to indicate that Krishna is exalting the path of Karma/Bhakti over Jnana. But a careful reading would reveal something else. In verse 12.2, though he says that the Karma/Bhakti Yogi is the most exalted, he does not say that he reaches him as he speaks for the jnani in the verses 12.3-4 (Those who contemplate on that which is not subject to decline-gain me)

In the next verse, Krishna unequivocally declares that the path of Jnana is much more complex than the path of Karma/Bhakti Yoga because one has to give up one's body as false. With Karma/Bhakti Yoga, the mind is prepared for recognizing the body as a mere superimposition on Atma.

Greater is the affliction for those whose minds are committed to what cannot be objectified, for an end that cannot be objectified is reached with difficulty by those identified with the body. (B.G. 12.5)

Even in verses where Krishna is speaking in the first-person singular, he is not speaking about himself as God but as Absolute Brahman. Therefore, this verse should make it clear where he clearly distinguishes between the world of Gods and his Absolute world.

Those who are committed to the gods reach the world of gods. Those who are committed to the manes reach the plane of the manes. Those who worship the spirits go to the realm of the spirits. Whereas those who worship me reach me. (B.G. 9.25)

But not everyone who is called to the task of realizing the Absolute/Brahman is ready for a path leading to the transcendence of all the finite elements in the personality. To some, it suggests the prospect of impoverishment or extinction. Hence, it is understandable that at a later time, other teachers, such as Ramanuja, Nimbarka, and Vallabhacarya, should have arisen and made a different synthesis of the Upanishadic teaching, regarding the highest result of it as a condition in which the soul retained its individuality. But it remained in perpetual proximity with and adoration of the Lord of the Universe, conceived in personal form and understood as the great whole of which the individual worshipper was a tiny part[1].

Shankara's View on Bhakti/Worship

But Sankara adhered to the principle of transcendence that had been enunciated in the earliest Upanishads.

"That which is not seen by the eye, but which beholds the activities of the eye — know that, verily, is the Absolute (Brahman) and not what people here adore" (Kena Up. 1.7 or 1.6)

He could not accept that deliverance from the bondage of illusion and plurality had been attained as long as the notion of any difference between the worshipper and the object of his worship remained. Hence, he regarded the theistic teachings of the ancient texts as provisional doctrine, aimed partly at introducing the student to the pure transcendent principle through clothing it in forms which he could readily conceive and partly at preserving him from the grosser errors of materialism and spiritual negligence. He did not regard them as statements of the final truth. Sankara's writings have been regarded as providing the classical formulation of Indian wisdom because of his strict adherence to the principle of transcendence. He alone could account for all the Upanishadic texts. None of the pantheistic and theistic commentators who followed him were able to give satisfactory explanations of the negative texts that deny all the Absolute's empirical predicates. And yet, as I have shown earlier in my Chapter "The Origin of Advaita," a tradition (sampradaya) which judged these negative statements to be the critical texts of the entire Veda had existed long before Sankara's day. [2]

The individual Upanishadic sages voiced their sublime intuitions in the language of myth and symbol. Since the verses of Upanishads are full of complexity and contradictions, as I mention in my Chapter "The Puzzle of the Upanishads," as a traditional commentator and apologist, committed to the task of presenting all the texts as harmonious expressions of a single view, Sankara was sometimes forced to translate the vivid imagery of the sages into the paler but more precise language of conceptual thought. Further, he had to subject their formulae to a degree of systematization. The scholars of the Upanishads merely condemned the world and its finite objects as paltry and insignificant (alpa) in comparison with the Infinite (bhuman4)[Chand. VII. xxiii. 1, xxiv. 1.] In their most inspired moments, however, they had spoken of the Absolute in purely negative terms as beyond all human predication. Sankara saw that all the intuitions of the earlier sages could be taken into account and presented as forming a single system if all plurality was regarded as totally illusory from the standpoint of the highest truth. He held that the Upanishadic texts, which smack of dualism, pluralism, or theism, are mere provisional affirmations of practical utility to the student. For what is non-dual by nature can only be communicated through texts which first assert its existence clothed in recognizable empirical characteristics and then subsequently deny these empirical characteristics. This was already a recognized principle amongst those who knew the true tradition (sampradiya-vid) for interpreting the Upanishads before Sankara's day [3], so he was not introducing anything new in applying it. [4]

Shankara: Vaishnavism and Shaivism

Determination of Shankara's Original Works

Despite Sankara's unequivocal non-dual stance, there are a number of devotional hymns and works attributed to Sankara, which again bewilder a seeker as to why a staunch Jnani likes Shankara should compose such works.

Determination of the authenticity of Śaṅkara's works is complicated on two counts: there are far too many to carry the conviction that an individual could have authored so much, and that, too, within such a short lifespan. So, the rift between the traditionalists and the modern researchers becomes even more expansive, with the latter narrowing them down to just a handful. Besides, skepticism also abounds regarding the broad spectrum of works that he is said to have composed.

G.C. Pande states that 'the different catalogs ascribe nearly 400 works of different kinds to Shaṅkara'. However, after assessing this problem exhaustively, taking into account the traditional view and the opinions of scholars, especially G.V. Kaviraj, Baldev Upadhyaya, S.K. Belvalkar, Hacker, and Mayeda[5], almost all works are met with skepticism. One can see that all are in agreement only about the authenticity of Śaṅkara's prasthānatraya commentaries (bhāṣyas). They are the commentaries on the ten classical Upaniṣads, namely the Bṛhadāraṇyaka, Chāndogya, Īśa, Kena (has two commentaries), Katha, Taittirīya, Aitareya, Muṇḍaka, Māṇḍūkya and Gauḍapāda's Kārikā on it, and the Praśna Upaniṣads, the Bhagavad-gītā and the Brahma-sūtra. Among the independent works (prakaraṇa), the Upadeśa Sāhasri, his commentary on the Adhyātmapaṭala of the Āpastamba-dharma-sūtra and the Yoga-sūtra-bhāṣya-vivaraṇa also meet with approval by the majority.

There are a number of devotional works attributed to Shankara like Dakṣiṇāmūrti-stotra (Mānasollāsa being Sureśvara's vārtika on it), Bhaja Govindam, Mānīsāpañcakam,

DaśaŚloki, Govindāṣṭakam, and the Harimīde-stotra. Also, there is a popular song called Nirvanashatkam attributed to Shankara, as well as a popular commentary of Viṣṇu-sahasranāma-stotra. Though the current Advaita tradition reveres them as compositions of Sankara, scholars are not unanimous in their opinion, as can be seen from the previous passages. These holy books talk about two Gods – Shiva and Vishnu. Did Sankara, being an Advaitin, worship any of these two Gods? The most reliable way is to look into his works agreed to be genuine undisputedly by all scholars – the prasthānatraya commentaries (bhāṣyas).

Shankara's References to Smriti Works – Puranas

Shankara, in common with most of his co-religionists, distinguished between the texts of the Veda (Sruti), regarded as eternal and inviolable, and the 'derivative' texts called 'Smriti,' traditional Sanskrit lore that was regarded as authoritative because derived directly or indirectly from Vedic authority, but also as fallible because of human origin, and therefore subject to correction when it could be shown to contradict the Veda. For Sankara, the essential Smriti texts were the Law Books (Dharma Sastra), notably those ascribed to Manu, Yajnavalkya, Gautama, and Apastamba, the two Epics (the Mahabharata and the Ramayana), and certain Puranas. Sankara only occasionally refers to the Ramayana or the Mahabharata, apart from the Twelfth Book (the Santi Parvan) and the Gita. He attributes the Mahabharata and all the Puranic texts he knew of collectively to Vyasa. It is impossible to conclude his spiritual affiliations from stray identifications of his quotations from the Puranas made by modem translators, as the verses he quotes are sometimes found in several different works[6]. The Visnu Purana, however, would appear to predominate. There are no references to the Bhagavata Purana, the most exemplary text of them all and the closest to Sankara in spirit and metaphysical outlook. It was probably composed shortly after his day and partly under the influence of his writings and perhaps of those of his earliest followers.[7] [8]

History Behind Worship of Gods – Shiva and Vishnu

These Smrti works, especially the Epics and Puranas, embody what amounts to a new form of religion that had already begun to rise and spread before 300 BC. And which for a long time flourished under Brahminical patronage in more or less amicable partnership with the strictly Vedic form of worship, and then gradually, during the Middle Ages, virtually came to supplant it. Greatly simplifying and omitting all reference to the importance of Brahmi at an earlier stage, we may speak of it as the religion of Visnu-worship (Vaishnavism) and Siva-worship (Shaivism).[9]

We have seen that already before the Upanishadic period; the Vedic priests had begun to lose respect for the ancient Vedic gods. As living presences, the deities were forgotten, while the priests occupied themselves with the meticulous performance of complicated ritual from which material benefits were expected eventually to flow. This mentality persisted in certain Brahminical circles. It was attacked in the Gita. [Bh.G. 11.41-49.] And it was represented in Sankara's own day by the Purva Mimamsakas, the professional technicians of the Vedic ritual, towards whom he was not sympathetic.

But not all the upper castes retained their interest in Vedic ritual. It must be remembered that, particularly after Alexander's invasion (327-325 BC), the north Indian plains had been regularly exposed to barbarian conquest. Some of the invaders settled and extended their patronage to Buddhism and Jainism, and other religions which rejected caste. The Brahmins and their upper-caste co-religionists responded by broadening the basis of their own support. Non-Aryan cults had always flourished among the humbler sections of society, and gradually many of them came to be adopted, in modified form, by the upper castes themselves. The Brahmins developed the legendary parts of their own traditions and absorbed some elements from local and non-Aryan cults. The outcome was a new body of religious tradition focused on the old Vedic deities Visnu and Siva, now elevated by their worshippers to the status of a supreme deity. Unlike Vedic ritualism, the new cults were predominantly devotional in character. Honour, not to say reverence and adoration, was restored to the deity. It is convenient to speak of those votaries of the new sects who accepted the old Vedic caste system and observed the code of the Law Books, the Smrti par excellence, as 'Smarta' Vaishnavas or Shaivas, to be distinguished from those Vaishnava and Shaiva sects which rejected the Vedic traditions outright. The new cults evolved their own forms of ritual, mainly consisting of image worship (puja) in temples, a form of religion unknown in the Vedic texts. [10]

New meditative techniques for gaining contact with the deity on the mental plane were also adopted. Amongst these may be included the practice of repetition of the Name of God with a rosary in such formulae (mantra) as 'Om namo Vasudevaya' or 'Om namah Sivaya', both attested before Sankara's day. The final goal of such worship was usually some form of intimate association with the deity after death, in his 'heaven' or 'world', together with perhaps a foretaste of this beatitude here below. [11]

Shankara's Writings: Earliest Surviving Synthesis of Upanishads and Vaishnavism and Shaivism

Shankara's writings provide the earliest surviving synthesis of the Upanishadic wisdom with the Vaishnava and Shaiva teachings of the Smriti. Hence, his followers are not unjustly regarded as a storehouse of compassion and Vedic, Smrti and Purana lore'. He did not regard the more recent practices taught in the Smrtis, such as temple worship or repetition of the Name of God, as forming part of the discipline of the monk who had embarked on the Upanishadic path to liberation.[12] But he held them to be efficacious for the preliminary purification of the mind. And it appears that his impulse to search for the Absolute on the Upanishadic path may well have owed something to a pious upbringing in a Smarta Vaishnava environment. There is little in his commentaries to connect him with Siva worship. But he invokes Narayana, equatable with Visnu, at the beginning of his Gita commentary in what the sub-commentator Anandagiri calls an obeisance to his chosen deity (ista-devata). And part of the verse in which he does so appears in the course of his statement of the doctrine of the Bhagavata/ Pancaratra school of Vaishnavas in his commentary on Brahma Sutra II.ii.42. He there says: 'There are parts of this (Pancaratra Vaishnava) doctrine which we do not deny. 'We do not deny that Narayana is the Supreme Being, beyond the Unmanifest Principle, widely acknowledged to be the supreme Self, the Self of all... Nor do we see anything wrong if anyone is inclined to worship the Lord (bhagavan) vehemently and one-pointedly by visits to His temple and the rest, for the adoration of the Lord is well-known to have been prescribed (as a preliminary discipline) in the Veda and Smrti'. [13] (Further, in the same para, he goes on to deny that any individual soul can be born from the supreme Self)

As elsewhere in Sankara's writings, knowledge and devotion, Jnana and Bhakti, are fused. Though, as mentioned earlier, we cannot say for sure that any of the devotional hymns attributed to Sankara are genuine, there can be little doubt that he had the capacity for composing devotional poetry of a high order. [14]

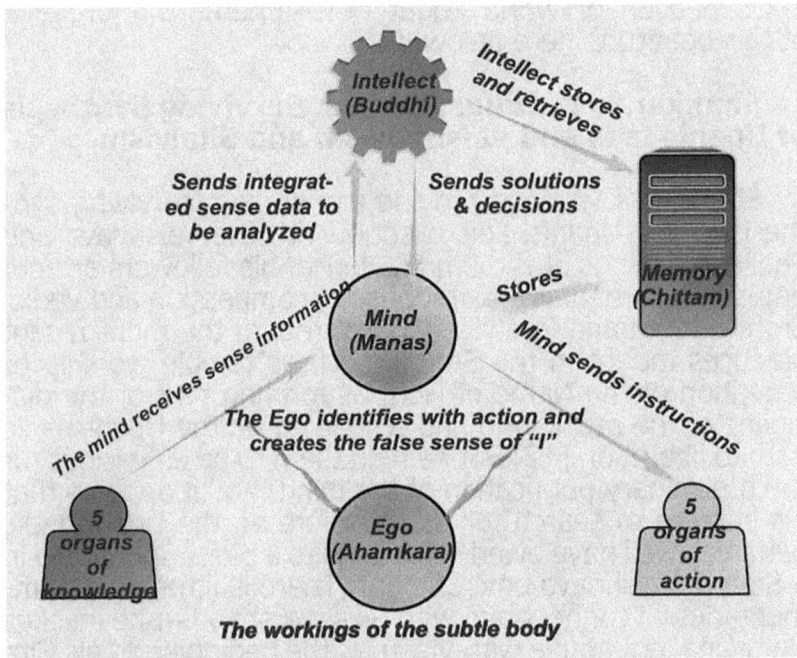

The workings of the subtle body

Did Shankara Worship Shiva and Vishnu?

Whether Sankara also worshipped Siva and Visnu must be accounted doubtful in the present state of our knowledge. We have seen that there is little evidence of it in his commentaries. But we have the verse commentary called the Manasollisa Varttika attributed to his pupil Suresvara on the Shaiva hymn called the Daksinamirti Stotra attributed to himself. On the one hand, the authenticity of the commentary is doubtful, and even if proven, there would still be, as its learned editor remarks, nothing in it to connect Sankara with the hymn. Indeed, the absence of any eulogistic references to Sankara is unparalleled in Suresvara's certainly original works. On the other hand, certain features of the comments suggest that Suresvara may have been its original author. And there is a passage in the Brahma Sutra Commentary of the early post-Sankara author Bhaskara. He appears to be recalling the image of a perforated pot inverted and placed over a light that occurs in the hymn and attributing it to Sankara.[15] Suppose the Manasollasa and the Daksinamirti Stotra are works of Suresvara and Sankara, respectively. In that case, this will point to a sojourn in Kashmir, as both speak the language of Kashmiri Shaivism in places. Thus, whereas Sahkara's connection with Vaishnavism is certain and emphatic, his connection with Shaivism is highly prob-lematic and, if it existed at all, may have occurred in Kashmir. [16]

Shankara Never Supported Shaivism Tantrika Worship

The more developed and independent form of Shaivism associated with the name 'Tantra' had already begun to flour-ish before Sankara's day. Although certain Tantrika hymns have come down falsely associated with his name, there is no trace of the influence of Tantrika ideas in his commentaries.

Tantrika ritual was 'anti-Vedic' in being specifically designed to supplant the Vedic ritual and meditation. Cer-tain branches of it included woman-worship in both its loftier and cruder forms. Sankara attacked the orgiastic variety of Tantrika worship as sinful according to Vedic law.[17][18]

Conclusion

So from all the evidence presented in this Chapter, it is safe to assume that Shankara never considered any form of Karma/Bhakti Yoga to lead to ultimate enlightenment. Also, despite the contradicting claims of the latter-day Dualist and Qualified Non-Dualist schools, we see that the srutis (Upanishads) and the smriti (Bhagavad Gita) do not speak about any dualistic action like worship/meditation/chanting as leading to ultimate enlightenment. Even when the Upa-nishadic texts smack of dualism, pluralism, or theism, they are mere provisional affirmations of practical utility to the student. The Brhadaranyaka verse I quoted at the beginning of this Chapter is one of the several verses scattered in different Upanishads which deny any creator God as the absolute reality. The survey of all undisputed works of Shankara, who is the earliest commentator on the prasthanatrayas whose writings are known to us, too, show that there is no conclusive evidence to prove that Shankara endorsed Karma/Bhakti Yoga or any action as a final means of liberation. True, as the Chapter illustrates, he showed that he shared some affinities with Vaishnavism. Yet, he was a faithful follower of the sampradaya of non-duality, which only accepts conditionings on Brahman provisionally for the sake of the student. Ultimately all of them have to be negated to intuit the final non-dual Brahman: God being conditioning to be negated like all other conditionings.

Notes

[1] – Sankara Source Book Volume 1 – Sankara on the Absolute by A. J. Alston (2004), page 1

[2] – Ibid, page 2

[3] – Bh.G.Bh. XIII. 13, trans. Shastri, 349. Such teachings may be traced as at least implicitly present in Sundara Pandya, cp. Kuppuswami Shastri in J.O.R.M., Vol.I., 6

[4] – Sankara Source Book Volume 1 – Sankara on the Absolute by A. J. Alston (2004), page 6

[5] – G.C. Pande, Life and Thought of Śaṅkarācārya, Delhi: Motilal Banarsidass, 1994.pp. 104–29

[6] – Hazra, 20, Note 31

[7] – Gail, 9-16; Hacker, Prahlada, 125 and 126.

[8] – Sankara Source Book Volume 1 – Sankara on the Absolute by A. J. Alston (2004), page 7

[9] – Ibid

[10] – Ibid, page 8

[11] – Ibid, page 9

[12] – Shankara refers to the repetition of the name in describing the Pancaratra discipline at B.S.Bh. II.ii.42 and in describing the practices appropriate for widowers and outcasts at B.S.Bh.III.iv.38. Probably it is included under the term 'other practices' in describing samradhana at B.S.Bh. III.ii.24, and understood as a preliminary purifying practice. Elsewhere in his writing, 'japa' and 'svadhyaya' probably refer exclusively to the repetition of Vedic mantrams and the syllable O.M., and not to the 'repetition of the Name' in the modem sense.

[13] – Sankara Source Book Volume 1 – Sankara on the Absolute by A. J. Alston (2004), page 9

[14] – Ibid, page 10

[15] – Bhaskara's B.S.Bh., 7. Note the introduction of the image at Brhad. Bh. I.v.17, trans. Madhavananda, 161.

[16] – Sankara Source Book Volume 1 – Sankara on the Absolute by A. J. Alston (2004), page 12

[17] – Anandagiri ad B.S.Bh.III.iv.II. See Hacker, Texte, 114, Note 2 and Madhusudana ad Sarvajnatman, III. 18.

[18] – Sankara Source Book Volume 1 – Sankara on the Absolute by A. J. Alston (2004), page 13

Consciousness is Everything (Part I)

Since origination is not a well-established fact, it is declared (by the Upanishads) that everything is birthless.

In this Chapter, I am presenting a journal of a student of the NEEV Advaita Study Facebook Group. He happens to be a 15 yr old boy studying in the 11th grade who discusses Advaita with me while doing his homework. Recently he sent me a journal, feverishly written, describing the understanding he gained about how everything, including himself, is in reality Consciousness, and he is not a person. The journal was quite long and, given his age, quite understandably a jumble of thoughts with gems of understanding buried in them. I am presenting his diary in this Chapter, removing extraneous material but leaving his language and expression untouched to give readers the genuine flavor of his understanding and expression. This sacrifices the clarity of concepts of Advaita. But I wanted to give a snapshot of the process of getting clarity in Advaita through my student's journal. At any rate, I have provided a clear account of Advaita concepts in my response.

In this Chapter is about my response to his journal, I show how uncannily he has managed to pack all the four Mahavakyas of Advaita. Mahavakyas of Advaita are "great statements" that serve as signposts for the journey of a seeker in the path of Advaita from ignorance to enlightenment. Thus, I use my student's journal as a base to explicate the four Mahavakyas and how they serve as signposts in the journey of a seeker.

In Part 2 of Chapter, I shall delve into the other aspect

of my student's journal, which is about the nature of the relationship between Consciousness, Mind, and God.

Krishna's Journal:
When Consciousness is projecting a suffering body-mind, the body-mind is coming, suffering, enjoying, and going. Whether the mind is ignorant, or enlightened, or whatever, it does not affect Consciousness. The same Consciousness is illumining the basic insects and the tigers and the animals and humans. There is no good or bad. All are working according to their own samskaras and karma and working as nature wills them to, as the Lord wills them to.

Not just a peaceful mind is Consciousness, but the CONSCIOUSNESS IS GROUND OR WHOLE OF REALITY. SUFFERING, HAPPINESS, EVERYTHING IS CONSCIOUSNESS. That's why Anurag sir says there is no "bliss of Brahman," as people understand it. For unenlightened people or enlightened people, CONSCIOUSNESS is the same. So there is something funny in saying, "I know that I am consciousness, but they do not know they are consciousness, so it is my duty to help them know they are consciousness" NO, they are already CONSCIOUSNESS. They ARE CONSCIOUSNESS.

The Jiva may be unenlightened, but there is no way to make the Jiva enlightened unless the machine permutation in that unit, that is, that particular Jiva dissolves enough or that the mind shuts down enough and says it is enlightened. But CONSCIOUSNESS IS EVER SAME, and this knowledge is coming to the unit jiva, the permutation in the machine.

The body-mind turning inward and losing its identification by itself lets the consciousness shine. The person never becomes Consciousness. It is not that the person is the Consciousness. No, I am the Consciousness watching the "person i" occur in the universe that is happening in the Consciousness. That I am, and all that happened, happened because it had to happen by His Will. Everything is just happening; responses are coming; people feel that they have free will, and he is thinking guiltily, maybe doubting his thoughts; but the mind that is questioning, the mind that is thinking, is itself a helpless part of the world. It is a coordinating system like the CPU of a computer, illumining and giving coherence to the functions. It is just a part of an organic whole (Universe), and this organic whole is illumined by Consciousness. So the whole is known by Consciousness; the mind is known by Consciousness, and the knowing function of the mind that knows, the known objects, and even the function of the mind that wonders why Consciousness is somehow illumining the mind and knowing the world through the mind ... is in reality/Consciousness's "knower" aspect.

Consciousness is the mind, and it is knowing everything at once as "I am consciousness." But it does not know anything; at the same time, it knows everything; it just - is. It is inexpressible, yes! But there is no mind that it will use to look through to the world like a telescope. No, it is just experiencing itself, and the infinite objects so-called that is all just itself through and through not little appearances or big appearances it is not like a vast space. It is reality: the ground of reality. No, no, not even that, just the reality.

So anyway, the mind is a coordinating system; and even right now, the guilt and the fear of being wrong that it is feeling for pursuing self-inquiry. A strange mystery is not being "of use to the world" somehow and presenting fear-based solutions and fear-based rejections of those solutions. It is both superficial and lacking any deeper layers, but with the power to invent deeper layers, the more it investigates because it works with the law of cause and effect. Even the investigation of the web of cause and effect is a part of cause and effect. So the guilty feeling, the urge to watch the insight moment, the suppression and the fear, the initial action and the sudden burst of activity after a long build-up, is all his infinite grace. Because his grace is ever-flowing. So even the guilt of thinking that thinking about this "long build-up" is undermining his grace is also a part of the web of cause and effect. Because if his grace is ever-flowing, then his grace is cause and effect!!! His grace is the vidya, Maya.

So the mind does not exist but as a mere constant flow of objects in Consciousness. Yes, so this tallies with the intuitions coming from contemplating the fact that there is no proof for the last moment's existence or this moment's presence by the time I write this and the next moment has begun. You can't define what "length of time" is a moment. It is a flow, so infinite flow is also infinite stillness! So observe the mind and surrender to Him. To the Lord.

Anurag:

As I read your journal, I could experience the excitement of discovery coursing through your veins. So now you are initiated into the gates of non-duality. It is a conceptual understanding of non-duality but a powerful one, undoubtedly going to affect your life fundamentally. And considering that you are all just 15 yrs old, I would say that what you have written and tried to explain is simply phenomenal. At 15 years, I was like a kitten whose eyes had not even opened to the world of spirituality, let alone the world of non-duality. Even when they did, I did not encounter the word "non-duality" in my spiritual journey till I was about 36 years old. Even amongst spiritual aspirants, to get a glimpse of even a conceptual understanding of non-duality is considerably rare. So before I proceed further with my response, I should let you know that whatever you have discovered and written in this journal is a rare gem that is bestowed to rare people at such an early age. Now it is up to you how to prize it, cultivate it further, and make it reach full fruition. But please do not allow this praise to lodge in your mind and become vanity. Conceptual understanding is one thing, a complete transformation so that understanding becomes part of the experience is a very long road with many dark nights.

Your understanding has already touched a very high level in this journal. I am only going to illustrate it further with concepts from Advaita. I am also going to take the understanding in the journal further. What you have written is almost touching the heights, but there is a conception of Lord, Isvara, or Creator that is still lurking, which is also transcended in the peak of Shankara's Advaita. I am not doing this to show a limitation in your understanding as you are already far, far ahead, considering your age, but I am doing this just for the sake of readers who can learn Advaita by going through this Chapter. Your journal provides a wonderful launching pad to speak about the highest truth of Advaita as it is revealed through the stages outlined by the four Mahavakyas of Advaita. I shall show how in your journal you have uncannily written about every single stage.

The Four Mahavakyas of Advaita

These four Mahavakyas – Statements of Ultimate Truth – chart the progress of a student as he/she assimilates the non-dual wisdom of Advaita. Your journal shows that you have finally broken through a dualistic framework of understanding reality and come to a non-dual understanding, as indicated by the first two Mahavakyas. You wrote:

"Whether the mind is ignorant, or enlightened, or whatever, it does not affect the Consciousness. The same Consciousness is illumining the basic insects and the tigers and the animals and humans."

"But was the Consciousness not there before too? Not just a peaceful mind is Consciousness, but the CONSCIOUSNESS IS GROUND OF WHOLE OF REALITY. SUFFERING, HAPPINESS, EVERYTHING IS CONSCIOUSNESS."

Your journal clearly indicates that you now see Consciousness is the primary reality and that you are actually that Consciousness in this very moment. In fact, you have always been Consciousness since that is the ultimate reality. Thus, whether you are enlightened or unenlightened, you are always Consciousness. This is something very difficult for people to understand because they take themselves to be a person and believe that they have to become a "better person" through enlightenment. But Advaita is saying something very amazing. It is saying that you have never been a person at any time. However, this understanding does make you a "person" free of all afflictive emotions and suffering eventually. The first Mahavakya makes you familiar with the ultimate truth – what it is? It says that you are not a person in essence but Consciousness/Brahman/Non-Dual Knowledge. I wrote in detail about this misunderstanding of people in my Chapter "Tat Tvam Asi – You are Brahman." In Advaita, Brahman is a synonym of Consciousness.

The Inconceivability of Brahman/Consciousness

Please note that Brahman/Consciousness here does not mean some substance or entity, or form. Brahman is frequently referred to as a Subject in Advaita. People get confused with this word. Since the word subject (without a capital 'S') usually refers to a person in common English, Brahman is often taken to be some form of the person. Brahman is inconceivable. It is not anything that the mind can conceive. This is very important to understand. Any conception of ultimate truth is not the ultimate truth. Brahman is just a word we used to communicate the Ultimate Truth.

The same can be called – Awareness, Consciousness, Self, Purusha, Atman, Turiya, Absolute or Ultimate – as long as we are sure that these words mean that they are "nirguna" or "attributeless. " Brahman is referred to as Subject in Advaita, only to indicate that Ultimate Truth can never be objectified and made an object of experience. However, we can speak about truth conceptually or objectively to teach as I am doing now. However, the experience of truth itself is inconceivable and ineffable. This verse from Mandukya Upanishad best brings out the inconceivability of Brahman. Ultimate reality, in this verse, is denoted as Turiya:

Nantah-prajnam na bahis-prajnam nobhayatah
prajnam na prajnana-ghanam na prajnam naprajnam,
adrstam-avyavaharyam-agrahyam-alaksanam
acintyam-avyapadesyam-ekatma-pratyaya-saram
prapanco-pasamam santam Sivam-advaitam
caturtham manyante sa atma sa vijneyah.

Verse 7: Turīya is not that which is conscious of the internal (subjective) world, nor that which is conscious of the external (objective) world, nor that which is conscious of both, nor that which is a mass all sentiency, nor that which is simple Consciousness, nor that which is insentient. (It is) unseen (by any sense organ), not related to anything, incomprehensible (by the mind), uninferable, unthinkable, indescribable, essentially of the nature of Consciousness5 constituting the Self alone, a negation of all phenomena, the Peaceful, all bliss and the Non-dual. This is what is known as the fourth (Turīya). This is the Ātman, and it has to be realized. ~ Mandukya Upanishad

You referred to this inconceivability in your journal here:

"Consciousness is the mind, and it knows everything at once as, "I am consciousness." But it does not know anything; at the same time, it knows everything; it just - is. It is inexpressible, yes! But there is no mind that it will use to look through to the world like a telescope. No, it is just experiencing itself, and the infinite objects so-called that is all just itself through and through not little appearances or big appearances it is not like a vast space. It is reality: the ground of reality. No, no, not even that, just the reality."

Through your words, one can witness the struggle your

mind is undergoing to grasp the inconceivable, to express the inexpressible. You start with many words of description, but towards the end of the para, you realize that the more the number of words you use or conditioning attributes you use, the further away you move away from reality. Thus, towards the end, you wisely resign by the phrase, "It is reality: the ground of reality. No, no, not even that, just the reality."

Suppose you compare what you have written with the verse from Mandukya Upanishad [Ma. Up.], you shall notice that Ma. Up. has made one refutation which you have included in your description of reality. It is in these lines of yours, "No, it is just experiencing itself, and the infinite objects so-called that is all just itself through and through. " Though you have also negated "knowing of objects" in these lines, "But it does not know anything; at the same time it knows everything;" There seems to be an uneasy tension in you to accommodate "not knowing anything" with "knowing everything." It's counter-intuitive. Generally, we would grant "all-knowingness" or omniscience a higher pedestal than "not knowing." This is where the non-dual instinct has to kick in. As jivas with limited knowledge, we are clamoring for power that comes from infinite knowledge. Thus, we set up a duality relation between the Jiva (an entity with limited knowledge) and Isvara/Lord/Creator (an entity with infinite knowledge). We cannot conceive of ultimate reality as total inaction. An Advaitin can see the tension of this duality running right through your journal. You end your journal with the words, "So observe the mind and surrender to Him. To the Lord." Despite your commendable and courageous attempt to decode duality, which you almost did, this duality between Brahman/Ultimate Reality and Isvara persists. And this difference makes all the difference between duality and non-duality. Because till there is an Isvara, there is a Jiva. Both go together.

Therefore, Ma. Up. in verse 7 quoted above, negates even "all-knowing" Isvara pithily by the words, "nor that which is simple Consciousness. " The note to this, provided by me at the end of the verse, expands its full meaning, denying ultimate reality to be an all-knowing Isvara too. Why? Because Isvara still knows objects. There is still a subject-object duality there. Therefore, the ultimate reality is knowledge without any object.

Prajnanam Brahman – Knowing Brahman

The first Mahavakya is called Lakshana Vakya because it is indicating the nature of Ultimate Reality as Non-Dual Consciousness. The Mandukya Upanishad, too, despite its resounding negations, helps to indicate the reality with the words "ekatma-pratyaya-saram" or "essentially of the nature of Consciousness." But we have to understand the word Consciousness, again, as what is called a "non-affirming negation." It means that the ultimate reality is non-void: it exists, and also, it is not inert like matter but of the nature of illuminating knowledge. Anandagiri, an ancient Advaitin, and commentator writing in his commentary to Mandukya Up. verse 7:

"The elimination of all the attributes may make Turīya appear as a void to the unwary student. Therefore, it is described as a positive existence which can be realized by spotting it as the changeless and the constant factor in the three states. The states, no doubt, do change, but there is a unity of the subject implied in the conscious experience of "I am that perceiver" common to all the three states."

So basically, Reality is Consciousness or Knowledge as such, wherein it has no objects to qualify. It is that knowledge that does not even have any duality as the Jiva and Isvara. The best way to put it, therefore, is that it is a "knowingness" or "Awareness." Metaphorically it can be said to be light. Chandogya Upanishad refers to knowing Brahman as "The Path of Light." In fact, some paths like Tibetan Dzogchen Buddhism also use the word light to describe ultimate reality. Unlike all knowledge that is split by the subject-object duality, this knowledge has no suffering because of lack of division. Thus, the Ma. Up. Verse 7 provides some other nonaffirming attributes to this knowledge. They are

Prapanca-opasanman – it is the absence of all plurality of the phenomenal world.

Santam – Since there is an absence of phenomena, there is an absence of all conflict.

Sivam – Since there is an absence of plurality, conflict is absent, and there is no conflict; there is bliss.

Advaitam – It is the reality that has no other. If we said "one," it would imply that there is "two." To seal this possibility, we say that this is the only reality.

Thus, we see that the only attributes we have given to the ultimate reality is not in terms of positive attributes but indicating it by denying positive attributes as Neti, Neti - not this, not this. This is the way Brahman/Ultimate Reality is taught, not only in Advaita but in all non-dual systems. By employing such a via negativa approach, the non-dual paths are trying to achieve the stillness of mind. When the mind ceases to conceptualize, duality ends, and non-dual reality is revealed.

So, if you see carefully, the four Mahavakyas are a beautiful map of a seeker's journey – the first Mahavakya or Lakshana Mahavakya is indicating ultimate reality as Prajnanam – non-dual knowledge/Consciousness. This is the part that you have assimilated conceptually to a great extent. (Of course, you still have to get clear about your confusion between Isvara and Brahman)

Tat Tvam Asi – You Are Brahman

I have talked about this in detail in my Chapter Tat Tvam Asi – You are Brahman. The knowledge in the first vakya is purely conceptual. It is indicating the nature of the ultimate reality so that one can define the path or the direction that we are supposed to take. In one sweep, it has negated the entire phenomenal world, as Vivekachudamani, verse 387 says, "Right from Brahma (God/Creator) to the most insignificant unicellular organisms, all as conditionings are quite unreal. Therefore, One should realize one's Self/Awareness as the only existent principle." This prepares the mind of the seeker to go within. It has been explained to the seeker that Brahman is not some objective reality that can be seen, known, or experienced. So now, naturally, the question arises, how can one get to the truth if it cannot be known, seen, or experienced?

With this, we come to the second Mahavakya of Advaita, which is called the Upadesha Vakya. Upadesha means the spiritual guidance or instruction given by the teacher. This is a very significant turn in the journey of a seeker. While a sincere seeker could have somewhat assimilated the "Lakshan Vakya" which defines reality as Consciousness or

Awareness through mere independent reading of scriptures, he shall still be at a loss to locate it. The inveterate tendency of the mind is to locate it as some object of experience or knowledge. This is because avidya or ignorance is the cause of the mind, so it is prior to the emergence of the mind. The mind is an offspring of ignorance. Through the mind, by the time one has come to know oneself as a Jiva or an "individual knowing subject" in a Jagat – plural world of objects, one is already in the realm created by ignorance after getting up from sleep. Thus, the conceptual mind, no matter how hard it tries, is going to be like a snake eating its tail. It is only the teacher – "the knower of Brahman" who has ended "avidya" in himself and who is well versed with the traditional teaching methodology of Advaita called Agama (Superimposition followed by Rescission/Cancellation), who can help the seeker understand the non-dual reality. I have written about this methodology in Chapter "Method of Upanishads to Convey Ultimate Reality: Brahman".

After this detour, we can come back to our question, "How can one get to the truth if it cannot be known, seen, or experienced?". The Lakshana Vakya has already conceptually eliminated all objects of knowledge and experience as truth, so there is only one candidate left, "YOU." "YOU ARE THE TRUTH." This is startling. I remember when I had the akhandakara vritti, which helped me reach Self-Realization (see Chapter "Self inquiry and insight into one's true nature/ Self in Advaita"), I felt really stupid and foolish. The truth was evident all along....in plain sight. Such is the nature of avidya. Later Advaita scholars used the word Maya for avidya more than perhaps Shankara did to bring out the "magical" nature of illusion. Maya fools you, tricks you like a magician. Of course, all this should not give the reader an illusion that one can simply hear the statement, "You are the Truth," and one shall reach Self Realization. One needs to have a qualified mind/adhikaritva to get Self Realization through mere listening of the statement the first time. If one has the qualifications, one reaches Self Realization instantly by listening to the second Mahavakya. Thus, Advaita is called Shabda Pramana. I have covered this in detail in my Chapter Enlightenment through Words.

For most of us, mere listening to the second Upadesha Mahavakya, does not do the trick. So there are three steps outlined in Jnana Yoga of Advaita – sravana/listening, manana/reflection and dialogue, nidhidhyasana – deep contemplation. If the first step fails, you go to the second; if even the second fails, you go to the third step, till you reach the final insight Aham Brahmasmi/"I am Awareness." During the Upadesha phase, where the student is receiving spiritual instructions from the teacher, various scriptures are studied, which continuously hammer home the point, "You are Awareness" through various methods or prakriyas. The primary method is, of course – superimposition and rescission – which I have stated. But since our minds are thick with subject-object duality, it needs an attack from multiple angles to understand that truth is not an object, but you are the truth and have always been the truth. One such method/prakriya is called the Avastha traya viveka, or knowing reality by examining the three states (waking, dreaming, and deep sleep). This technique is the kingpin of all prakriyas in Advaita. This is what we find in the Mandukya Upanishad. Hence, in the commentary to Ma. Up. Verse 7. Shankara writes:

"Hence it (Turīya) is "unseen"; and because it is unseen therefore it is "incomprehensible." Turiya cannot be apprehended by the organs of action. It is "uninferable" because there is no common characteristic for its inference. Therefore Turīya is "unthinkable" and hence "indescribable" (by words). It is "essentially of the nature of consciousness consisting of Self." Turīya should be known by spotting that Consciousness that never changes in the three states, viz., waking, etc., and whose nature is that of a Unitary Self. " ~ Mandukya Karika Bhashya by Shankaracharya

Or as Anandagiri in his commentary on the same verse mentions:

The states, no doubt, do change, but there is a unity of the subject implied in the conscious experience of "I am that perceiver" common to all the three states."

Basically, it is conveying what the second Upadesha Mahavakya is saying. Let us see how. The dreamer, sleeper and waker, are phenomenally so different that none of them can be you. Yet, you do not have a broken perception of yourself. In your waking state, you still consider that "YOU" were the same who slept and dreamt and who is awake now. This unchanging Witness of all three states is "YOU," and this

"YOU" is nothing but Turiya/Brahman/Consciousness/Awareness/Non-Dual Knowledge. You are not the waker, dreamer, or sleeper. You are not the body/mind/intellect that appears and dissolves in these states. I have covered all this in detail in my Chapter "Turiya : The Fourth State of Consciousness."

Now, the exciting thing is that you have issued the "Upadesha Vakya – You are Brahman" in your journal in these words of yours.

"So there is something funny in saying, "I know that I am consciousness, but they do not know they are consciousness, so it is my duty to help them know they are consciousness" NO, they are already CONSCIOUSNESS. They ARE CONSCIOUSNESS."

Aham Brahmasmi – I am Brahman

But the question is, how far did you get to understanding the second Mahavakya. You have written in your journal:
"The person never becomes Consciousness. It is not that the person is the Consciousness. No, I am the Consciousness watching the "person i" occur in the universe also occurring in the Consciousness. That I am."
This is the final Anubhava Vakya. You have written this without going through the third vakya or the Abhyasa Vakya.
So in a flash of inspiration, you have touched the final Mahavakya, which speaks about the final insight. But your statement is not an insight; quite far from being steady wisdom. Nonetheless, as I said at the beginning of this Chapter, at your age, it is very commendable that you are even thinking about these matters, let alone understand them.

Ayam Atma Brahma – This Self is Brahman

You have to go through the second Mahavakya, which means that the teacher has to unravel the teachings from many angles through different prakriyas/methods. Then, or along with it, comes the third or Abhyasa Mahavakya – the practice part. This part has to do mainly with mañana/reflection/dialogue and nidhidhyasana/deep contemplation. This is a long journey of purification of mind through jnana yoga. The mind of a seeker has got a lot of rajas/dissipativeness. A mere conceptual understanding reached in flashes is not enough. The mind has to become sattvic/pure and harmonious. When it comes to a sufficiently sattvic state, then one sees the reflection of Self in the sattvic intellect during meditation.

This is the point when the mind says, "This Self is Brahman," and further becomes ripe for the final insight of the fourth Mahavakya – I am Brahman, which you have written in your journal. This part of the journey is what I cover in the three inquiries on my Facebook Groups – Psycho-Philosophical Inquiry, Meditative Inquiry, and Advaitic Inquiry. One can read more about it on "Stages of Self Inquiry" page. This is, in most cases, a very long phase in the journey of a seeker. To your credit, you have captured this journey too in your journal in these words of yours:

"The jiva may be unenlightened, but there is no way to make the jiva enlightened unless the machine permutation in that unit, that is, that particular jiva dissolves enough or that the mind shuts down enough and says it is enlightened."

One must understand this phase of the journey, which involves meditation, that meditation involves the meditator and the object of meditation. Thus, it is an action involving a subject-object duality. It is an action, cannot be the means to liberation. The means to liberation is Self Knowledge that comes through like a flash of akhandakara vritti, "I am Brahman," which I have mentioned earlier in the Chapter. (see Chapter "Self-inquiry") Action always leads to the production of something. But the Self is not a thing. It is not produced. It is ever-existent. So the means to Self is not any action like meditation but knowledge. You are already Self; you have to know it. Meditation is only a means to make the mind subtle enough to discriminate between Self and not-Self. In his introduction to Chandogya Upanishad Bhashya, Shankara writes:

"These forms of Meditation and Worship bring about the purity of mind and character and thereby become illuminative of the real nature of things; to this extent, they are helpful in bringing about the Cognition6 of the One without a second. In as much as they are based upon a substratum, they are also easier of accomplishment. It is for these reasons that the Upanishads, first of all, sets forth these forms of

Meditation and Worship." ~ Chandogya Upanishad Bhashya, Shankaracharya

Consciousness is Everything (Part II)

In this Chapter, I would like to delve into the highest peak of Advaita: Ajativada. Gaudapada propounded the doctrine in Mandukya Karika. It reveals something quite unbelievable: It states that in the Absolute sense, the world, including oneself, is devoid of changes or mutations like birth, growth, death, etc. (Janmadivikiirarahita), as also it is devoid of all duality (Prapanchopashama). All this is verily Atman/Consciousness/Awareness/Self/Brahman alone. CREATION NEVER HAPPENED. I have written about it in my Chapter "Turiya : The Fourth State of Consciousness & End of Suffering". In that Chapter, my emphasis was more on helping the reader understand how the Mandukya Upanishad, through the analysis of the three states of waking, dreaming and sleep. This helps one know that the ultimate reality is the unborn non-dual reality, as described above, and how the phenomenal world is only real. I had written in my conclusion to this Chapter:

Analysis of the Three States and Turiya/Atman/Brahman/Non-Dual Reality

The Three Bodies

The first task of Mandukya Karika is to establish the nature of reality through the analysis of three states of waking, dreaming, and deep sleep. Since I have already done this in detail in my Chapter, "Turiya : The Fourth State of Consciousness & End of Suffering," I shall just do a lightning review of it here.

To go into the three states, we need first to understand the five sheaths or three bodies a Jiva is supposed to be composed of. "Composed of" is a shorthand way of saying that the "Jiva is Brahman conditioned by the three bodies/five sheaths." I shall give a detailed explanation of this later. I mentioned this point here intentionally to undercut the tendency in a reader's Mind to attribute any "substantiality" to any "phenomena." To deny a "substance attribute" to any phenomena and to show that all phenomena are nothing but dream-like "appearances" of a single reality called Brahman is, after all, the purpose of this Chapter.

All Jivas have a Gross Body which is made up of matter, a Subtle Body which is the Mind, and a Causal Body or Bliss Body because it is the body closest to Brahman and thus reflects the Bliss of Brahman. The Causal Body is given the name "Causal" because it is the cause for the projection of the other two bodies – subtle and gross. While we can perceive the gross body as our physical body and the subtle body as thoughts and internal images, we cannot perceive the Causal Body as it is formless. The Causal Body is likened to the seed which projects/ sprouts into the shoot of the subtle body and the tree of the gross body in the waking and dreaming states because it has got vasanas/memory of past lives stored in it according to which the Subtle and Gross bodies are projected. In the sleep state, there is only the Causal Body with the other two bodies withdrawn into it.

The Three States

According to Mandukya, the three states of Waking, Dreaming, and Deep Sleep are nothing but the worlds we experience because of the projection or withdrawal of the three bodies mentioned above. When we are in the Sleep State, we are in the Causal Body, which is formless. When we come to the dream state, the Causal Body has projected the Subtle Body, and when we come to the waking state, the Causal Body has also projected the Gross Body.

Based on the three states, one can now understand the phenomenal nature of the sleeper, dreamer, and waker. The term "vasanas" means memory. Through the stored vasanas, the Causal Body projects the other two bodies.

Analysis of the Three States

Having understood the above concepts we can go into

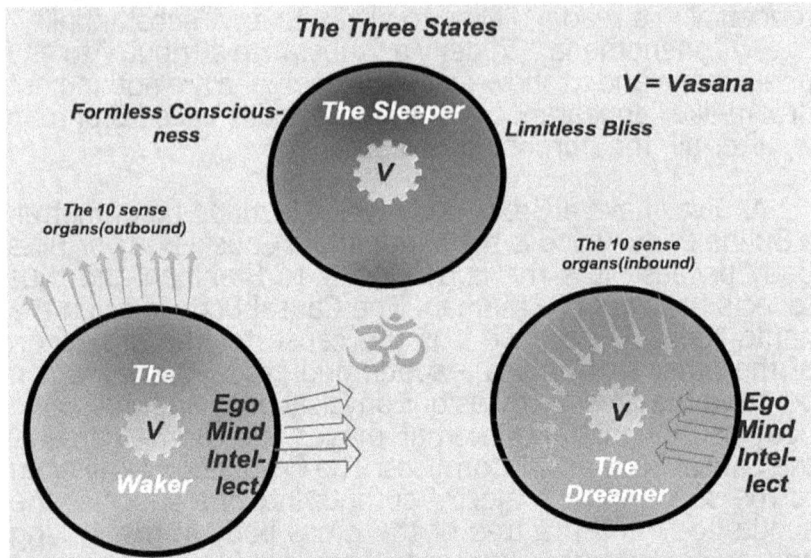

The Three States

how the Mandukya Upanishad analyses them to reveal Turiya/Brahman/Non-Dual Reality. The Upanishad asks one to appreciate the following by analysing the three states.

All three states appear and disappear to a common Seer/ Witness/Experiencer. In one's life, one intuitively assumes that one is the same waker, dreamer and sleeper even though the worlds of the sleeper, dreamer and waker are entirely different. What makes one assume that the same "I" persisted through the three states, even though one's ego-identity kept changing from being a waker to someone else as a dreamer (One may have become a child in one's dreams but is an adult as a waker) to no-one as a sleeper? When one wakes up from dream or sleep how does one have a memory of the dreamer and the sleeper? Memory is always about an experience. If there was no experiencer in the sleep state like we have in the dream and waking state, then who experienced the sleep state, which appears as a memory (I slept well) in the waking state?

Can the waking state, dream state or sleep state be real because all three states keep changing and the reality within one state, cancels the reality within another state? In the waking and dream states there is a phenomenal world of forms but in sleep state the entire phenomenal world including one's mind and body are wiped out? Can the phenomenal world which includes one's mind and body be real if it is absent in one of the three states?

The first point establishes the fact that the real "I" is not whom we are assuming ourselves to be – "The Waker". This is because it is absent in two of the three states. Reality can never cease to exist. When I get up, I don't feel that I am a different being from the one who slept and the one who dreamt. My sense of being is continuous. Neither the waker, dreamer or sleeper can be the one responsible for my continuous sense of being. It has to be something that is existent in all three states. What is it? It is Awareness/Consciousness/Witness/Turiya which is NOT the individual experiencer present in the waking and dream state and which is lost in the sleep state. Awareness/Consciousness/Witness/Turiya is the Ultimate Experiencer which persists even in the sleep state. This is our real "I"/Self. The second point establishes that the phenomenal world of objects, including our body-mind, we experience in the waking and dream states cannot be real because they are absent in the sleep state. Combining the two we can say in negative terms – "I am NOT the Body-Mind" or in positive terms, I can say – "I am Self/Awareness/Witness/Brahman/Atman/Turiya/Non-Dual Knowledge" which is beyond the three states of waking, sleeping and dreaming.

The final point one needs to appreciate is that the ultimate reality being formless, non-dual and beyond space and time (because it is Witness to the projection of space-time and the phenomenal world of forms in the waking and dream states and their dissolution in the sleep state) it cannot ever be said to be born. Thus, Ultimate Reality in Advaita is called Aja or unborn or birthless. All entities of relative existence possess six characteristics, such as birth, duration, growth, change, decay and death. Brahman/Self/Witness/Awareness is free from them.

The waking state experiencer is called Vishva, the dreaming state experiencer is called Taijasa, and the sleep state experiencer is called Prajna. None of them is who I am. I AM TURIYA/Brahman/Awareness on which appear Vishva, Taijas, and Prajna and the three sates of Waking, Dreaming, and Sleeping.

A Very Big Disclaimer – Brahman is not a Substance/Entity

Many individuals, Advaitins, and especially Buddhists think that the words Self/Turiya/Brahman/Atman indicate some "substantial" entity. It is ridiculous for anyone to think so, given the fact that Advaita establishes the Ultimate Reality after negating the world of forms (physical/gross and mental/subtle) as well as the formless world (causal). Gaudapada defines Ultimate Reality as Non-Dual Knowledge – which is the synonym for the words Consciousness or Awareness. Thus, we have the verse:

Verse 3.33: "The knowledge (Jñānam) which is unborn and free from all imaginations is ever inseparable from the knowable. The immutable and birthless Brahman is the sole object of knowledge. The birthless is known by the birthless."

Shankara's Commentary: The Knowers of Brahman describe the knowledge, i.e., the mere essence of thought, which is unborn and free from all imaginations as non-different from Brahman, the ultimate Reality, which is also the object of knowledge. This is supported by such Scriptural passages as, "Like heat from fire, knowledge (Jñānam) is never absent from the knower (Ātman)," "Brahman is Knowledge and Bliss," "Brahman is Reality, Knowledge and Infinity," etc.

Anandagiri's Gloss: The Jñānam or knowledge is the same as Brahman; otherwise, no knowledge would be able to tell us what Brahman is. Darkness cannot illumine the sun. Only the light of the sun, which is the sun itself, can illumine the sun.

Who/What is Isvara/God?: Maya

My student Krishna makes constant references to Isvara, the Lord who controls and directs the activities of different Jivas. Who is this Isvara or Lord? He is nothing but the Causal Body or Prajna. The following verse Mandukya verse and commentary by Shankara makes it quite clear:

Verse 5. "That is the state of deep sleep wherein the sleeper does not desire any objects nor does he see any dream. The third quarter (Pāda) is the Prājña whose sphere is deep sleep, in whom all (experiences) become unified or undifferentiated, who is verily, a mass of consciousness entire, who is full of Bliss and who experiences Bliss, and who is the path leading to the knowledge (of the two other states). "

Verse6: "This is the Lord of all; this is the knower of all; this is the controller within; this is the source of all, and this is that from which all things originate and in which they finally disappear. "

Shankara's commentary: This, in its natural state, is the Lord (Īśvara) of all. All, that is to say, of the entire physical and super-physical universe. He (Īśvara) is not something separate from the universe as others hold. The Śruti also says, "O good one, Prāṇa (Prājña or Īśvara) is that in which the mind is bound."

Our previous discussion on the three bodies would have made the above evident. The Causal Body is the source of the Subtle and Gross Worlds; thus, it is called Isvara. It contains the vasanas/memory/source code for the projection of the other two bodies and their corresponding worlds. (A dialogue on this can be found in my Chapter: "The Place of Devotion/Bhakti in Shankara Advaita"

So the analysis of the three states and the three bodies should make it clear to a reader that the world we experience is nothing but Brahman/Turiya/Awareness conditioned with the Causal Body/Isvara, which is nothing but a collection of past impressions stretching back to beginningless time. This Causal Body/Isvara is also called Maya.

Creation Theories

Gaudapada examines Maya once again through the analysis of various creation theories arising from the root concept of cause and effect. Maya is then also shown to be this false conception of cause and effect. It shall be shown that the beginning of all vasanas is in the first false root conception of cause and effect, which keeps proliferating. This is because a vasana is nothing but a stored experience. All experience is only possible when the non-dual, partless reality is imagined to split into two. This first imagined split into duality is caused by imagining a cause-effect transformation. Thereafter, all dualities are overlaid on it: a process called prapancha/conceptual proliferation/vasana build up.

It is the common experience of all of us that all phenomena, as noted earlier, share the following six characteristics – "birth, duration, growth, change, decay, and death." We all see people being born and people dying. We plant a seed, and we see it spouting into a shoot and then into a tree. In short, every effect we see has to have a cause. If I see a tree, I infer that it must have been born from seed. Similarly, if we see a world – as an effect – we look for its cause.

The most plausible explanation that comes to our mind is that all phenomena are born from a changeless Ultimate Reality or two changeless Ultimate Realities. The Upanishads at many places also seem to support such creation theories. For example, at many places, the Upanishads have spoken about "That from which all these beings emanate," "As small sparks (come out) from fire," "The Ākāśa has evolved from that which is this Ātman," "It created heat" etc.

But the above does not exhaust the possibility of creation theories. It is actually just the beginning of a long list of creation theories that have been advanced by different schools, both those who consider the Vedas to be their authority and those who don't. In the Mandukya Karika, Gaudapada compiles a list of creation theories in the following verses.

Verse 1.6: "It is the firm conclusion [of wise men] that [there must be] an origin of all existing entities. Prana creates the universe [and] Purusa creates separately the rays of consciousness (i.e, the individual jivas)."

[It is indicated by the above verse that there are two manifestors, namely, the Puruṣa and the Prāṇa. The Puruṣa manifests the Jīvas and Prāṇa the inanimate objects. From the empirical standpoint we see two kinds of manifestations, viz., the sentient and the insentient. Therefore, we naturally ascribe these to two manifestors, viz., Puruṣa and Prāṇa. (As the general principle of causality is that the like produces the like.)]

Verse 1.7: "Those who think of (the process of) creation believe it to be the manifestation of the superhuman power of God; while others look upon it as of the same nature as dream and illusion."

Verse 1.8: "Those who affirm (the existence of the) created objects attribute this manifestation to the mere will of God, while those who look upon time as real declare time to be the manifestor of all beings. "

Verse 1.9: "Others think that the manifestation is for the purpose of enjoyment (of God) while still others attribute it to mere diversion (on the part of God), Rut it is the very nature of the Effulgent Being (Ātman) (for), what other desire is possible for Him whose desire is always in the state of fulfilment? "

The theories above can be broadly divided into two types of creation theories:

Cosmological Theories:

Creation is caused by two eternal principles (like Purusa and Prana) (Dualistic Atheism)

Creation is manifestation of the divine power of God (1. 7). (Monotheism)

Creation is manifestation of the nature of dream or illusion (1. 7). (Mayavada)

Creation is manifestation of the Divine Will which cannot but be fulfilled (1. 8).

Creation is manifestation which proceeds from "Time". Īśvara is indifferent about it (1. 8).

The above Cosmological theories can be classified more generally into Causation and Teleological Theories, which I shall be listed below. All Causation theories share the assumption that there is an ultimate timeless, changeless reality or cause (one or two) that gives rise to the world. The Ultimate Reality may have different names and characteristics and maybe theistic or atheistic, existent or non-existent.

Teleological Theories:

These are theories relating to or involving the explanation of phenomena in terms of the purpose they serve rather than of the cause by which they arise.

Creation is for the purpose of the enjoyment of God. (1.9)
Creation is an act of God's sport. (1.9)

Refutation of all Creation/Causation Theories

The teleological theories are negated by Gaudapada in

verse 1.9 itself, by saying that "What could be the desire for manifestation on the part of Brahman whose desires are ever in a state of fulfillment?" No will can cause creation because a will implies an effort to gratify some unsatiated desire. Brahman is Bliss which means the absence of all wants. Therefore, the Divine Will Cannot be the cause of the universe.

Next, the Cosmological/Causation Theories are refuted by Gaudapada in Verses 4.3 – 4.10

All those who believe in the act of creation are dualists because they talk about the existence of two reals: the unchanging Cause and the changing Effect. In the proceeding verses, Gaudapada goes on to show the untenability of all Causation theories, which imply dualism. The very fact he notes first is, since there are many contradicting theories of dualists for the origination of the universe, this in itself is an indication of an inherent flaw/weakness in creation theories. The dualists dispute with each other and simply destroy each other's position: thus, unwittingly, they aid in establishing his Ajativada by their mutual contradiction.

Verse 3.3. "Quarrelling among themselves, some disputants postulate that an existing entity undergoes evolution, whereas other disputants, proud of their understandings, maintain that evolution proceeds from a non-existing entity. "
The above verse is hinting towards the first two of the whole range of Cosmological theories of causation held by different schools in the list below.
     Arambha-vada – The theory (of atomic agglomeration) that the effect, which is something newly produced, does not exist in the cause, held by Nyaya and Vaisheshika Schools. It is similar to modern scientific theories of creation.
     Parinama-vada – The theory of real transformation, based on the fact that the effect, though phenomenally different, is substantially identical with the cause and pre-exists latently in it; held by Samkhya and Vishishtadavaita schools in different variants. See Note for a detailed explanation
     Vivarta-vada – The theory of apparent transformation or of false appearance accepted by Gaudapada from a certain standpoint
     Pratityasamutpada-vada – the theory of dependent origination of Buddhism – There is nothing permanent, noth-

ing substantial, no unique individual self in the nature of becoming and existence because everything is a result of "dependent origination." There are no independent objects and independent subjects; there is fundamental emptiness in all phenomena and experiences. Gaudapada and Shankaracharya consider it as nihilism, but this is not the view held by many schools of Buddhism.

These theories cover all possible cause-effect relationships of duality.

Cause and effect are identical (the former exists in the latter)

Cause and effect are absolutely different

Cause and effect are both absolutely different and identical

Cause and effect are neither absolutely different nor identical

By negating the first two theories, the third is automatically negated. The fourth option does not need to be negated because it itself is the denial of any cause-effect relationship; therefore, things happen randomly.

After stating the disputing Cosmological theories of Causation, Gaudapada says regally.

Verse 4.5. "We approve the Ajāti or non-creation declared by them. We do not quarrel with them. Now, hear from us (the Ultimate Reality), which is free from all disputations. "

Basically, he is trying to say here that, with regard to causality, we accept that theory that is not refuted by any party but which must be admitted by all, viz., Ajāti.

Then with a single strike of his hammer, he blows to pieces the first two creation theories in these verses:

Verse 4.6/3.20: "The disputants (i.e., the dualists) contend that the ever-unborn (changeless) entity (Ātman) undergoes a change. How does an entity which is changeless and immortal partake of the nature of the mortal?"

Shankara's Commentary: Some interpreters of the Upaniṣads, who are garrulous and who put on the airs of the Knowers of Brahman, admit that the Reality—the Ātman—which is by nature ever-unborn (changeless) and immortal, really passes into birth (i.e., becomes the universe). If according to them, the Ātman really passes into birth, it must undergo destruction. But, how is it possible for the Ātman, which is, by its very nature, ever-unborn (changeless) and immortal to become mortal (jivas) and be subject to destruction? It can never become mortal, which is contrary to its very nature.

Thus gone into smoke are the first two cosmological theories of causation: Arambha-vada and Parinama-Vada. Next we come to Vivarta-vada. Some people say that Gaudapada was talking only Ajati-vada while Shankara toned it down to Vivarta-Vada. This is not at all true. This contention is based on the misreading of the Mandukya Karika. Vivarta-Vada is nothing but the term later Advaitins used to call Gauadapada's view of the world as Vaitathya (false/unreal), which is the heading of his Chapter 2 of Mandukya Karika. The culprit is the word Maya, which is used both by Advaita and Buddhism. The confusion arises because both these schools use the same word differently.

I shall now proceed to show that Gaudapada was asserting Vivarta-vada and Advaita's conception of Maya, though from a provisional standpoint. Gaudapada states this categorically in verse 3.24: "From such Scriptural passages as, "There is no multiplicity in Ātman," "Indra through Māyā," we know that the Ātman, though ever unborn, verily appears to have become many (only) through Māyā." Gaudapada being a Vedantin cannot go against the authority of the scriptures. The confusion is that in certain verses, he denies "Maya," even as the cause of apparent creation. I shall show that in these passages, his denial of Maya is the way it is conceived in Buddhist scriptures rather than rejecting the Upanishadic notion of the word. From an absolute standpoint, he, of course, denies Maya and Vivartavada.

Vivartavada from a Relative Standpoint

We have to go back to our discussion of the three states I talked about at the beginning of this Chapter. We need to remember how we established that the three states are unreal because they change and cancel each other's reality. Further, we said they all appear to the unchanging Witness/ Self/Atman/Turiya/Non-Dual Reality. We have already demolished any "real" causation to take place because it is absurd to think that an immortal, changeless entity can modify itself to become a mortal entity like all Jivas and undergo destruction. So the only option now left for us is to think that the Atman/Non-Dual Reality has not "really" given any birth but "appears" to do so. Thus, Gaudapada says:

Verse 2.11: If the objects cognized in both the conditions (of dream and of waking) be illusory, who cognizes all these (illusory objects) and who again imagines them?

Verse2.12: Ātman, the self-luminous, through the power of his own Māyā, imagines in himself by himself (all the objects that the subject experiences within or without). He alone is the cognizer of the objects (so created). This is the decision of the Vedānta.

To explain how Atman can imagine a diversified world of all objects due to Maya, Gaudapada gives the following example.

Verse 2.17. As the rope, whose nature is not really known, is imagined in the dark to be a snake, a water-line, etc., so also is the Ātman imagined (in various ways).

The above is an example of Vivartavada. A rope being "imagined" like a snake. The rope did not give any natural birth to a real snake. The rope only "apparently" appears as a snake. The appearance is based on the imagination/memory of the mind. The same is the case for Atman. Taking this example, further Gaudapada says:

Verse 2.19." The Ātman is imagined as Prāṇa and other endless objects. This is due to Māyā (ignorance) of the luminous (Ātman itself) by which It is (as it were) deluded. "

Shankara's (commentary): If it is definitely ascertained that Ātman is verily one, how could it be imagined as endless objects like Prāṇa, etc., having the characteristics of the phenomenal experience? It is thus explained:—This is due to the Māyā (ignorance) inhering in the luminous Ātman. As the illusion conjured up by the juggler makes the very clear sky appears covered with trees blooming with flowers and leaves, so does this luminous Ātman become deluded, as it were, by his own Māyā. "My Māyā cannot be easily got over" declares the Gītā.

The commentary of Shankara supplies another example of a magician creating a delusory appearance of a clear sky covered with trees and blooming with flowers. The sky never actually created these appearances, but they were merely imagined in the sky. A more common and universal example would be seeing the color blue in the sky even though the sky or space does not have any color. Now let us understand how the Atman imagines the world.

Verse 2.16: First of all, is imagined the Jīva (the embodied being) and then are imagined the various entities, objective and subjective, are perceived. As is (one's) knowledge, so is (one's) memory of it.

Shankara's (commentary): What is the source of the imagination of various objects, subjective and objective, that are perceived and appear to be related to one another as cause and effect? It is thus explained:—The Jīva is of the nature of cause and effect and is further characterized by such ideas as "I do this, I am happy and miserable." Such Jīva is, at first, imagined in the Ātman, which is pure and devoid of any such characteristics, like the imagination of a snake in a rope. Then for the knowledge of the Jīva are imagined various existent entities, both subjective and objective, such as Prāṇa, etc., constituting different ideas such as the agent, action, and the result (of action). What is the cause of this imagination?

It is thus explained:—It, the Jīva, who is the product of imagination and competent to effect further vision, has its memory determined by its inherent knowledge. That is to say, and its ability is always followed by memory, similar to that knowledge. Hence, the knowledge of the idea of cause results from the knowledge of the idea of the effect. Then follows the memory of both cause and effect. This memory is followed by its knowledge which results in the various states of knowledge characterized by action, actor, and the effect. These are followed by their memory, which, in its turn, is followed by the states of knowledge. In this way are imagined various objects, subjective and objective, which are perceived and seen to be related to one another as cause and effect.

Shankara's commentary above bears a striking resemblance to what my student Krishna wrote in his journal. Therefore, I am quoting him here:

"So anyway the mind is a coordinating system. and even right now, the guilt and the fear of being wrong that it is feeling for pursuing self-inquiry and not being "of use to the world" somehow, and presenting fear-based solutions and fear-based rejections of those solutions is a strange mystery. It is both superficial and lacking any deeper layers, but with the power to invent deeper layers, the more it investigates because it works with the law of cause and effect. Even the investigation of the web of cause and effect is a part of cause and effect."

It's to his enormous credit that he could grasp this at such an early age of 15 yrs. What Shankara is trying to say above is that the Jiva/subject is nothing but the imagination of Atman by Atman, the way a snake is imagined on a rope. After Atman imagines itself as Jiva, then for the sake of the Jiva/subject other subjects and objects too are imagined by Atman. This is how we get the appearance of a plural world. A rope has no parts. But when the snake is projected on it, the snake has various parts like the head, body, and tail. In the case of the world, the Jiva is first imagined by Maya, then the Jiva further imagines ideas like actor, action, and results of action. This means that the Jiva imagines itself to be an actor doing action and reaping the consequences of their actions. These imaginations are what Krishna's journal (my student) alluding to when he speaks of guilt, fear of being wrong, etc. He further says that all these ideas are nothing but the mind which is "superficial, "nonetheless with the "power to invent deeper layers. " And then finally, with a master-stroke of sheer brilliance, he writes that the superficial nature of the mind is "because it works with the law of cause and effect. Even the investigation of the web of cause and effect is a part of cause and effect." In saying so, Krishna almost anticipates Ajativada. This is what the great Shankara mentions in the commentary above. See this:

"It, the Jīva, who is the product of imagination and competent to effect further imagination, has its memory determined by its own inherent knowledge. That is to say, its knowledge is always followed by memory, similar to that knowledge. Hence, the knowledge of the idea of cause results in the knowledge of the idea of the effect. Then fol-lows the memory of both cause and effect. This memory is followed by its knowledge which results in the various states of knowledge characterized by action, actor, and the effect. These are followed by their memory, which, in its turn, is followed by the states of knowledge. "

The above lines may appear confusing but what they are saying is something very simple. It says that the Jiva is a product of wrong knowledge superimposed on Atman. What is the wrong knowledge? The knowledge of "Cause and Effect." The wrong knowledge that "I" as a Jiva (effect) was born from Atman (cause)." Now all knowledge is followed by a memory that is similar to the knowledge that creates it. The knowledge that inheres in the Jiva or rather creates Jivahood is the wrong knowledge of "Cause and Effect"; thus, this wrong knowledge of cause and effect becomes a memory for the Jiva, and he constructs further knowledge based on this memory. This knowledge creates further memory of cause and effect, which further reinforces the wrong primary knowledge. The whole re-iterative cycle of cause and effect can be shown with the help of the following diagram:

Anandagiri, in his Tika/gloss/explanation to the above commentary of verse 2.16, clarifies it beautifully:

"It is seen from everyday experience that the idea of satisfaction follows the idea of food and drink. One is not possible in the absence of the other. Following this method of agreement and difference, we imagine this. The idea of knowledge of food, etc., which is the cause, follows the idea of the knowledge of satisfaction which is the effect. The next day, we get the memory of this cause and effect experienced on the previous day. Then we have the idea of duty which may be described as a result of the previous experience. Accordingly, we begin the act of cooking, etc., with the help of rice, fuel, etc.

After eating the food thus prepared, we derive certain definite states of knowledge characterized by the idea of sat-isfaction, etc. This satisfaction inheres in us as the memory which stimulates us, the next day, to similar action. We perform the action, which is followed by an identical result. Thus ideas succeed one another and appear to be related as cause and effect. That these ideas need not have any counterpart in the gross physical world of the waking state can be understood by the analysis of the dream experiences. As a matter of fact, it cannot be rationally proved that even, in the waking state, an idea can produce a corresponding effect in the world perceived to exist outside of us."

With reference to our discussion of the three bodies and the three states of sleep, waking, and dreaming, we are now in the position of understanding them in terms of Cause and Effect. Thus as Gaudapada says:

Verse 1.11: "Viśva (Waker) and Taijasa (Dreamer) are conditioned by cause and effect. But Prājña (Sleeper) is conditioned by cause alone. These two (cause and effect) do not exist in Turīya.

Anandagiri's Gloss: Causal state/Body/Prajna is that in which we do not know the Truth. From it follows the result/effect, which is the misapprehension of Truth. It is because one does not know the rope one mistakes it for the snake. Prājña, or the state of non-apprehension as such, is said to be the cause of the Viśva(Waker) and Taijasa(Dreamer) or the states of misapprehension. In dream and waking states, there are both non-apprehension and misapprehension of Reality. But in a deep sleep, there is only non-apprehension. As a matter of fact, these two conditions, misapprehension and non-apprehension, cannot be experienced separately. They have been differently classified only to facilitate understanding.

It must be clear from the above discussion how:

The Cause of Creation/Plurality is nothing but having wrong knowledge of Cause and Effect called Avidya. This Avidya conceals the right knowledge that the Atman was never born and, therefore, there are no Cause and Effect phenomena in operation.

The wrong knowledge of Cause and Effect/Avidya causes the effect or Causal Body/Maya which further creates the effects: Dreamer(Taijasa) along with dream world and the Waker(Visva) along with waking world.

The cycle of cause and effect started by Avidya-Maya keeps reinforcing itself.

Gaudapada rounds off his discussion on Avidya-Maya (wrong knowledge of Cause & Effect) with it being the sole reason for us to perceive a plural world of phenomena when in fact, there is only Atman/Brahman, with the verse:

Verse 3.19. This unborn (changeless, non-dual Brahman) appears to undergo modification only on account of Māyā (illusion) and not otherwise. For, if this modification were real, the Immortal (Brahman) would become mortal.

And finally:
Verse 4.56. As long as there is faith in causality, the (endless) chain of birth and death (samsara) will be there. When that faith is destroyed (by knowledge) birth and death (samsara) become non-existent.

To summarize, non-origination, non-birth, or the negation of the concept of causality strikes at the root of dualistic conceptual thought. The concept of birth or causation suggests duality in all its forms of relation. Cause and effect is the example that stands for the other relations within time, space, and causality, such as subject-object, substance-attribute, and so forth. Instead of dealing with multiple examples of dualistic relations, he confines himself to fully exploring this one proposition and negating it by showing that it is Maya.

Seeming Negation of Vivartavada

After asserting Vivartavada or Avidya-Maya as the cause of the apparent birth of the phenomenal world, Gaudapada seems to negate Maya too. Here are two verses. In the first, he posits Maya, and in the second one, he negates it.
Verse 3.27. "That which is ever-existent appears to pass into birth through illusion (Māyā) and not from the standpoint of Reality. He who thinks that this passing into birth is real asserts, as a matter of fact, that what is born is born again (and so on without end)."

The above verse gives another logic as to why the Atman cannot give birth to anything real. However, this verse is quoted by me here to show that Gaudapada accepts the illusory birth of the world through ignorance/Maya. Shankaracharya's comment on this verse reads:

Shankaracharya's Comment: Brahman or Ātman, however, does not really create the universe nor transform itself into the universe, as the rope does not really create the snake, nor does it become the snake. The appearance of creation is due to ignorance. Therefore the theory of Māyā or vivarta, which posits a real Ātman is the best explanation of the universe when such universe is recognized as a fact.

And soon after the preceding verse, Gaudapada writes this:

Verse 3.28. The unreal cannot be born either really or through Māyā. For the son of a barren woman is born neither in reality nor in illusion.

Shankara's Commentary: There are those who hold that all entities are unreal, that the non-existent produces this world. But the production, by the non-existent, of anything either in reality or in illusion, is not possible, for we know nothing like it in our experience. As the son of a barren woman is not seen to be born either really or through Māyā, the theory of the non-existence of things is, in truth, untenable.

Anandagiri's Gloss: In truth—In case the Ātman is a Reality, the passing into birth may be explained by Māyā; but in this case, even that explanation cannot hold, for there is no evidence in our actual experience to justify the presumption that either something comes out of nothing or nothing comes out of something.

A careful reading of the above comments shows that what is being rejected is not actually Vivartavada's conception of Maya or the "seeming appearance" of the Atman as the world through ignorance. What is being rejected is the concept of Maya in the school of Buddhism, which claims that Maya-like creation happens out of nothing or avoid.

The Early Buddhist Texts contain some references to illusion/Maya, the most well known of which is the Phenapiṇḍūpama Sutta in Pali (and with a Chinese Agama parallel at SĀ 265) which states:

Suppose, monks, that a magician (māyākāro) or a magician's apprentice (māyākārantevāsī) would display a magical illusion (māyaṃ) at a crossroads. A man with good sight would inspect it, ponder, and carefully investigate it, and it would appear to him to be void (rittaka), hollow (tucchaka), coreless (asāraka). For what core (sāro) could there be in a magical illusion (māyāya)? So too, monks, whatever kind of cognition there is, whether past, future, or present, internal or external, gross or subtle, inferior or superior, far or near: a monk inspects it, ponders it, and carefully investigates it, and it would appear to him to be void (rittaka), hollow (tuc-chaka), coreless (asāraka). For what core (sāro) could there be in cognition?7

Gaudapada's objection is to this conception of Maya, which shows creation happening from a "void" or "nothing-ness", which denies any real substratum that persists for the illusion to manifest itself, like a rope for a snake and the Atman for the world, or, in the above example, a "magician" for the magic trick.

In his commentary to verse 2.12 (quoted earlier), Shan-kara explains this very clearly:

Shankara's Commentary to Verse 2.12: The self-luminous Ātman himself, by his own Māyā, imagines in himself the dif-ferent objects to be described hereafter. It is like imagining the snake, etc., in the rope, etc. He himself cognizes them, as he has imagined them. There is no other substratum of knowledge and memory. The aim of Vedānta is to declare that knowledge and memory are not without, support as the Buddhistic nihilists maintain.

Thus, the above attack is to Buddhist's conception of creation happening from avoid. It is an attack leveled at their concept of Emptiness and Pratityasamputpada-vada or Dependent Origination. According to me, this attack seems to be based on a misinterpretation of the Buddhist doctrine of Emptiness or Sunyavada and Pratityasamputpada-vada. I shall deal with this in another Chapter.

Ajativada from the Ultimate Viewpoint

The question naturally arises that if Vivartavda has been shown to be the accepted philosophy for Gaudapada, then why is he so famous for Ajativada. The answer is simple theoretically, but there is a world of difference experientially. Ajativada and Vivartavada are explanations given from two different standpoints of reality. Anandagiri, in his gloss of verse 2.19, says, "Māyā as the explanation of the manifold is from, the causal standpoint. Even when the Ātman appears to be transformed into the universe, it does not, in reality, lose its non-dual character." This terse statement explains everything. Vivartavada is spoken from the empirical/causal standpoint of viewing the world constituted by Jiva-Jagat-Isvara, which is from the standpoint of ignorance. It is provisional teaching for realizing Self/Atman/Brahman as Witness. From the Ultimate Standpoint, the standpoint of Atman itself or the Jivanmukta, the Atman never got transformed into any world, never into the trio of Jiva-Jagat-Isvara, so even the division of Witness and objects does not exist. This is Ajativada. As Gaudapada intimates to us in this verse.

Verse 2.35: "By the wise, who is free from attachment, fear and anger and who are well versed in the meaning of the Vedas, this (Ātman) has been verily realized as totally devoid of all imaginations (such as those of Prāna, etc.), free from the illusion of the manifold, and non-dual."

Another point to bear, because the mind's tendency to objectify reality is compelling, is that Maya itself is not something existent. Thus, Gaudapada clarifies in the following verses:

Verse 4.58: "Those Jivas said to be born by convention are not born in reality. Their birth is like Maya, and that Maya itself does not exist"
Shankara's commentary to this verse clarifies this matter beyond doubt:

Shankara's Commentary: Those, again, who imagine the birth of the Jīvas and other entities, do so only through Samvrti or the power of ignorance as stated in the preceding Kārikā. The Jīvas are seen to be born only through ignorance. But from the standpoint of the Supreme Reality, no such birth is possible. This (supposed) birth of the Jīvas is, through ignorance, described above, is like the birth of objects through illusion (Māyā).
(Opponent)—Then there must be something real known as Māyā or illusion?
(Reply)—It is not so. That Māyā or illusion is never existent. Māyā, or illusion, is the name we give to something which does not (really) exist (but which is perceived).
Maya is thus the creative and elusive principle. It does not have independent ontological status as it is not an entity or a reality having a substance of its own. Brahman is the only real (sat). As such, Maya is a riddle to the intellect. It is indeterminable and unthinkable. But when the Absolute

is directly realized in anubhava, there is no Maya to be explained, for Maya does not really exist.

Now I quote the most famous statement of Ajativada found in the Mandukya Karika, along with Shankara's commentary, which beautifully summarizes the entire Chapter.

"Verse2.32. There is no dissolution, no birth, none in bondage, none aspiring for wisdom, no seeker of liberation, and none liberated. This is the absolute truth."

Shankara's Commentary: When duality is perceived to be illusory, and Atman alone is known as the sole Reality, then it is clearly established that all our experiences, ordinary or religious (Vedic), verily pertain to the domain of ignorance. Then one perceives that there is no dissolution, i.e., destruction (from the standpoint of Reality); no birth or creation, i.e., coming into existence; no one in bondage, i.e., no worldly being; no pupilage, i.e., no one adopting means for the attainment of liberation; no seeker after liberation, and no one free from bondage (as bondage does not exist). The Ultimate Truth is that the stage of bondage, etc., cannot exist in the absence of creation and destruction. How can it be said that there is neither creation nor destruction? It is thus replied:—There is no duality (at any time). The absence of duality is indicated by such Scriptural passages as, "When duality appears to exist...." "One who appears to see multiplicity...." "All this is verily Atman." "Atman is one and without a second." "All that exists is verily the Atman," etc. Birth or death can be predicated only on what exists and never on what does not exist, such as the horns of a hare, etc. That which is non-dual (Advaita) can never be said to be born or destroyed.

That it should be non-dual and at the same time subject to birth and death is a contradiction in terms. It has already been said that our dual experience characterized by (the activities of) Prāṇa, etc., is a mere illusion having Atman for its substratum, as the snake imagined in the rope which is its substratum. The imagination characterized by the appearance of the snake in the rope cannot be produced from nor dissolved in the rope (i.e., in any external object), or dissolved in mind, nor even in both (i.e., the rope and the mind). Thus duality being non-different from mental (subjective) imagination (cannot have a beginning or an end). Duality is not perceived when one's mental activities are controlled (as in Samādhi) or in a deep sleep. Therefore, it is established that duality is a mere illusion of the mind. Hence, it is well said that the Ultimate Reality is the absence of destruction, etc., on account of the non-existence of duality (which exists only in the imagination of the mind).

Even Ajativada is a Description from the Empirical Reality

After the vast terrain that we have covered and come to the ultimate, is there anything left to say? Yes. We must negate the last word and enter into total silence as the ultimate description of non-dual silence. Thus, Gaudapada is careful to last vada/viewpoint from us so that we enter that viewless experience from where the mind turns back speechless.

Atman is called unborn (Aja) from the standpoint of the illusory empirical experiences. However, it is, honestly speaking, not even unborn. - Gaudapada, Mandukya Karika, Verse 4.74

The Problem with Becoming

Psychological Becoming as Cause of Conflict

One of the causes of suffering is conflict. Self-inquiry is about examining the root cause of conflict. Unfortunately, instead of helping us explore, discover, and uproot the cause of this problem, our society conditions and promotes competition in myriad ways. While the patterns are countless, self-inquiry can trace all these various proliferating ways of conflict to a single source: psychological becoming.

What is psychological becoming, and how it causes suffering?

There are two causes of suffering that we experience – physiological and psychological. Physiological suffering is the one we experience bodily as a disease or injury. On the other hand, psychological suffering is what we experience mentally as emotions and feelings. This classification has to be taken with some degree of fluidity because physiological suffering in our unexamined consciousness leads to psychological suffering. Psychological suffering in our unexamined consciousness leads to physiological suffering or clinical diseases like depression, diabetes, etc.

Physiological suffering is a phenomenon related to the senses. When a sense-related phenomenon is registered in one's memory, it becomes a psychological phenomenon. So to distinguish between these two different forms, let us call the sense related suffering, pain, and psychological phenomenon as suffering. When pain is registered and stored in memory, it becomes the root of suffering. Well, this requires a little explanation. Pain is an experience of the present. It is fleeting and happens in chronological time. Someone slaps me across the face; I get a burning and tingling sensation in my cheeks, which arises and subsides in a matter of minutes. The pain in itself does not constitute suffering. When we internalize and store this sensation of pain in our memory, psychologically as "insult," or when we interpret this pain based on our memory, psychologically as "insult," that constitutes psychological suffering. Had there been no memory operation at the moment of experiencing the slap, there would only be an instantaneous physical pain but no psychological suffering.

From this, we can see that the root of suffering is memory. All experiences we have in life are stored in the form of pain and pleasure in our memory. Rather than playing just a passive storage function, this memory actively intervenes in every moment of experience. Not only interpreting it and giving it a psychological value in terms of pain and pleasure but also predisposing one to act in the future to avoid pain and pursue pleasure. So we can see that memory and psychological time are the same thing. It is the memory that stores an experience as past. It is the memory that interprets an experience in the present based on this past experience. It is the memory that predisposes us to create an experience in the future based on the past experience. So psychological past, present, and future time are constructs of memory. If there were no psychological memory, there would be no psychological past, present, and future. We would only register chronological time, the way we record the passage from day tonight. We would only report the facts of events rather than the psychological value of pain and pleasure we ascribe to events.

If there was no psychological memory, will there be a psychological future? If we examine all our activities in our daily lives, very little of it has to do with the basic survival of our organism: meeting the basic physiological comforts of food, clothing, and shelter. Instead, almost all our activities and thoughts are directed towards a future. We are all the time having goals, plans, ambitions to become someone. We want to be rich, famous, respectable, knowledgeable, powerful, wise, or enlightened: in a nutshell, we are all involved in the process of psychological becoming. This movement of psychological becoming defines our entire life, its meaning, and purpose.

And we have seen that the basis of this psychological becoming is in psychological memory, which stores all the complex experiences of our life in terms of pain and pleasure, then projects a future to maximize enjoyment and minimize pain. Thus, all psychological becoming: materialistic, psychological, intellectual, or spiritual is an action to maximize pleasure and reduce pain. Socially we may differentiate this pleasure-seeking in terms of lower and higher, calling spiritual pursuits higher than material pursuits. Still, essentially, they all constitute the movement of seeking and securing the experience of pleasure. I am not saying that this differentiation is pointless. It has its value in relative terms, but one cannot get ultimate freedom until one has denied the entire gamut of psychological becoming. In the journey of understanding and negation of psychological becoming, the pleasures are stacked vertically from material to emotional to intellectual to spiritual.

One moves from being materialistic to being spiritual like water gets hotter when heated from 0 degrees C to 100 degrees C. Nonetheless, the phase remains the same. Water at 0 degrees C is still water at 100 degrees C. A material person is still seeking pleasure as much as a spiritual person. The shift occurs beyond 100 degrees when there is a complete phase change. Water heated after 100 degrees C changes to water vapor: liberating from its liquid state.

In the same way, a spiritual person is freed from suffering only when he gives up all notions of becoming: when he is freed from the state of seeking anything. There is a phase change in him too. He ceases to be a person because a person is nothing but psychological memory. When all his psychological memory is boiled out through understanding and insight, no "him" remains psychologically. One does not fail to appreciate that water at 0 degrees C or 50 degrees C, or 99 degrees C does not boil and becomes vapor. But water at 99 degrees C is closer to becoming water vapor than water at 50 degrees C or 0 degrees C. Analogously, a spiritual person is more comparable to psychological freedom than a materialistic person. A person who, as a thinker, has worked through his material, emotional and social needs is much closer to attaining freedom than one who is caught in meeting these needs.

I know I will make matters more complicated by saying this, but if I don't, I will leave the readers with a very linear sense of the whole process of freedom, which is nothing short of a lie. All models, systems, and constructs are lies if they purport to be a path and guarantee of freedom. They would be more honest if they claim that they are just facilitating inquiry towards freedom. If I state that a spiritual person is closer to freedom than a materialistic person, it is not in any absolute or literal sense. Water can and does boil at a temperature below 100 degrees C at higher altitudes, lower air pressure. So the ultimate phase change of water is dependent not only on temperature but also on ambient pressure.

At higher pressure, water would not boil even at 100 degrees C. Similarly, to say that a spiritual person is closer to freedom than a materialistic person, in simplistic terms, is to create a very grave error. This error perpetrates suffering and does not lead to freedom. A person wearing saffron robes, denouncing sex and family, leaving all possessions and becoming a monk or an ascetic, who is well versed with the scriptures, may not be more spiritual than a person who lives with a family, having sex, having material comforts and pleasures. What I mean by a spiritual person is not a social role. A spiritual person in a social position may be more ambitious and power-seeking than a simple materialistic person. He may be more bound to scripture and tradition than a worldly who has an open and inquiring mind. A spiritual person, the way I use the term, has a profound interest in freedom and understanding life: who devotes his life, time, and energies to question, ponder, reflect, think and meditate on topics like human freedom, suffering, creativity, truth, and love. All this is born out of an intrinsic love rather than a role-play. Unlike so many modern gurus who have just achieved some intellect and psychic experiences, who veil their search for power and fame in a hundred different garbs in the name of teaching, a truly spiritual person does not mind being anonymous.

Now, where is the suffering in all this psychological becoming in experiential terms? When one is in a state of psychological becoming, one constantly has an unworded yet constant feeling of being deficient; This is mainly unconscious for almost all who have become lost in society and all its movements, institutions, and organizations. The deficiency expresses itself in the conscious as intentions, goals, and ambitions. When one is ambitious, one is always in a state of effort. There is a constant conflict between what is and what should be. I am poor, but I want to be rich. I am unknown and anonymous, but I want to be known and famous. I am powerless, but I want to be powerful. I am bored, but I want to feel stimulated and entertained. I feel empty and meaningless in life, but I want to create a meaningful and purposeful life. I have vices, but I want to be virtuous. I do not know the truth, but I want to know the truth. I am mortal, but I want to be immortal. So every moment, there is a conflict between what is and what it should be. And this, as I have tried to show, ranges from the most worldly to the most spiritual desires. At every moment and every level of one's consciousness, there is a conflict created by what one is and what one wants to be. This conflict not only plays out in one's mind but also in one's relationships at work, family, and society. The desire to become plays out on a global scale in terms of war and the clash of nations; this is the depth and scale of what constitutes the suffering of psychological becoming: our society is a daily living monument of this.

At present, our society fosters psychological becoming, so it actively encourages, promotes, and rewards psychological becoming. In essence, our current society is a recipe for the creation and perpetuation of suffering. One who inquires into freedom realizes the factors of psychological becoming in society – expressed in its cultures, religions, organizations, and institutions – breaks away from them: which means one drops out of the stream of society. This breaking away frees one from all the clutter that keeps one's conscious mind engaged with the world. Once the conscious has become free from psychological becoming, there is silence in one's mind and life for the deeper unconscious to reveal itself in one's self-inquiry.

The Purusharthas (Aims of Human Life) and Psychological Becoming

Most people not-self realized suffer from the sensation of limitation and incompleteness. And therefore, they try to rid themselves of this inadequacy. And almost universally, the solution is trying to change one's current situation by acquiring more security (Artha) or pleasures (Kama).

In Advaita, one comes to know that there are four purusharthas or four aims of human life: dharma (virtue/duty), Artha (wealth/security), kama (pleasure), and moksha (liberation from suffering). An average person in society pursues the first three aims exclusively to varying degrees. The fulfillment of the first three aims necessarily involves the pursuit of temporary and transient objects. Not only that, invariably, a person's desires involve him in the net of things that are often contradictory to each other. Because of these reasons, a person's mind locked in following the first three aims is always in a state of frustrations, contradictions, and confusion. Of such a mind, is involved only in the aims of dharma, artha, and kama, to the exclusion of moksha the Bhagavad Gita says,
Verse 2.41: Concerning this moksha, Arjuna, the descendant of Kurus! There is a single, well-ascertained understanding. The notions of those who lack discrimination are many-branched and innumerable indeed.

Effectively, the Bhagavad Gita is trying to say that till a person has not made moksha as an aim, his mind is "many branched" or scattered in all directions. A person who has made moksha a drive has a focused mind with a "single and well-ascertained understanding." Why is it so? Because moksha is not about the pursuit of transient objects. It is about "attaining" that which is beyond all forms.

Difference Between Dharma (Virtue/Righteous

Conduct) and Adhyatma (Spirituality)

The most exciting thing to note above is that even dharma (righteous actions, duties, good deeds) is a part of psychological becoming and, therefore, a seed of conflict, if not pursued along with moksha. And it is precisely for this point that I have endeavored with such a long introduction. Most people conflate spirituality with dharma. In Indian philosophy, spirituality is given another name called adhyatma. Adhyatma is a compound Sanskrit word made of Adhi (concerning) and Atma (soul). So adhyatma means concerning the soul. Adhyatma is also the discipline of knowledge that leads to spiritual wisdom and eventually to moksha or liberation. It is considered to be the best kind of knowledge. This knowledge, adhyatma, pertains to the Self and deals with the discernment between the Self and the non-Self. Adhyatma is the knowledge concerning Atman and the path to be adopted in order to attain the knowledge of Atman. This knowledge is considered to be eternal. Adhyatma also refers to the exposition or explanation about the nature of the supreme reality, Brahman. One's leaning towards the study of scriptures and one's effort to understand one's true nature, Atman, is also called adhyatma.

Dharma as a Means of Psychological Becoming

Thus, dharma could be a step to adhyatma, but it is not adhyatma. In fact, the unbridled pursuit of dharma can actually become a hindrance to adhyatma. Gita makes no bones about this fact, as we can see in the following verses.

Verses 2.42&43: Partha! The non-discriminating people, who remain engrossed in karma enjoined by the Veda and its results, who argue that there is nothing other than this, who is full of desires with heaven as their highest goal, utter these flowery words that talk of many special rituals meant for the attainment of pleasures and power and results in the form of better births.

Verse 2.45: The subject matter of the Vedas is related to the three variable qualities (of material nature). Arjuna! Be one who is free from the hold of these three-fold qualities, from the sorrow of pairs of opposites; be one who is ever established in truth, who is free from the anxieties of acquiring and protecting, and who is situated in Self.

The "karma enjoined by the Vedas" in verse 2.42 can be interpreted, both as rituals to be performed to get better birth in next life, or in a more contemporary way to mean doing moral acts in the hope of accruing good karma for the future/future birth. Thus, it is talking of doing moral acts (dharma) for securing a better future. The verse 2.43 states in Advaitic terminology that the subject matter of the Vedas (referring only to the Karma Kanda portion of the Vedas or the part of Vedas which deals only with the science of actions/rituals and their results) deals only with "three variable qualities of material nature." This means that the Karma Kanda part of the Vedas deals only with the three Gunas (sattva, tamas, and rajas) or constituents that make up material nature.

Rajas is a doing and projecting function.
Sattva is thinking, knowing, and perceiving function
Tamas is dull and inert, not able to know or do.

Thus, dharma-oriented action deals only with material nature, which is ever-changing and transient. Whereas adhyatma deals not with transient and ever-changing nature but the knowledge of the eternal Self. From this difference, one can easily fathom that dharma leads only to psychological becoming, whereas adhyatma leads to infinite wisdom, which is the end of all psychological becoming. The Bhagavad Gita nails it when it says:

Verse 2.50: One who is endowed with the sameness of mind gives up both punya (virtue) and papa (vice) here, in this world.

Verse 2.53: When your mind is no longer distracted by the Vedas, which present various means and ends to be gained, it will remain steady, firmly established in the Self. Then you will gain self-knowledge.

Thus, Self Inquiry is not about gaining any object, including dharma/virtue, which involves one in any form of psychological becoming but the attainment of Self Knowledge which is beyond all forms and their duality. I have written about this in greater detail in my Chapter A life of meditation.

Stages in Self Inquiry

When a person begins inquiry, he moves from the outer

to the inner. The ancient spiritual also addressed the external levels of consciousness and then gradually moved through the internal ranks until one reaches the ultimate datum beyond which no movement is possible. For example, in Advaita, one first does Karma Yoga (in any of its forms – Bhakti Yoga, Raja Yoga, Tantra Yoga, etc.). Then, the seeker's mind is sufficiently mature, one shift to Jnana Yoga. A similar movement is seen in other paths too. For instance, Buddhism talks about – sila (morality), samadhi (calming of mind), and prajna (transcendental insight). Patanjali's Yoga school talks about asthanga yoga or eight-limbed yoga – yama and niyama (rules of conduct), asana, pranayama (body purification), pratyahara (withdrawing mind from senses), and dhyana, dharana, samadhi (concentration, meditation and final dissolution of mind). As illustrated in the previous paragraph, we can see that in all paths, virtue is the means to the ultimate end rather than being the end in itself.

However, the path which I teach starts directly from Jnana Yoga. This may not be suitable for all personality types. Thus, a seeker has to choose whether they can follow the path of direct Jnana Yoga that I teach. In this path, one does not begin with cultivating virtue since it is only a provisional requirement.

Krishnamurti

About Truth Being a Pathless Land and The Reason for a Path

In one of my debates, someone told me that Truth is a Pathless Land; no path can lead to Truth. He was quite right. No approach can lead to Truth because You Are Truth. But my saying that You Are Truth/You Are Brahman/Tat Tvam Asi does not move a hair in your body. Why? Because you did not train your intellect for this. It is full of rajas and tamas. Self does not require enlightenment. It is the intellect that requires sophistication. The mind reflects the Self. In all reflection cases, you see that the quality of the reflecting surface determines the quality of the image reflected. If the reflecting surface is imperfect in any way, the quality of the image reflected is inadequate in a corresponding manner. So even though there is one sun, we see as many suns as there are reflecting surfaces. So, for example, we get one kind of reflection of the light in muddy water, one in moving water, and one in pure transparent water.

Similarly, the Self, in different ways, reflects in the intellects of other Jivas/persons depending upon the reflecting quality of intellect, which, in turn, relies on the degree of sattva present in it. Rajas create an excited, turbid, and dissipated intelligence, whereas Tamas creates a dull mind. Sattva develops a calm, transparent intellect. So all practices form a path to polish your intellect to receive the reflection of Self. In traditional Advaita, if your mind is sattvic enough, and the teacher says, "You Are Truth/Self/Brahman/Witness/Awareness," you will get Self Realization in one shot, just by hearing this. Some people, due to the force of their karma, actually require very little practice. Those graced by their past karma with exceptionally sattvic intellects get enlightened just by hearing this statement—the Aitareya Upanishad talks of Vamadeva, who was born enlightened in the womb.

"While I was in the womb, I knew all the births of the gods. A hundred walls made of steel protected me. I burst out of them with the speed of a hawk," Vamadeva spoke this verse while lying in the womb."

Aitareya Upanishad, Verse 2.1.5

Shankara again mentions this in his Brahma Sutra Bhashya. The commentary by Shankara is as follows:
"The Yogi, striving assiduously, purified of taint, gradually gaining perfection through many births, then reaches the highest goal" (Ibid 6. 45). Moreover, knowledge sometimes fructifies in the next life is known from the life of Vamadeva, who possessed knowledge even while he was in the womb. This shows that it must have resulted from his past actions, for he could not have practiced any Vidyas in the womb. Therefore, knowledge did not manifest in his previous life owing to obstruction. Removing the obstacle when he was in the womb, knowledge fructified as a result of his past Sadhana." Brahmasutra Bhashya, Verse 3.4.51

Problems With Neo-Advaita Like Approaches

But very few are blessed with such karma. Most have to practice to attain a sattvic intellect. Some people listen to the teachings of Krishnamurti or the higher education of Advaita, Dzogchen, etc., and say that no practice is required at all. In general, this is not correct. That is a deception of the mind. Many neo-Advaita teachers and Satsang teachers work on this principle that there is no requirement for practice. Just sit in the Satsang, listen to a teacher, and the insight shall dawn at some point, paralyzing the mind. On the one hand, the seeker is bursting with rajas, seeing himself as a thinker/ doer/experiencer and lurching forward to seek and find. On the other hand, you have these Neo-Advaita and other New Age Satsnaga teachers telling seekers that all practices are a mark of your ignorance.

The Wisdom of Advaita Teaching Methodology: Alternate Superimposition and Recension/Cancellation

The great teachings like Advaita, which has the wisdom of centuries, realize the predicament of students. From the ultimate viewpoint, they know that the phenomenal world is an illusion and that all actions happen only in fantasy. For example, we have this verse from Gaudapada,
"There is neither dissolution, nor birth: neither anyone in bondage, nor any aspirant for wisdom; neither can there be anyone who hankers after liberation, nor any liberated as such. This alone is the Supreme Truth." Mandukya Upanishad, Karika, Verse 2.32

And further, relating to the futility of all knowledge of the scriptures, we have this verse from Bhagavad Gita.
"For the Brāhmaṇa who knows the self, all the Vedas are of only so much use as a small reservoir is when there is flood everywhere." Bhagavad Gita Verse 2.46

These quotes show that the seeker, the teacher, and the teachings are all an illusion from the ultimate point of view. But it also realizes that for a seeker stuck with ignorance that this phenomenal world is real. To accommodate both views and resolve this seeming dilemma, Shankara evolved a two-fold view of reality. He spoke of

Ultimate Reality/ Paramarthika Satya: Reality conceived from the ultimate viewpoint, Self/Brahman/Awareness/Formless. From this viewpoint, the phenomenal world is mithya or only apparently real like a dream. This is the viewpoint of a Jnani or Self Realized Beings.

Conventional/EmpiricalReality/Vyavaharika Satya: Reality is conceived by people who are ignorant about the ultimate reality and take this phenomenal world of forms as the only reality as materialists do.,

The teacher of traditional Advaita. Wielding the proper method of Advaita learned from the scriptures helps the seeker move up the stages from conventional reality to the ultimate Truth, in a graded manner, through a sophisticated teaching methodology of Advaita called Alternate Superimposition followed by Recension/Cancellation. Thus, the teacher does not perplex a newcomer seeker with the ultimate statements of Advaita I quoted above. Instead, for the sake of the student, the teacher first accepts that this world is real and the seeker is an actual thinker/doer/experiencer entity. After that, through a series of investigations starting from grosser conventional reality, the teacher helps the student understand and negate the reality of each level, rising to subtler levels till they can deny no other phenomenal reality. And Awareness shines due to its Self-revelatory nature. This process is beautifully explained by Shankara here:

"He who knows It, the Self-described above, as such, as the fearless Brahman, becomes the fearless Brahman. This is the purport of the whole Upaniṣad put in a nutshell. It is to bring home this purport that the ideas of projection, maintenance, dissolution, etc., as well as those of action. Its factors and results were superimposed on the Self, by negation- eliminating the superimposed attributes through a process of 'Not this, not this'—the Truth has been made known. Still, he never says that the letters are the leaf, ink, lines, etc.; similarly, in this exposition, the one entity, Brahman, has been taught through various means such as the projection (of the universe). Eliminating the differences created by those hypothetical means summed up the Truth as 'Not this, not this.' In the end, knowledge, further clarified to be undifferentiated, together with its result, has been concluded in this paragraph."

Krishnamurti's teachings as a preliminary to Advaita's Jnana Yoga in My Teaching Methodology

You need to provide the question to which I have provided this answer in the comment section as that will give the context to the reader.

I use Krishnamurti's teachings to prepare for the Jnana Yoga of Advaita. Krishnamurti can be seen in a neo-Advaitic light, but he was not that. He talked of 'no practice' and 'no effort' but did talk of effort to become aware. He spoke of putting his words to practice, but his approach is very subtle and requires more than average sattvic intellect to follow him. This also explains why his teachings are not popular among the masses. I don't teach Karma yoga or Bhakti Yoga or Raja Yoga, as is done in traditional Advaita, which are the basic steps to prepare the intellect for most. I start directly with a 'form of Jnana Yoga' found in the teachings of J Krishnamurti. One person had joined our Neev Advaita Study group and was very enthusiastic. But then he discovered Karma Yoga in the Advaita teachings which talks about sacrificing your work to God. He fell so much in love with that that he left the group, saying that he is not ready for Jnana Yoga right now, as he is enjoying the Karma Yoga. I did not resist him at all.

On the contrary, I encouraged him and wished him all the best. My wife, who lived with me for twenty-five years, having a dialogue with me every day. has moved away into the path of intense Bhakti Yoga to the extent that she has given up married life and lives separately, following her practices. So this 'path' thing is significant as it determines the nature of your practice.

There Are Even Practices in Jnana Yoga of Advaita

Practice is required to make your intellect ready or sattvic enough to understand that you are the Truth. Even in the final Jnana Yoga of Advaita, there are 'practices', if you do not get Self Realized by mere listening or 'shravana '. Then one has to do other practices of manana/reflection/dialogue and nidhidhyasana/deep contemplation. In my journey, I did not have to proceed till nidhidhyasana or deep meditation. The insight came through after shravana and manana only. Same was the case with others who got Self Realization in the NEEV Advaita Study group.

As you can see, the practices get subtler and subtler till finally, you understand your True nature as Self had always existed, and all your methods never made any dent in it. Your practices only helped you get a true reflection of Self. At the point of insight, the distinction between reflection and the source of reflection, Self, is overcome – The intellect knows itself as Self.

Finally, a person comes to Self Inquiry to escape suffering. Is this an escape, as you have asked in your question? Some say that even a desire to escape hell is, after all, a desire. The answer is that once Truth is known, even this desire ends. Suffering happens as an illusion. Once you get up from the dream, you don't bother about whatever you did or did not do there. After Self Inquiry is over, you wake up to your eternal nature, which you are permanently and has always been free from suffering.

Choiceless Awareness of 'What Is' and the Question of Ethics

(You need to put the question of the questioner, to which I have responded, otherwise a reader shall not get the context)

You have to understand that Krishnamurti uses the word Awareness differently from how Advaita uses it. For Advaita, Awareness is the ultimate reality. For Krishnamurti, Awareness is the process through which the mind is understood. In my system, to avoid this confusion, I use 'choiceless awareness of what is when talking about it as a process like Krishnamurti does. And simply the word Awareness with a capital' A', when I am talking about it in terms of Advaita: as an ultimate reality-Awareness. In the way Krishnamurti uses the word, and, in the way which you should understand it, as of now is, that it has its intelligence. When you are watching anger, there is a complex web of thoughts that come. It's not just one unidirectional flow of thoughts. For example, if you are thinking of throwing and damaging stuff, that is one thought. Simultaneously, another idea could arise, telling you the consequences of what will happen when you damage property. This does not mean that the second thought is much wiser than the first thought. When we are choicelessly aware, we are not choosing between ideas, judging between them, saying that this thought is wise and unwise. We are just looking at all our thoughts. We are not even bothered about looking at our thoughts to decide what action needs to be taken. Because if we do that, then we shall have to judge and choose between ideas. And we choose thoughts only based on past conditioning, so we can never examine the whole network of thought. We are not able to watch the entire network of anger. We suppress anger out of fear, out of our desire to be respectable. So the network of fear and anger remains. If we do not subdue, then what happens? You plunged into the unknown. Within your mind and with all your relationships, you come into a zone of unknown. You are no longer playing by the rules and codes of conduct, norms, and acceptable behavior set by society.

You become a rebel. And one is very afraid of being a rebel, losing relationships, being seen as an angry person, insulting, and losing reputation. Whatever I have said is not something that you have to agree with. See for yourself whether what I am saying is true or not? All people have anger, but they either suppress it, dissipate it, or substitute it with other concepts like God, chanting, etc. All these are only temporary measures. The only way to end anger or whole of thought is to watch it choicelessly. Look at what happens to you the moment I say this? Most probably, there is a fear. What fear? The fear of losing all control, of becoming an impulsive animal. What happens the moment you get this fear? You pull back. Isn't it? You get back into the game of control. There is a split between the thinker and the thought—the thinker trying to control thought because of fear. Now, the question is, why did you come to self-inquiry? To become a respectable member of society or to know Truth at all costs. To understand the Truth, you have to pay the price. This is not a journey of acquisition. It is a journey of ending, of dying to all of the thought and its acquisitions: it implies the ending of all acquisition, including virtue.

So when you are opening out to choiceless Awareness, is it a dumb act, or is it an act of great intelligence? The basis of choiceless Awareness of what is is the desire to know yourself honestly, to see through all falsity. Is this intention, a dumb intention, or an intelligent intention? If the purpose is wise, can it produce dumb acts? A socially respectable person is dotting all the i's and crossing all the t's, maybe a darling for the family or society. A ruthless, ambitious person is an object of envy and adoration for the family and the masses. These so-called successful, respectable, and adored people who follow all etiquettes are, in fact, dumb.

Choiceless Awareness of 'what is' will certainly not going to take you down this path. You shall go to that path which is your most actual intention. If you intend to know the highest indisputable Truth, you will move to that, and if you want to become respectable and gain power, you will move to that even within the field of spirituality. If you wish to seek experiences, you will move to that. All traditional paths start with ethics, as I mentioned before. But I don't start with ethics because ethics anyway is a step, not the aim. I like Krishnamurti's teachings because they don't start with ethics but start just a grade lower than the ultimate Truth. But not all can start here. It may be a shorter climb up the mountain of falsity to the peak of Truth, but it is a very steep climb. Most people prefer a gentler ascent, starting with ethics, gradually moving up the stages. So what you have mentioned as the Yoga view of 'saying no no' is a beginning step of that path which moves through eight stages. In the ultimate stage, Even Yoga transcends the world of virtue and vice as its end is the same as that of Krishnamurti's teachings: ending of all thought. With Krishnamurti, while we cannot directly compare with Patanjali's Yoga system, but in a general sort of way. I can say that we enter several stages above: almost in the fifth stage of Yoga, called pratyahara, or even in its sixth stage called dhyana.

The uniqueness of Krishnamurti's Teachings

Now, coming to the last part of your question:
3.) Question: "Also, I think (not sure) I've read of a Yogic method of "purifying the mind" by saying "no, no" as soon as unwanted tendencies pop up. Is that suppression?"

My Response: I have already answered in my comment related to your first question that 'choiceless Awareness of what is' which a means for purification of mind only. Not only this, at the end of my comment to the second part of your question, I have mentioned that this method of Krishnamurti is almost the fifth or sixth stage of Patanjali's Yoga in a very general sort of way. I am not very familiar with many Buddhist teachings, but they teach the same practice: mindfulness, etc. There is a school called Dzogchen school in Buddhism, which, according to some, contains the highest teachings of Tibetan Buddhism, also talks of choiceless Awareness of 'what is. Of course, most of these schools talk about this in a set up of monks and renunciates. So the complexities are significantly reduced. However, to Krishnamurti's credit, he taught this in the setup of the non-ascetic world most of us live in. Thus, his teachings are unique, even if his process exists in other schools. His instructions cover all the issues we face as people in society, which is lacking in the teachings of similar Buddhist schools.

Krishnamurti and Choiceless Awareness of "What Is"

In my opinion, J Krishnamurti, whose teachings I followed and teach for the first part of my self-inquiry, came up with a distinctive form of psychological Jnana Yoga, not taught by anyone before him. He delivered his teachings in deceptively plain and straightforward layman's English without technical terms and concepts. This method engenders a feeling in a seeker that self-inquiry is not something out of this world or an impenetrable mountain. The crux of his teachings is that one must be choicelessly aware of '" what is." Meaning that to know one's mind, one must not condemn, justify, control, or modify thought. This was the simple one-line teaching that he unfolded for sixty years of his teaching life.

Psychological Becoming and the Division of the Thinker and Thought in the Teachings of Krishnamurti

Through his penetrating analysis of human thought and psychology, Krishnamurti showed that the ultimate root of conflict in humans is between the thinker and the thought. Thought, he said, played mischief by splitting itself into the thinker and thought. The thinker becomes a stable center for impermanent thought – directing it, controlling it, and modifying it according to its conditioning. As one plumbs into the depths of his teachings, the seeker understands that ultimately it is the division between the thinker and the thought that fuels psychological becoming. One identifies oneself with the thinker and considers thought to be something other than oneself. Once this division is made, the machinery of conflict is set running. The thinker is the entity that wants to become something psychologically – rich, famous, virtuous, knowledgeable, or enlightened. Because of desire, the thinker is always controlling thought. This control of desire, our society calls virtue.

But one can easily see that control is not freedom. It is like a dam holding a large volume of water that can leak any time, or even burst. We have seen in previous paragraphs, virtue is based on the desire for a happy future, in this life or the next. And wherever there is desire, there is also fear. So the division between thinker and thought is a creation or manifestation of fear/desire. Till the time we address the root of this fear/desire, there can be no freedom. Virtue/control, as we have seen, is not the solution. Instead, it is an effect of a deeper problem of fear/desire. In freedom, there is no need for any control or effort. It has to be effortless. As the Ashtavakara Gita remarks with great subtlety:

"Verse 18.52: The conduct of the wise man, which is unrestricted by motive, shines being free from pretense, but not the affected calmness of the deluded person whose mind is attached."

Difference Between Krishnamurti and Advaita as a Solution to Ending of Suffering

While Krishnamurti and Advaita have a lot in common, they differ in their ultimate solution to suffering and methodology. In creating my teaching methodology, I have kept the common points between Krishnamurti and Advaita and left out those that conflict. This borrowing from different schools is accepted and endorsed by Shankara himself to the extent that the borrowed stuff does not contradict the shrutis/scriptures (Upanishads) of Advaita.

For Krishnamurti, the solution to ending suffering is ending all psychological thought, what is technically called manonasha (ending of psychological mind) and vasanakshaya (ending of all binding desires) in the Yoga school. Though Krishnamurti would detest his teachings being classified according to any tradition, I can firmly contend that his teachings fall under a school I term Yoga-Advaita. We can find an excellent description of the methodology of these schools in two Advaita textbooks – Vivekachudamani and Jivanmuktiviveka. As the name suggests, this school combines the teachings of Advaita and Yoga.

The difference between Advaita and Yoga-Advaita is that In Yoga, the ending of mind is considered enlightenment because the mind is considered real. Only a real thing has to be ended in order to end its binding. An unreal thing does not need to be ended to finish its binding. Only knowledge about its real nature ends all binding. Consider the example of a man misperceiving a snake (which is only real) on a rope. In Advaita, one does not have to kill the snake on the rope; one needs to know that the snake was just an apparent superimposition on it. In Yoga, one has to kill the snake or the mind to reach liberation because it considers them real. Yoga Advaita is a school that accepts Advaita because it feels Self Knowledge to be the cause of liberation but then adds the Yoga program to Self Knowledge. Stating that one must end the mind and desires if one wants self-actualization in this very life. Otherwise, the remaining vasanas can cause future births. Shankara has refuted this view in his commentaries.

So in Advaita, it is not about ending the mind but knowing that everything is Self that is the solution to suffering. I follow Krishnamurti in the first stage (psycho-philosophical stage) of self-inquiry (Jnana Yoga) and then shift the student to Advaita (metaphysical stage) when I discern ripeness in his/her mind to begin comprehending the dialectics of Advaita.

Enlightenment is not about acquiring dharma (virtue), which is a feature of the phenomenal world of the three Gunas, but about adhyatma – knowing the eternal reality beyond the three Gunas. You can never make the transient phenomenal world eternal or convert the dualistic samsara into non-dual Brahman/Self. Spirituality is about knowing the transcendent, eternal Self rather than purifying the phenomenal Self (psychological becoming). There is a verse from Avdhuta Gita which brings this out beautifully, "Verse 1.48: The Self indeed does not become pure through the practice of six-limbed Yoga. It indeed is not purified by the destruction of the mind. It certainly is not made pure by the instructions of the teacher. It is itself the truth. It is itself the illumined one. "

Even though the eternal reality is ever-present, it is clouded by ignorance. To penetrate this ignorance, one needs to follow a path with definite stages, as I have mentioned in the introduction. The first stage of the path is to acquire a sattvic intellect.

In Advaita, what is required, is not precisely a dharmic mind but a sattvic mind. Though dharma and sattva usually seem to be conflated by people, I treat them separately. For me, dharma is a social reality, whereas sattva is an individual psychological reality. Dharma often comes in the way of self-inquiry. For instance, I may want to pursue self-inquiry, but my parents would like me to land a good-paying corporate job. So this leads to conflict. As mentioned in the Introduction, Bhagavad Gita verses 2.41, 2.42, and 2.43, a mind with moksha as its aim, is automatically resolved (focused). Whereas a mind with dharma and karma as its objective is "many branched" (dissipated). Therefore, if moksha is your strongest desire, you already have a sattvic mind which will collaborate with you in self-inquiry.

After the above points are clear, I am providing the gist of how one deals with the conflict between the thinker and the thought, which happens in two stages.

First Stage: Psycho-Philosophical Inquiry – Understanding the Conditionings of the Thinker through Choiceless Awareness of "What Is" – This is a reasonably long stage. For me, it took about seventeen years which is by no means the standard amount of time. It all depends upon your karma load. I mentioned it to show that the preparation time is much longer than the second stage, where one enters into the insight stage of penetrating the conflict between the thinker and the thought. This stage is where one is learning to shift from being a Thinker trying to analyze and solve problems to being a silent Observer passively observing the movements of the mind rather than trying to solve them. It is the stage where one learns to shift from all forms of psychological becoming to being.

The processes of this stage are facilitated by reading the

teachings of Krishnamurti, reflecting upon them, having a dialogue about them with a teacher, and starting your practice of choiceless awareness of 'what is.' All three practices have to be undertaken together. These practices are what Jnana Yoga (Yoga of Knowledge) all about

Reading
Reflection/Dialogue/Journal Writing
Contemplation/Choiceless Awareness of 'What Is'

These are the practices of Advaita, which I have lifted and applied to the teachings of J Krishnamurti as they work fine with his teachings too. The NEEV Psycho-Philosophy Facebook Group, which I run , is the place where all these processes take place.

Second Stage: Advaitic Inquiry – You (Self/Awareness) Are Not The Thinker and the Thoughts. After one has gained sufficient maturity of mind, and   one has seen through all forms of psychological becoming and become an Observer rather than a Thinker then one is qualified to move to Advaitic inquiry. Not that Advaita does not require the thinker: it does but in a very definite way.

In my Chapter Enlightenment through Words, I have provided the actual method of how the teaching of Advaita engenders enlightenment in the student. It is not any reasoning that can help you get the liberating insight of Advaita but only the reasoning in line with the scriptures, wielded by a teacher who is a knower of Brahman. That can help you with the final liberating insight that frees you from being a thinker/doer/observer/experiencer to being Self/Awareness/ Witness. In my Chapter: Self-inquiry and insight into our true nature/Self in Advaita, I have described how this shift happened. All these processes are facilitated in the second Facebook group that I run: NEEV Advaita Study Group. The same Reading, Reflection/Dialogue, Contemplation methods are followed here, but this time with Advaita literature.

I end my Chapter with a brief pictorial representation of how you are Self and not the thinker and the thoughts, which is just for your preliminary knowledge. The in-depth understanding of this model requires an elaborate unfolding of the teachings of Advaita.

The Five Sheaths Model

The five-sheath model is one of the tools employed by Advaita to help a seeker get liberation. The pic above shows the five sheaths that are 'superimposed' on Self. Advaita helps a seeker to discriminate between the five sheaths and the Self/Witness of the five sheaths. So Advaita resolves the conflict between the thinker and thought by showing that both the thinker (Intellect Sheath/Vijnanamaya Kosha) and the thought (Mental Sheath/Manomaya Kosha) are objects to You/Self/Witness/Awareness rather than You being them. You are free from the thinker and thoughts in your true nature as Self, so there is no point bothering them. Just like the smoke never dirties the space, no thoughts or actions ever taint You/ Self.

The last lines I wrote above refers to Seer-Seen Discrimination in Advaita.

Law 1. I am different from whatever I witness
Law 2. I, the witness, am always free from the attributes of the object.

EndNote:
Annamaya kosha, "food" sheath (Anna)
Pranamaya kosha, "energy" sheath (Prana)
Manomaya kosha "mind" sheath (Manas)
Vijñānamaya kosha, "discernment" or "Knowledge" sheath (Vigynana)
Anandamaya kosha, "bliss" sheath (Ananda)

Turiya : The Fourth State of Consciousness

Introduction

As normal human beings going about our daily lives, chasing dreams, getting happy, or grieving over life's inscrutable experiences, we are all aware of three states of Consciousness – waking, dream sleep, and deep sleep. They are so much part and parcel of our lives, so much taken for granted, we can hardly imagine a treasure concealed by these three states. However, for a person who has devoted himself to solving life's paradoxes – life's dualities of birth and death, pain and pleasure, peace and suffering – the careful study of these very, taken for granted, three states of Consciousness, lies a fourth state. This fourth state of Consciousness has the answer to all the riddles of a self inquirer. In Advaita Vedanta, this fourth state of Consciousness is called Turiya or the Eternal Self/ Witness/ Consciousness.

Mandukya Upanishad of Vedanta: A Testament to its power in Self Inquiry

The fourth state of Consciousness is mentioned in the Mandukya Upanishad of Vedanta school. In my own journey of self-inquiry, it was the most important Upanishad that lead me to the insight into the fourth state of Consciousness – Turiya/Eternal Self/ Witness/Consciousness. An insight into this state spells the end of the active seeking kind of self-inquiry, even though it is the shortest of all the Upanishads. It is listed as number 6 in the Muktikā canon of 108 Upanishads. The fact that this Upanishad proved to be the most significant text for my own journey of Self inquiry through Advaita is not entirely surprising.

Historically, the Muktika canon, which is part of a dialogue between Rama and Hanuman of Ramayana, underscores its power in self-inquiry. Rama proposes to teach Vedanta to Hanumana, saying.

"Even by reading one verse of them [any Upanishad] with devotion, one gets the status of union with me, hard to get even by sages."

Hanuman enquires about the different kinds of "liberation" (Mukti, hence the name of the Upanishad) and the following dialogue ensues.

Rama : The only real type [of liberation] is Kaivalya

Hanumana: But by what means is the Kaivalya kind of Moksha got?

Rama: The Mandukya is enough; if knowledge is not got from it, then study the Ten Upanishads. Getting knowledge very soon, you will reach my abode. If certainty is not got even then, study the 32 Upanishads and stop. If desiring Moksha without the body, read the 108 Upanishads.

Mandukya Upanishad as a text for Self inquiry and ending suffering in Advaita Vedanta

The primary purpose of self-inquiry is the permanent end of suffering. Through various stages in one's self-inquiry journey, one understands that the root cause of suffering is that one takes oneself to be this limited mind-body-intellect as one's Self. This apparatus of mind-body-intellect is constantly changing, constantly subject to the dualities of pains and pleasures, and experiences birth and death.

For an inquirer, death is a very great paradox of life. death puts a big question mark on all our life projects. For example, what is the point of our chasing of dreams and achievements when they all end in death? Not only that, just a step further comes up the big existential question, "What is the point and meaning of the whole of life and living, if all has to end one day in death?"

Well, the answer to all these questions is found in the Upanishads. The Mandukya Upanishad, in particular, is the favorite book for the student of Advaita Vedanta, as it relies totally on rational self-inquiry. In its twelve terse prose paragraphs, Mandukya Upanishad reveals the secret of life that resolves all suffering and paradoxes facing a human being. The meanings of the twelve verses are unpacked by a commentary by Gaudapada, who authored Mandukya Karika. The founder of Advaita Vedanta – Shankaracharya, was Gaudapada disciple's disciple.

Advaita Vedanta, a school of non-dual self-inquiry that I follow, leads a seeker to the state of Turiya/Eternal Witness, which is unborn, undying, and partless. According to it, our true Self is not what we take to be – the mind-body-intellect complex. Instead, our true Self is Turiya/Eternal Witness of the mind-body-intellect, also the Eternal Witness of the entire universe. Because of beginningless ignorance, we have identified ourselves with the mortal, limited, and changing – body-mind-intellect. The truth is that we are immortal – unborn, undying, and unchanging.

The Mandukya Upanishad, along with the Mandukya Karika brings home to the seeker this bewildering point through a very rational process of self-inquiry. The truth of our immortality is hidden in plain sight. It is available for all of us to see if we wish to because the nature of truth is that it never ceases to exist. The difference between truth and suffering is just this. Suffering may not have a beginning, but it has an end because it is not real. On the other hand, being real has no beginning and no end; therefore, it never ceases to exist even when it is superimposed by suffering.

Turiya – Fourth State of Consciousness: Not an Additional State (Nirvikalpa Samadhi etc.)

Every human being, as I noted in the beginning, is aware of three states of Consciousness – the waking state, dream sleep state, and deep sleep state. But what every human being is not aware of is that all these three states are actually superimpositions on the fourth state of Consciousness which is called Turiya/Eternal Witness. The reader should, however, not be confused by these numbers to believe that there are four different kinds of Consciousness. As I go along, the reader shall understand that there is fundamentally only one Consciousness, which appears as the three states of waking, dream sleep, and deep sleep. The number four does not represent a numerical quantity but a modality. The fourth state of Consciousness is the substrate of the other three states of Consciousness, not something in addition to the other three states. It subsists in all three states. One can imagine it as a screen over which the other three states of Consciousness roll over like a movie. A movie, which is a changing set of images, cannot be viewed without a changeless background. Turiya is the changeless background over which the three states of waking, dreamless sleep, and deep sleep appear to be projected as changing entities.

This is something important to understand as we go along. There are schools of Yoga that interpret Turiya to be a state of Nirvikalpa Samadhi, a special state of object-less Consciousness. This is not how it is taken in Advaita Vedanta. Nirvikalpa Samadhi is a special state of objectless Consciousness reached in meditation. Its uniqueness lies in the fact that there it is a state of awareness where there is no thought. The mind is held in abeyance, and one comes to see after the samadhi has subsided that one did not exist as a mind-body-intellect at that time. The samadhi gives one proof that one is actually not the mind-body-intellect.

However, notwithstanding the uniqueness of this sama-dhi, the fact is that it is an experience that one goes in and comes out of. So essentially, it is no different from the other states of waking, dream sleep, and deep sleep. Turiya/Awareness/Consciousness in Advaita is that which is never absent at any time. It is just concealed from us because of ignorance. Once an inquirer gets an insight into its existence, it stands revealed.

Self Inquiry/Analysis into Three States of Sleep, Dream Sleep, and Deep Sleep

Advaita Vedanta is a school of Vedanta that teaches that all suffering can come to an end by a rational process of examining the nature of suffering, which leads to a supra-rational insight that we are not the body/mind/intellect that was born and that is going to die. It does not posit any God or Creator or any system of belief. It also does not require the inquirer to practice any act like chanting, meditation, con-centration, pranayama, Yoga, etc. It is therefore also called the direct path to liberation. (It sounds like a cool deal but let me inform the reader that it is acknowledged as the toughest path in the Bhagavad Gita)The Mandukya Upanishad (MKU) along with the Mandukya Karika (MK), therefore, is a favorite for Advaita Vedanta. There is no talk of any God or Creator or practice. Even when it does talk of God, it talks only pro-visionally and not as some deity or personal God. The God of MKU and MK is nothing but Maya – a power of illusion that projects a phenomenal world which only apparently exists. The only thing that MKU does is to analyze the three states of waking, dream sleep, and deep sleep to reveal that they do not and cannot exist without Turiya/Eternal Witness or Eternal Consciousness and that these three states are fun-damentally unreal and non-existent. It reaches the baffling and stupendous conclusion that Turiya/Eternal Self/Witness/Consciousness is the only thing that exists.

With the aid of MKU and MU, the analysis of the three states of waking, dream sleep, and deep sleep, we real-ize the following. I am not going into quoting and making comments on MK and MKU, rather rendering the concepts in them into a format that is elaborate and yet simple for a reader to assimilate.

The universe as a real external entity with multiple subjects and objects occurs only in the waking state of Consciousness. Here one is aware of oneself as a body-mind-intellect self. There is a hard duality between self/subject and other objects.

In the dream state of Consciousness, the entire universe which was outside of us is now within us. Here one is no longer aware of one's body. The dreamer/ a single subject, which is just our mind, creates the entire universe, which seems as real as the universe in the waking state. The subject-object duality is still there but less dualistic. Subject and object are now in the same plane, like the mirror and the image in it. It is clear that here the subject has created the objects, in fact, the entire universe. The mind has created the universe.

The dream state shows that the time and space of the waking state are not objective realities independent of the mind; as in this state, the time and space of the waking state are compressed. The dream state shows that the body is a projection of the mind because the body does not exist at all in the dream state. Also, the body is not a real entity as it does not exist in the dream state. The body exists in the mind, not the other way around.

Finally, the dream state shows that the self-identity we hold on to in our waking state is also changing. For example, in my dreams, till date, I dream of myself as being a student in my school days. When I get up, paraphrasing Zhuangzi, the Taoist sage, I may ask, "Am I the man dreaming myself to be the school student, or am I the school student dreaming myself to be the man?"

In the deep sleep state – mind, body, universe, space, and time – all vanish. One is aware of nothing or no-thing. Paradoxically and precisely because of this, this state holds the key to the riddle of our suffering.

The deep sleep state reveals that the mind is also not a real entity as it does not exist in the deep sleep state. Here there is no mind; there is no universe, no time and space. So the sleep state is the originator of mind, body, universe, time, and space. Since there is no subject and no object in a deep sleep, the subject-object duality completely vanishes. So even the subject-object duality which is present in our waking state is not a reality as it does not exist in the sleep state. Since there is no mind, thought, the universe, and suffering, sleep is a state of no experience, yet Bliss – a state free of all suffering. A beleaguered king, a beggar, a sick man, a worried man, a dying man, all are freed from the suffering of every kind in sleep.

Though body, mind, intellect, universe, time, and space all come to an end, something still exists. What is it? After one wakes up from deep sleep, one has the memory of having slept well, of a feeling of refreshment. Also, one is aware that during sleep, one saw no-thing. There was an awareness operating even when everything else had subsided; the awareness of having slept well and of having seen no-thing/no-objects, which is available as a memory in the waking state. This background awareness, which is conscious of even the sleep state, is Turiya/Awareness/Consciousness (Please note I am using the terms Consciousness and Awareness synonymously)

Conclusions of Analysis into the three states – Understanding Turiya and Maya

For a mind which is tuned to self-inquiry, all this analysis would point to the following stupendous conclusions.

The mind-body-intellect cannot be one's true Self because they are changing entities in the three states. In a deep sleep state, they are entirely absent. Our sense of Self is constant. It never changes. Even when one wakes up from sleep, one feels himself/herself to be the same unchanged Self. If our true Self was mind-body-intellect, then this could not be the case, as these do not persist in all three states. Even in sleep, there was a self that was aware of not seeing objects and which felt bliss/no suffering.

Since our sense of Self is constant across the three states, it cannot be the body-mind-intellect with which we are identified because body-mind-intellect is completely absent in the deep sleep state. This means that we have wrongly identified our Self with body-mind-intellect. In Advaita, this wrong identification with our body-mind-intellect is called avidya.

Our true Self is that which exists in all three states. Now, what exists in all three states? Is it not the background awareness or Consciousness which witnesses all these three states. This background awareness/consciousness/witness is the only thing that exists at all moments at all times and is, therefore, our true Self. This true Self/Consciousness/ Awareness is called Turiya in Mandukya Upanishad.

What is the nature of Turiya? It is eternal Existence-Consciousness(Witness)-Bliss or Sat-Chit-Ananda as they say in Advaita. How? While the three states of waking, dream sleep, and deep sleep are changing and mutually exclusive to each other (meaning one state cannot exist in the presence of the other state and one state cancels the other state), it is only Turiya that exists in all three states. So it is eternal existence. Since it is aware of even the sleep state, where time and space are absent, it is beyond time and space and change. Also, Turiya is Aware of or Conscious of all three states, so it is eternal Consciousness. Finally, Turiya is unchanging because it has no subject-object duality. Being beyond space and time, it is not made up of any parts. Since it has no parts, no change, and therefore no experience, there is no suffering in it. Moreover, after one wakes up, one is aware of the Bliss of sleep caused by no experience. So Turiya is also eternal Bliss.

So our true Self is Turiya or Eternal Existence-Consciousness-Bliss. We are identified with the mortal mind-body-intellect as our Self because of ignorance which conceals our true Self as Turiya in broad daylight. This power of ignorance is called Maya, and this is the root causes us suffering.

Maya causes us to see ourselves as a body-mind-intellect apparatus that is born in a universe and which is going to die. Maya is the power that superimposes the mind-body-intellect and the resulting universe of space-time-objects on our true Self/Turiya, which is Eternal-Consciousness-Bliss. Maya creates the universe and our mind and body where none exist in reality. It does so by its power of delusion. Just like we are deluded in seeing a rope to be a snake in the absence of light, we are deluded to see a universe of objective forms, by Maya, where none exists. The forms are nothing but

Consciousness. But because due to ignorance, we see an objective and real universe and ourselves as a limited being in this universe, we suffer from fears and desires.

Like the rope appearing a snake causes fear and suffering, Maya causes us to fear and suffer by projecting an objective individual and the universe. When we shine a light on the rope and see that it was not a snake, all fear and suffering are dispelled. In the same way, Maya and suffering are dispelled by the light of Self -Knowledge gained through inquiry.

Maya is unreal because it ends with knowledge. A real thing can never end. The Self/Turiya is real because it never ends. It is unborn and undying. When the snake was seen on the rope and when the rope was seen as a rope after the delusion of the snake on it was removed, the rope remained unchanged. In the same way, Turiya/Self remains unchanged as the three states of waking, dream sleep, and deep sleep is projected on it cyclically or when Maya ceases.

Therefore we are the true Self/Turiya all the time. Even when delusion projects the snake on the rope, the rope was present as it was. After the delusion ended, the rope continues to exist as it was. There was no production of a new Self or state. Only because of Maya, we are thinking ourself to be the mind-body-intellect. Once the thought of Maya ends, we know ourselves as Eternal Self/Turiya, and suffering ends.

No amount of beating the snake on the rope with a stick can end our fear. Similarly, no amount of action can end suffering. Just as when we shine a torch on the rope and examine it closely, we come to know of the delusion of snake, and it ends, in the same way, only knowledge of our true Self/Turiya through self-inquiry can end suffering.

My intention in this Chapter was to show how the study of analysis of the three states of waking, dream sleep, and deep sleep as revealed in Mandukya Upanishad and Mandukya Karika can lead one to recognize our true Self as Turiya/True Self/ Eternal Existence-Consciousness – Bliss. This is how we can permanently end suffering. There are three steps involved here.

Sravana (Listening/Reading) – getting indirect knowledge of Self/Turiya

Manana (Deep & Sustained Reflection) – getting an insight/direct knowledge of Self/Turiya

Nidhidhyasana (Contemplation)– Abiding as Self/Turiya till the knowledge gets converted gradually into a full-blown experiential realization of eternal existence-consciousness-bliss.

For those who are interested in the process of getting direct knowledge/insight into Turiya/Self, they may read the Chapter "Self inquiry and insight into one's true nature in Advaita"

However, I hope that I have been able to fully illustrate the meaning of Turiya and how it ends suffering permanently. If the reader has any doubts, they may feel free to write back to me with doubts or question

Self-inquiry

The Way It Happens in Advaita Vedanta

For those who have rambled long enough in the corridors of spirituality, especially non-dual spirituality, self-inquiry is a familiar word, if not rare. A google search for the term will return the results of Ramana Maharishi's "method" of self-inquiry, which begins with asking the question, "Who am I ?" Even Wikipedia, for some reason, devotes its page on self-inquiry exclusively to Ramana, which in my opinion, is a very myopic statement of facts.

This leads to a ubiquitous notion among people new to self-inquiry, even those who have spent several years in this endeavour, that there is one form of self-inquiry. The notion of self-inquiry is found in several schools of Buddhism, as also in the Advaita Vedanta school of Hinduism.

The complexity and perplexity of this matter do not end here. Even among those who talk about eternal, non-dual Self, different individuals teach different methods. For example, the trio of Ramana Maharshi, Nisargadatta Maharaj, and Atmananda Menon all talk about the same truth. Still, the process of inquiry taught by each one of them is unique.

Though they all can be loosely called to be representatives of the school of Advaita Vedanta, their instructions for self-inquiry are quite different from the traditional school of Advaita Vedanta: which bases itself on three texts of Upanishads, Brahmasutras and Bhagavad Gita.

In my journey of self-inquiry, I stumbled into traditional Advaita in 2012. At that time, I did not have the wisdom I have today about different paths and teachings. Looking back, I can say that all my previous years of sadhana/spiritual practice with the teachings of J Krishnamurti had landed me automatically to the doorstep of Advaita – the highest teaching of non-duality in the Hindu school of thought.

Self-inquiry in Advaita

I will describe the manner of self-inquiry I underwent in traditional Advaita, and not through any of the individual teachings of Ramana, Nisargadatta, or Atmananda. What I am going to describe is the way self-inquiry is done traditionally in the school of Advaita (found in Gaudapada's Mandukya Karika and later in Shankaracharya), through three processes of

Sravana – Listening/reading of scriptures

Manana – Reflection/dialogue on scriptures till all doubts cease

Nidhidhyasana – Contemplation on truth ascertained through manana/reflection for arising of non-dual insight.

The qualifications required of a seeker for self-inquiry in Advaita

This process of self-inquiry is called Jnana Yoga/ Knowledge Yoga in Advaita, and one has to be an adhikari/a qualified aspirant, before coming to Jnana Yoga. This is something that modern seekers sometimes overlook. Not everyone has the proper orientation to inquiry. Most are seeking some form of psychological solution to their problems. Self-inquiry is not a solution to problems of mundane life. Though it does solve them eventually, it is quite disruptive and disturbing in the beginning. It is going to demand and involve you in a way that can disrupt your livelihood, family, and other pursuits.

Realizing the predilection of immature seekers to jump to

self-inquiry, Advaita enjoins seekers to first achieve a certain set of qualifications before coming to Jnana Yoga; else, one has to do Karma Yoga/Yoga of Action, which develops these qualities in the seeker. The set of qualities for a seeker to enter Jnana Yoga are

Viveka/Discrimination – the ability to differentiate between what is true and what is false.

Vairagya/ Dispassion – lack of attachment to mundane ends of life – duties, wealth, and gross pleasures

Shad Sampat/ wealth of six virtues – sama/control of mind, dama/control of mind, upariti /life activities reduced to bare essentials, titiksha/endurance to opposites of experiences, shraddha/faith in scriptures, and samadhana/constancy of purpose to reach liberation.

Mumukshutva – Intense desire for liberation

I never did Karma Yoga. I was following Krishnamurti's teachings of self-inquiry for seventeen years before I came to Advaita. My Krishnamurti style of self-inquiry had already developed the above qualities. The result was, when I came in contact with Advaita, within no time, the teachings precipitated the insight – I am Witness/Self – for me.

The mechanism for self-inquiry and insight into true Self in Advaita

This is how traditional Advaita works. For a mind that is sufficiently prepared, the mere exposition of the scriptural truths of Advaita by a teacher results in the awakening of insight in such a mind about one's true Self. I did not even go to a teacher or search for any teacher. Advaita says that one does not need to search for a teacher actively: when one is ready, the teacher appears. In my case, the teacher did not even appear physically. I was reading the writings of one Advaita teacher – James Swartz, very intensely for a week. I was reading others too, but for some reason, I felt an inexplicable pull towards his writings only. One day, while reading one of his Chapters, the insight about my true Self just flashed in me. The Chapter was to do with something called akhandakara vritti in Advaita.

Before I can go into what it is, I have to briefly go into the central premise of liberation in Advaita. According to traditional Advaita, the root cause of our suffering is the ignorance of our true nature. In our ignorance, we identify ourselves with our phenomenal self . This phenomenal self – in Advaita – is the apparatus of body, mind, and intellect. Because we take our Self to be the body-mind-intellect apparatus, we are subject to suffering. The body-mind-intellect apparatus is a limited, changing identity subjected to the duality of pain and pleasure, birth and death. The solution to our riddle of suffering, as per Advaita, is to realize that we are not this limited, changing apparatus of body-mind-intellect. We are actually the eternal, formless Self/Witness which is aware of the impermanent and changing body-mind-intellect apparatus.

In our ignorance, we mistake our true Self/Witness to be the mind-body-intellect. I consider myself to be Anurag which is a body that was born and which is going to die. But Advaita says that I am not the body. I am that to which the body-Anurag appears. I am the eternal, formless Self/Witness. The body is a form that appears in the formless Self/Witness and which dissolves back in the formless/Witness. So the Self/Witness is the eternal subject. What I take as myself – body-mind-intellect apparatus – is actually an object to the eternal Self/Witness.

All our suffering is related to the wrong identification of our eternal Self/subject with impermanent objects: body-mind-intellect. The solution is to reclaim our true Self through knowledge. There is no action required. The Self as eternal, unborn, and undying always exists. It is just clouded by ignorance like the clouds shield the sun. The sun never ceases to shine. Ignorance is nothing but wrong knowledge. Once we get the right knowledge, we see the sun, which had always been shining.

So Advaita acts as the source of knowledge that dispels the ignorance of our true nature. One may validly ask at this point, why is it that anyone and everyone who reads Advaita does not get liberated with the insight of eternal Self? The reason is simple. For any knowledge to be assimilated, we need two things

Valid source/object of knowledge

Valid sense organ/subject for assimilating the knowledge

For instance, if we want to know the color of a rose, we have to have a pair of functioning eyes. I cannot know the color of a rose through my ears. Once an 'object to be known' is placed in front of the 'valid knowing subject', there is an immediate arising of knowledge. No other extraneous effort is required. But if there is any limitation in the object or subject, true knowledge does not arise. Suppose there is a defect in my eyes, I shall not be able to get the knowledge of a rose through my eyes, even if it is placed in front of them. In the case of Advaita, the object to be known is the Self through teachings/scriptures/words; the subject that has to know/assimilate this object is the intellect, and the knowledge to be assimilated is the nature of one's true Self/Witness. Suppose my intellect is sufficiently prepared, without any psychological defects, when a competent teacher enunciates the teachings/ scripture/words, in that case, knowledge of one's true Self/insight happens spontaneously and effortlessly. But if there is a psychological defect in the intellect in the form of doubt, lack of motivation: the lack of four qualifications I mentioned earlier etc., insight does not awaken. In such a case, one has to 'purify' one's intellect through Karma Yoga or keep doing Sravana/Listening/ Reading, Manana/Dialogue/Reflection and Nidhidhyasana/ Contemplation till the insight arises.

The akhandakara vritti – The unbroken thought

In my case, as I said earlier, my mind was already prepared through seventeen years of Krishnamurti style self-inquiry and the knowledge of the basic framework of Advaita. So when I was reading the Chapter on akhandakara vritti by my teacher (whom I did not even know by that point), the insight about my true Self/Witness just flashed. So let us go into what this is akhandakara vritti.

In Advaita, one is initially trained to separate the true subject and objects which are mixed up in ordinary consciousness. This is called the process of viveka/discrimination. Discrimination is about differentiating the changing objects from the unchanging subject When we begin, we start with identifying and negating objects. Thus all things which we can perceive and which change are objects. I have an unbroken experience of Self, so I cannot be something changing. Something changing will have gaps: but I do not feel as though I exist sometimes and do not exist at some times.

Also, I cannot perceive something which is me: there will be no difference between perceiver and perceived, hence no perception. I can only perceive something which is outside of me. We can perceive our body, so we are not the body; Similarly, we can perceive our mind in the form of feelings and thoughts, so we are not our feelings and thoughts too. The last and most difficult object to discern is the thinker/doer/experiencer. I take myself, Anurag, as the thinker/doer/experiencer. Because of this, I am constantly caught in the process of life – avoiding pain and pursuing pleasure in all its myriad forms, including life and death.

So all thoughts we usually have are called vishayakara vritti, meaning they are object-oriented thoughts. They have a duality between subject and object. Thus, in ignorance, one says, "I am feeling anger/angry". There is a subject, "I," and there is an object, "anger." In ignorance, I take this subject, "I," which is experiencing anger, to be myself. The teachings of Mandukya Upanishad – the most highly revered textbook of Advaita – elucidates the three states of – waking, dreaming, and deep sleep – to show that even this "I" – the thinker/doer/experiences, which we take as our permanent Self, is actually not permanent: it modifies in the dream state, and completely vanishes in the deep sleep state. Mandukya Upanishad then talks about Self/Witness being the only thing that is present in all three states. Once a seeker has grasped this, he is ready for the arising of akhandakara vritti. One starts looking for Self/Witness in one's experience, which is not an object, and which does not change. This prepares the ground for the last and most subtle discrimination to be made between the thinker/doer/experiencer and Witness/Self.

The meaning of akhandakara vritti is "unbroken thought", which means that this is a thought, which, unlike vishayakara vritti, does not have a subject-object duality, or 'broken-ness.' In akhandakara vritti the subject and object are the same; when it appears spontaneously in one's mind, it breaks the ignorance of our false self and reveals the true Self simultaneously. So when I was reading about akhandakara vritti, in the Chapter written by James Swartz , I suddenly had an akhandakara vritti in my own mind, which was in the form of "I am awareness."

If one examines this thought, it says that the subject "I" of the sentence is the same as the object "awareness" in the sentence, but this awareness is actually the non-dual, eternal metaphysical subject I was seeking in my inquiry: and I am That. The object of my inquiry, paradoxically, turns out to be "me" – the subject. The eternal Self that I was seeking is the one who was witnessing all this seeking and the seeker. So an immediate shift in my identity took place. Instead of me – Anurag – looking out for awareness in my experience, I became awareness looking at Anurag as an object/experience in awareness.

The fruits of this insight

The insight was phenomenal. It gave me a freedom that I had never experienced in all my years. It was not any experience. Experience comes and goes in time: insight is permanent. It was not the end of bad times for me. I faced a huge crisis in years to come, especially in the end of 2016. Please read my Chapter – "Prarabdha Karma After Self Realization" for a deeper ending of this issue. But nothing ever touched me fundamentally. As Self/Witness, I had found a sanctuary which is described in Ashtavakra Gita, one of my favorites, by King Janaka as

In me, the shoreless ocean, let the waves of the universe rise and fall as they will. I am neither enhanced nor diminished.
Chapter 7, Verse 2 – Ashtavakra Gita

I must definitely add here that this is not the final stage of liberation in Advaita. This is called the "I Am" stage, in short "I Am Brahman" or the Witness stage. The final stage is "Everything is Brahman," which comes when the notion of the Witness collapses with further deconstructions.

Stages of Self Inquiry

Theoretically speaking, if one has the prerequisites in terms of enormous zeal for self-inquiry, enormous dedication to make it the only important thing in one's life, one does not need a teacher in person. The books and writings should do. I did not have any appointed teacher throughout my own journey. I did have a number of philosophical dialogues with some teachers online in order to discuss certain very subtle issues. For my post Witness stage I had a lot of online dialogues with Greg Goode – Teacher of Direct Path. Nonetheless, I can say that a large part of my journey was almost without a teacher in person: just the books and the teachings. But this scenario is extremely rare.

For the majority of people, I have seen that they benefit rather than require the active support and guidance of a teacher. The rule of thumb is that if you are very serious in your self-inquiry, the teacher shall appear at the right time. It may not be one single individual, and it may not be a teacher who hands truth to you. I encountered several people in my journey who taught me a step or two in the direction of the final destination. They all came to answer, it seems to me in retrospect, those questions I was holding most intensely at that time. So one definitely needs to have a lot of dialogues with like-minded people in one's journey of self-inquiry, apart from one's personal readings. There are also the rare and genuine teachers who can ferry you across the ocean of samsara – right from one shore to the other.

Choosing One's Path

Inexperienced seekers labor under the illusion that all paths lead to the same truth. However, non-dual paths are completely different from dualistic paths in terms of the ultimate reality. Even among non-dual paths, the practices of different paths may be diametrically opposed to each other. For example, almost every seeker believes that spirituality is to do with meditation. This is the case mostly for Yoga based schools and devotion-based schools. In many non-dual inquiry-based schools, the emphasis is more on transformative knowledge; meditation is an invaluable aid (for mental stabilization) but not the direct means to liberation. (For further understanding, one may read my Chapter Enlightenment through Words. Nowadays, the teachings of Yoga schools are mixed with the teachings of Shankara-Gaudpada Advaita Vedanta.

Every path is different depending upon whether it is dual or non-dual.

Every path has a different methodology for reaching its goal. At times these methodologies or practices conflict with each other.

One must study the path carefully and see if it suits their purpose. For instance, those inclined to bhakti very strongly may not be inclined to Advaita Vedanta of Shankara/Gaudapada unless they are willing to consider God as a helpful illusion at an initial stage of their journey to arrive at non-dual Awareness.

The Beginning of Self Inquiry

Self-inquiry begins when one has an inexplicable and inextinguishable desire to gain freedom from all suffering. Vedanta shows that human life has four main aims: Dharma (Duties), Artha (Wealth), Kama (Pleasure), and Moksha (Freedom). The first three aims are actions that result in impermanent results. Being impermanent and transitory in nature, we are unwittingly tied to this 'wheel of activity/ samsara': both in this life and in the next, through the cycle of karma/action, death and rebirth.

Once an individual comes to understand the futility of the first three aims of Dharma, Artha, Kama vaguely and begins questioning them to find if there is something beyond this mechanical process of desire and suffering we call life, the fourth aim of Moksha appears on the horizon. Self-inquiry, thus, kicks in when one is discontented with all the goods that life has to offer. If the self-inquiry is really genuine, one shall leave no stone unturned to ultimately end the teeming discontent of life.

Stages in My Self Inquiry

My journey of self-inquiry till now is in four phases. These inquiries are arranged in hierarchical order as –
1.) Psycho-philosophical Inquiries – Understanding self

and world/Ending duality of thinker and thought

    2.) Meditative Inquiries – Developing Qualifications for Advaita

    Inquiry/Observer Stage

    3.) Advaitic/Direct Path Inquiries – Knowledge of Non-Dual Awareness

    Witness Stage – I am Brahman/Awareness – Vivartavada Stage

    4.) The collapse of Witness Stage – Everything is Brahman/Awareness – Ajativada Stage

    Common to all these inquiries are the three processes of Jnana Yoga/Knowledge Yoga, called:

    Sravana/Reading of Scriptures/spiritual literature

    Manana/Reflecting on them so that no doubts remain

    Nidhidhyasana/Contemplating on the truths ascertained through reflection

    These processes remain the same, but they became more profound as self-inquiry progresses.

    1.) Psycho-philosophical Inquiry (Lasted twenty years for me)

    This stage is about psychological preparation of mind: freeing itself from all worldly engagements of Dharma (Duties), Artha (Wealth), Kama (Pleasure), and orienting it towards Moksha (Enlightenment). For this stage, the psychological teachings of J Krishnamurti and Ken Wilber benefited me most.

    Krishnamurti's inquiries are pretty demanding, unsettling, and penetrating. They are meant to question the ego and free it from all its commitments and attachments to all worldly projects, going deeper into the mind and ultimately asking the very nature of thought. In my case, it took me about twenty years to get finished with all the psychological bindings to the world.

    The primary purpose of all psycho-philosophical inquiries is to understand that the root reason for all conflicts one faces in the world is due to the gap between 'what is' and 'what should be'. Our society conditions us from childhood to the path of psychological becoming. Society prepares us to become rich, famous, influential, knowledgeable, or erudite. The gap one fuels this constant becoming perceives between 'what one is' and 'what one should be' as conditioned by society. Once one understands that all these aims of life create a conflict of constant becoming and grant only temporary happiness, one shifts his journey from becoming to being: from the socially conditioned compulsion of becoming to the silence of understanding being. This is also where the duality between the thinker and the thought ends because the thought is 'what is and the thinker is 'what should be'.

Coming to this realization is the basis of further and deeper self-inquiry. Until one is involved psychologically in any social organizations or institutions, either materialistically, socially, ethically, or spiritually, one is a soul torn apart or perpetually trying to manage the conflicting demands of work, society, and relationships. The energy of such a mind is divided and dissipated. At some point, one has to decide to devote oneself wholeheartedly to self-inquiry and align all one's life activities along this axis. This process of cutting down all energy dissipating activities, doing only necessary ones, and utilizing the rest of time for self-inquiry is called upariti in Advaita.

Ken Wilber's stages of development of consciousness were a crucial tool for me to chart my journey. Krishnamurti highly negates a developmental approach, but I felt the need for such a map, and Ken Wilber's Integral Theory Model filled this need for me beautifully. It was this model that finally led me to Advaita later on. Strictly speaking, it is the spiral dynamics model of his Integral Theory that appealed to me most, which was originally developed by Dr. Clare Grave's emergent cyclical levels of existence.

All these psycho-philosophical inquiries result in steering our minds and senses away from their perpetual engagement in the outer world of becoming and fixing them on the ultimate aim of Moksha/Liberation. This steering away from the phenomenal world by mind and senses is called sama/withdrawal of mind and dama/withdrawal of senses in Advaita.

2.) Meditative Inquiry – Developing Qualifications for

Advaita Inquiry – Observer Stage

I used Krishnamurti's teachings of "Choiceless Awareness of What Is in the meditative inquiry. " This is a mode of
non-judgemental observation of thought which one comes to
when one is sincerely and deeply interested in understanding
the mind rather than merely superficially solving psychological problems through analysis. At this stage, gradually,
samadhana/one-pointed focus in self-inquiry is achieved;
what happens automatically is, instead of using our mind as
an instrument for acquiring objects and experiences, meditative inquiry trains awareness to the activities of the mind
itself. Thus, the mind turns back to look at itself instead of
looking out at objects.

Thus, a meditative inquiry is a process of learning about
the mind while it is acting in its daily life of work and relationships, without making any choice – "Choiceless Awareness
of What Is". Initially, when one's mind is still active in the
world, choiceless awareness implies facing all the dualities
of life – pleasure and pain, praise and insult, good and bad,
right and wrong, happiness and sorrow – without modifying or escaping any of them. This phase is called titiksha/
endurance of opposites in Advaita.

Titiksha neutralizes all likes and dislikes, thereby silencing
most of the movements of the mind. With this, one develops
vairagya/dispassion towards most actions of outer life to gain
wealth, success, and pleasure or fulfill social duties. Thus,
the inquiry becomes the only theme in one's life, even physically. This stage is a deeper stage of the mind developing
upariti/ total attention to thought free from outer objects.
The moment the mind enters the zone of thought, free from
all outer objects, it has come to the most profound form of
inquiry – Philosophical Inquiry/Advaitic Inquiry. Here, the
higher mind or buddhi/starts playing the predominant role.

3.) Advaitic Inquiry – Jnani/Witness Stage: "I am Brah-
man/Awareness" Stage and Vivartavada

Once the mind has become psychologically mature –
or in the words of Advaita school – an adhikari (qualified
seeker), it becomes fit for an intense philosophical inquiry
into the nature of truth and non-duality. At this stage come

the teachings of Advaita Vedanta – a traditional Indian school of Non-Duality.

Advaita's central teaching is that the root of all suffering is our ignorance about the ultimate nature of our reality. Relying on the revealed Knowledge of Srutis/scriptures called Upanishads, Vivartavada of Shankara shows that due to metaphysical Ignorance/Maya, we take ourselves to be this limited mind/body/intellect. But with the help of the teachings in the scriptures, along with a qualified teacher who knows the traditional way of teaching, a seeker is systematically led to the Knowledge that he is not the limited mind/body/intellect which takes birth, dies, subject to suffering and endless cycles of birth and rebirth. In actuality, we are Self/Brahman/Sat-Chit-Ananda or Eternal Existence–Consciousness-Bliss. We are immortal, unborn, and undying.

The traditional method of teaching Advaita starts by accepting the falsities that are superimposed on a seeker's mind. Gradually, one by one, peeling these layers through a process of negation, till all layers of falsity superimposed on one's true nature are discriminated.

Self-Knowledge being self-luminous reveals itself, and the seeker gains direct Knowledge of his true nature as Self/Brahman/Awareness/Witness. The primary tool used for this operation, as noted earlier, is the seeker's higher mind or intellect (called Buddhi in Advaita). Thus, this path requires a very sharp intellect. Only through such a keen Buddhi/intellect does one possess the Viveka/discriminatory power to isolate Self/Awareness/Witness from all false layers of identification. Thus, a mind which has passed all the previous stages I have outlined is at last engaged in the subtlest contemplation/Nidhidhyasana to discriminate between Awareness and all the objects that appear to Awareness. The most subtle object to be discriminated against is the thinker-doer-experiencer, the individual subject we take ourselves to be.

As one continues in this contemplation/Nidhidhyasana, at some point – a thought called the Akhandakara Vritti flashes in the mind. At that very instant, Self/Awareness/Witness/Brahman, on which the thinker-doer-experiencer that had been superimposed like a film on a screen, is revealed, and one's identity shifts from being the mortal thinker-doer-experiencer to being eternal Self/Awareness/Witness/Brahman.

In this stage, all thoughts, feelings, sensations, body, and mind appear to Witness. So Witness is not a personal seer. Instead, it is that to which the entire universe appears and disappears, including one's own body and mind.

According to Shankara, a person at this stage is a Jnani – a person who is Self Realized. While a Jnani is freed from the sufferings of two kinds of Karma – Sanchita Karma/stored Karma of past lives and Agami Karma/Karma resulting from future actions.

He still has to experience Prarabdha Karma/Karma, which has produced the current birth of the body and which has already become operative. When the Prarabdha Karma wears out completely, his body drops, and the Jnani dies. Shankara gives these explanations in his commentary of Chandogya Upanishad (6.14.2) and in his Brahmasutra Bhashya (4.1.15). Thus, in Shankara's scheme of Vivartavada, full enlightenment happens only in the time of death, when all Prarabdha Karma is exhausted, and the Jnani attains Videhamukti – the fall of the body.

In Vivartavada, Awareness is the eternal Witness. There is still a duality between the Witness and the world, which Shankara shows to be Maya. This duality between the Witness and Maya ends only on death with the exhaustion of all Prarabdha Karma. However, in his commentaries, like in Brhadaranyaka Upanishad (3.5.1 & 4.3.20) and Bhagavad Gita Bhashya (6.27), Shankara talks about Jivanmukti or liberation while living. Several other Advaita books like Vivekachudamani, Aparoksha Anubhuti, and Atma Bodha too, talk of Jivanmukti or the end of prarabdha karma while living. I also got very intrigued when I came across the Direct Path book of Greg Goode and noticed that he talks of the dissolution of the Witness too and the complete ending of duality between Awareness and the world (of objects) while alive, through the continuation of further inquiry. This curiosity made me go to Ajativada of Gaudapada and the Direct Path. Before moving to Ajativada however, a seeker has to spend a considerable time in the Witness stage for its stabilization. Only when one has become very stable in the Witness will the Witness be ready for deconstruction. In the

Witness stabilization phase, I have demarcated two stages.

*Note – While in this section, I have associated Shankara with Vivartavada in which one comes to the realization – "I am Awareness/Self/Witness", it does not mean that Shankara's teachings or commentaries were restricted to Vivartavada. It is just that a bulk of his teachings focus on Vivartavada and the Witness. However, in his commentaries to several verses of the Upanishads and Bhagavad Gita, Shankara also touches Ajativada, or the highest truth in Advaita – "Everything is Brahman" and Jivanmukti, as also mentioned above. Shankara explained his philosophy at an empirical level from the perspective of Vivartavada and from an absolute level in terms of Ajativada, though Gaudpada's focus was entirely on Ajativada, which I have discussed below.

4.) Advaitic and Direct Path Inquiry – Collapse of Witness Stage: "Everything is Brahman/Awareness" and Ajativada

Out of curiosity to understand the dissolution of Witness, I had several online conversations with my friend and guide Greg Goode, who finally led me to Ajativada of Gaudapada found in his Mandukya Karika. He also opened my way to the Direct Path teachings of Sri Atmananda Krishna Menon, a modern unfolding of Ajativada. In all of them, I found what I was looking for, a self-inquiry approach to deconstructing the subject-object duality completely. Greg Goode has authored some excellent books on Direct Path, with even more incisive and detailed deconstruction of subject-object duality than one comes across in the original teachings of Atmananda. Of course, Greg directly derives the main principles from Atmananda.

In Ajativada one realizes that Brahman/Awareness never gives birth to, or even "appears" as the plural world, the latter being the case in Vivartavada. Ajativada means the creation of the world never happened even in an illusory way, so even Maya of Vivartavada is rejected; it is seen that this very world is Brahman/Awareness itself, unlike the case in Vivartavada where the word is seen or caused as an unreal appearance of Awareness. All causality is deconstructed in Ajativada. Thus, we have the following verses.

All this before is immortal Brahman; certainly, all behind is Brahman; all to the south and to the north; all below and all alone stretched out, i.e., extended, all this is certainly Brahman, the highest.~ Mundaka Upanishad, Verse 2.2.11

And Shankara (ascribed to him) in his commentary to this verse says:

That which is before us and which, in the eyes of the ignorant, appears to be not Brahman is certainly Brahman. Similarly, what is behind us; so, that to the south; so, that to the north; so, that below, and that above and all that is extended everywhere in the form of effect, appearing otherwise than Brahman and possessed of name and form. Why say much? All this vast universe is Brahman, certainly. All perception otherwise than as Brahman is mere ignorance, just as the perception of a serpent in a rope. The declaration of the Vedas is that the one Brahman alone is really true.

Thus, the Witness is seen through as the most subtle superimposition on Awareness in the teachings of Direct Path. Once a seeker, who has stabilized in the Witness stage, enters Ajativada and Direct Path, further inquiry into the seeming duality between the Witness and objects dissolves the last standing subject-object duality. The construct of Witness collapses, and everything is then seen as Awareness without any subject and object duality. All phenomena that were taken as objects appearing to a Witness are seen to be insubstantial Awareness itself without any seer. In Ajativada, one realizes the following statements of Gaudapada from Mandukya Karika.

Verse 3.48: No Jiva is ever born. There does not exist any cause which can produce it. This is the highest Truth that nothing is born.
Verse 4.91: All Dharmās (phenomena) by their nature are well determined as enlightened from the very beginning (adibuddha). One who has such self-sufficiency is fit for the deathless state.
Verse 4.92: All Dharmās indeed are quiescent from the very beginning, unoriginated, and happy by nature itself, homogeneous, and non-separate, [Reality is] fearless and unoriginated sameness.

These statements show that "Sat/deathless – Chit/consciousness – Ananda/bliss" is the very nature of everything in the world, right from the beginning of self-inquiry, which was only obscured from one's view due to ignorance. Our previously existent and deluded view that the world consists of substantial, self-existent subjects and objects/phenomena is sublated.

Greg Goode clarifies this stage in terms of the collapse of the Witness aspect of Awareness:
"When your experience isn't characterized by comings and goings, Awareness has no witnessing aspect. This is referred to as 'pure consciousness,' or 'consciousness without objects.' Through deep, experiential inquiry, the witnessing aspect becomes more and more salient and then becomes more and more subtle. Finally, the witnessing aspect collapses or fades away. This point is sometimes referred to as 'non-dual realization' or 'self-realization.'"
~ After Awareness – The End of the Path

Speaking about this stage in a similar vein, Gaudapada says in Mandukya Karika:
Verse 3.32: When the mind does not imagine on account of the Knowledge of the Truth, which is Ātman, then it ceases to be mind and becomes free from all idea of cognition, for want of objects to be cognized.

Commentary by Shankara (ascribed to him) :

How does the mind become naught? It is thus replied:—The Ātman alone is the Reality like the clay; as in the Śruti passage, "All modifications are mere names arising from efforts of speech. The clay alone is real." That Knowledge of the Reality of Ātman comes through the Scripture and the teacher. The mind having attained to that Knowledge, does not imagine, as there remains nothing to be imagined. The mind then is like fire when there is no fuel to burn. When the mind thus does no longer imagine, it ceases to be mind; that is, the mind, for want of any object to be cognized, becomes free from all cognition.

The above actually corresponds to the stage of amanastam – No Mind. Both the quotes of Greg Goode and Gaudapada combined show that the Witness collapse occurs when one reaches the state of no-mind due to discrimination possessed by a seeker of Self Knowledge, which ends the perception of inherently existing objects. In Shankara's system of Vivartavada, total ignorance is destroyed only on death, but Ajativada shows the possibility of total ending of ignorance, thus the total ending of all duality while living.

Thus, this stage brings to an end the seer-seen duality.

After Non-Dual Realization

As mentioned in Gaudapada's Mandukya Karika, the state of no-mind brings about the total end of suffering. Nothing needs to be done after this. We have the following verses:

Verse 3.36: (This Brahman is) birthless, free from sleep and dream, without name and form, ever-effulgent and omniscient. Nothing has to be done in any way (with respect to Brahman). [after knowing it]

Verse 3.38: In that Brahman which is free from all acts of the mind, there is neither any idea of acceptance nor any idea of giving up (of anything). Established in the Atman (Self), Knowledge attains to the state of birthlessness and sameness, that is to say, changelessness.

Shankara, in his commentary to Brhadaranyaka Upanishad, says the same: once all object perception has ended due to Self Knowledge, and the insight "All is Brahman/ Awareness" arises, it marks the end of all self-inquiry and actions.

Verse 3.5.1: "Therefore, having risen above desires, he should strive to stand based on the strength of direct knowledge of the Self .... 'Strength' here refers to the total elimination of vision of objects, an elimination which is achieved through Knowledge of the Self. The phrase 'He should strive to stand based on the strength of the Self' means that he should strive to remain in the state where the vision of objects is eliminated... Then he becomes a silent contemplative sage (muni), that is to say, a yogi, through pondering (mañana). The phrase 'the preparations for contemplative sagehood means the perfection of wisdom and strength, understood respectively as Knowledge of the Self and elimination of all notion of the not-self. Sagehood is the culminating point and final result of the elimination of all notions of the not-self. When this has been achieved, the Brahmin has done all that needs to be done. The idea 'All is the Absolute' arises. "

No One Gets Enlightened

What needs to be understood is that no individual gained enlightenment, even though people would call him a Jivan-mukta – enlightened one from an empirical perspective. But from the ultimate viewpoint, since everything was always Brahman or nature of Awareness, the whole journey of an individual progressing from Ignorance to Enlightenment was just a dream, an illusory appearance [Individual-Creator-Creation never existed in Reality]. Thus, Gaudapada says in Mandukya Karika:

Verse 2.32: There is neither dissolution, nor birth: neither anyone in bondage, nor any aspirant for wisdom; neither can there be anyone who hankers after liberation, nor any liberated as such. This alone is the Supreme Truth

Shankara explains this verse:
This verse sums up the meaning of the chapter. When duality is perceived to be illusory, and Ātman alone is known as the sole Reality, then it is clearly established that all our experiences, ordinary or religious (Vedic), verily pertain to the domain of ignorance. Then one perceives that there is no dissolution, i.e., destruction (from the standpoint of Reality); no birth or creation, i.e., coming into existence; no one in bondage, i.e., no worldly being; no pupilage, i.e., no one adopting means for the attainment of liberation; no seeker after liberation, and no one free from bondage (as bondage does not exist). The Ultimate Truth is that the stage of bondage, etc., cannot exist in the absence of creation and destruction. How can it be said that there is neither creation nor destruction? It is thus replied:—There is no duality (at any time). The absence of duality is indicated by such Scriptural passages as, "When duality appears to exist...." "One who appears to see multiplicity...." "All this is verily Ātman." "Ātman is one and without a second." "All that exists is verily the Ātman," etc. Birth or death can be predicated only of that which exists and never of what does not exist, such as the horns of a hare, etc. That which is non-dual (Advaita) can never be said to be born or destroyed.

The emptiness of Awareness: Awareness is a Non-Affirming Conceptual Designation for the Nature of Reality/Phenomena

When the Witness collapses, signaling the end of all subject-object duality, we understand that Awareness is not some "substance," "thing," "attribute," "process," or "relation." While all this was clear in the Witness stage itself, Awareness was conceptualized as "Eternal Subject," "Witness," etc., as opposed to changing forms/objects of the world in Vivarta-vada of Shankara, which is an "essence" view of Awareness. (Though, most commonly, Shankara translates Awareness as non-dual Knowledge, which is its most profound meaning and remains unchanged even after the Witness collapses). Vivartavada was provisional teaching created by Shankara to first know Brahman/Awareness as existent. Later on, he says, this teaching is retracted, to know Brahman/Awareness in its true nature beyond all causality, and beyond existence and non-existence, in Ajativada. This process of superimposing an attribute to Brahman/Awareness and then later retracting it is the traditional way of teaching in Advaita called adhyaropa-apavada. In his commentary to Katha Upanishad, Shankara says:

He should be known to exist and also as he really is. Of these two, to him who knows him to exist [first], his real nature becomes revealed. [later]~ Katha Upanishad, Verse 2.3.14

Shankara's Commentary:

Therefore, having abandoned the theory of those who argue for non-existence, the Atman should be known as existing, as productive of effects and conditioned by intelligence. But when the Atman is devoid of that and subject to no modification (an effect has no existence independent of the cause); as the sruti says, 'a modification is a mere matter of speech and name; that it is mud is alone true,' then, is the true nature of the Atman [known] – unconditioned, devoid of indicative marks, and incapable of being thought of, as existent or non-existent. In that nature also, 'the atman should be known' follows. Of these two of the conditioned and the unconditioned, i.e., known as existence and its true nature; the genitive case has the force of Nirdharana, i.e., determining; of the Atman previously known as merely existent, i.e., of the Atman known by the belief in its existence produced by its limitations, i.e., its perceived effects. Afterward, the real nature of the Atman is subject to no condition, different from both the known and the unknown, i.e., the manifested universe and the prakriti, one without a second, and indicated by the srutis 'not this, not that, etc.,' 'not gross, not subtle, not short 'in the invisible, bodiless, supportless, etc.,' faces him who had previously realized it as existent.

The above commentary by Shankara clearly shows that first Atman/Awareness is realized to be existent (as productive of effects and conditioned by intelligence) as in the Witness stage of Vivartavada. This is the essence view of Atman, conditioned by causality. Then, later on, this very knower of Atman realizes it as beyond known and unknown, beyond existence and non-existence when unconditioned by causality. This is realizing the true nature of Atman/Awareness.

Thus, with the collapse of Witness, the essence view of Awareness also drops. The Witness realization had seen through the illusion of a personal self as subject. In contrast, the collapse of Witness realization sees through the illusion of an impersonal Self as a Subject. In the Direct Path, Witnessing Awareness is taken as a tool to examine all objects that appear to it. These were helpful conceptions to negate all other forms of duality before finally obliterating the subject-object duality. It's like you first sweep all the dirt of a room into a neat pile, and then you sweep out the pile away itself. So, in the end, one is not left with any Awareness as an essence, substance, or view. You sweep the room/view clean of all dirt of duality without any pile of dirt/duality remaining in the end.

Everything is Brahman/Awareness means that all phenomena are Brahman/Awareness. It means that there are no foreground phenomena separate from a background of unchanging Brahman/Awareness as a subject or essence. Nor does it mean that Awareness is some substance that is molding phenomena the way gold is molded into different ornaments. Awareness is a "non-affirming" description of the nature of phenomena/appearances. It is a non-affirming empty designation that negates all four extreme views of the existence of phenomena. Thus, talking about Awareness, Gaudapada says in Mandukya Karika:

"Verse 4.83. Childish persons verily cover It (fail to know It) by predicating of It such attributes as existence, non-existence, existence and non-existence and absolute non-existence, derived respectively from their notion of change, immovability, a combination of both and absolute negation."

A Note on the Path of Jnana Yoga Followed by Me

In my path of Jnana Yoga I have followed various paths which have been closely aligned with each other. I started out with J Krishnamurti, moved to Advaita, and then finally to a variant of Advaita called Direct Path. I jumped the raft of a path whenever I did not find teaching serving my purpose and predilection, which leans heavily towards deconstructive philosophical inquiry and contemplation rather than Yoga-based approaches, which demand any form of repetitive activity.

"That path alone, by following which a man becomes grounded in the Knowledge of the Reality, is the right path for him. There is no one single path which suits all alike."

This is what Sureshwaracharya, the great disciple of Shankara says. No attempt needs to be made to reconcile the different methods followed in the paths I have listed. There may be no difficulty if one can carefully discern the point of view underlying each prakriya/method listed in the

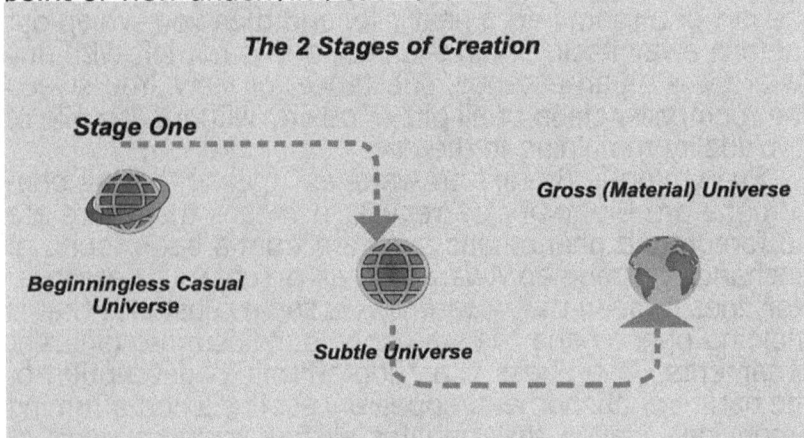

The 2 Stages of Creation

Stage One

Gross (Material) Universe

Beginningless Casual Universe

Subtle Universe

different paths. If this is not possible, one need only hold fast to the method which appeals to one. This is a very subtle point that can be understood by a student who is very far advanced in the journey of non-duality.

If anyone is interested in asking questions or even making

comments on self-inquiry from me, please visit my NEEV Psycho-Physical Inquiry and NEEV Advaita pages on Facebook, depending on your level of understanding.

Tat Tvam Asi – You are Brahman

One of the five great sayings (mahakavyas) of Vedanta, which proclaims the highest truth of Non-Duality or Advaita is "Thou art That" – Tat Tvam Asi, occurring in the Chandogya Upanishad in 6.8.7. Here "Tat" refers to Brahman/Self. So in the most common sense rendering of the statement, it means – "You are Brahman." This saying is not saying, "You must 'become' Brahman." What it says is that *one is already Brahman. Such is the case and one just has to know it to be so.*

I had to bold and italicize the last lines of this paragraph because even when it is clearly stated, people cannot overcome this notion of "becoming." This exists in the most advanced 'practitioners' of Advaita. This notion of "becoming" is Maya, which keeps one tied to doership. This Maya is tough to overcome, a fact anticipated and stated, both by Gaudapada and Shankaracharya, the foremost preceptors of the Advaita tradition.

This sense of Maya or "becoming" or "doership" is so powerful and so blinding that even after the Mahavakya says this to be the case; even after I shall show that all forms of doing are Maya; after giving all forms of quotes, logic, and arguments: the notion of Maya/becoming/doership is very hard to root out. The Bhagavad Gita gives words to this predicament in verse,
"Among thousands of men, one perchance strives for perfection; even among those successful strivers, only one perchance knows Me in essence." - Bhagavad Gita, Chapter 7.3

Difference between Jnana and Yoga

Thus the vast majority of seekers, due to the operation of Maya, start out their spiritual 'journey' as doers. Vedanta already states that "You are Brahman," so the very fact that one has to "do a journey" is an illusion. The entire journey of seeking is an illusion because one is already Brahman. So the whole journey is in Maya towards what end – towards Jnana – to know that one is, one was, and one shall ever be Brahman and nothing else. This is Jnana. It has to be appreciated by the reader that no new fact is created or no new status is being gained; only knowledge of an existing fact is being gained. One is already Brahman, and one comes to know that one is essentially Brahman. In fact, to a qualified mind, this knowledge can be gained just through the hearing/sravana of the Mahavakya.

This is illustrated in a well-known Advaitic story called the Tenth Man.

Story of the Tenth Man

"A guru entrusted to his senior student the responsibility of conducting a group of students to a place across the river and bringing them back. He told him: "You are ten in all. Ensure that all the ten return". The group left and chose to swim across the swollen river after discarding the ferry. After they reached the other bank, the senior student lined them up and counted them. Being engrossed in the counting of others, he missed counting himself and counted only up to nine. Filled with the worry whether one had not been swept away in the river, he asked another to check. But he committed the same mistake as he was also in a similar mental frame.

They concluded that one has been lost in the waters of the river and were in tears. An old man passing by enquired about the problem and counted them and found that they were ten when appraised of it. He told them that they were ten in all and that no one has been lost. Trust in the words of the passer-by gave them the indirect knowledge of the existence of the tenth man. They stopped weeping, and the old man asked the senior student to count them again to know it by himself. But he missed counting himself, as before. Then the old man revealed to him, "You are the tenth man." The senior student instantly had direct knowledge of the missing man and jumped with joy. The problem was the ignorance of the tenth man, and when the student was told in the proper context that he was himself the solution to his problem, the dropping of ignorance and solving of the problem were immediate. So is the dropping of being a doer/enjoyer/experiencer by the eligible person on his being told, after creating the context for it, that he is none other than Brahman."

The story illustrates that the tenth man was not missing at any time, not even at the time when only nine were being counted. What was required was not the creation of the tenth man but sravana/hearing of the knowledge that the tenth man was himself.

However, under the delusion of Maya, people take themselves to be "doers," forever in search of the tenth man, through some action or experience. But no amount of their "doing" (counting in this story) is going to release them of their suffering that one man is missing or that the Self is missing.

So Vedanta, understanding this problem, accepts the Maya of "doership" and "becoming" to be superimposed on the seeker's essential Self. After that, it systematically leads the seeker by carefully negating all the seeker's notions of "doership" to the most subtle levels until they arrive at the jnana/knowledge that he is essentially Atma/Self/Witness or a "non-doer." To attain, the doer has to submit himself to the teachings of a person who has realized the Self. It can only begin with trust in the words of a Self Realized teacher. There is no other way. In the story of the Tenth Man, the old passer-by was the teacher who could see Ten Men when all others, deluded amongst themselves, were constantly counting only nine men. In life, without the teacher, one shall continue making the same mistake because all doing starts with the "wrong knowledge" of being a doer. No matter how much one does, one cannot start with the wrong knowledge (the tenth man is missing) and end in the right place (no one is missing). And as illustrated by the story, when one gets the right knowledge, one comes to know that one himself was what he was searching for. So there was no need to "do" anything but just gain an understanding of it from a qualified teacher – established in Self Knowledge.

How does Vedanta address the movement from doing to jnana/knowledge? The first thing it does is to give the proper knowledge. Because knowledge is the problem, Vedanta does not bring it out as a secret at last. Instead, it is the very first thing it places in front of the seeker. Right at the beginning of Krishna's discourse to Arjuna, we hear

"They have an end, it is said, these bodies of the embodied-Self. The Self is Eternal, Indestructible, Incomprehensible. Therefore fight. O Bharata "– Bhagavad Gita, Verse 2.18

The knowledge of Self is given first. So the seeker is prepared for the fact that he is actually eternal, indestructible Self, right at the beginning itself. Advaita starts out with this fact of knowledge itself. It lays out the aim of its program as knowledge of what you already are. Whilst dualistic approaches start out with the notion of attainment: one has to attain something which one does not possess.

But in the case of Advaita, the unprepared mind of a seeker, even though he hears this, he gets only indirect knowledge. So how does one convert this indirect knowledge to direct knowledge?

This is "done" by the process of Yoga. Yoga is about doing. Yoga in Advaita is called an "indirect" means of knowledge because through specific – meaning – scripture-directed forms of doing – the doer/Yogi comes to Jnana/knowledge.

Jnani – The Actionless Actor

Once the Yogi becomes a Jnani, all "doership" is canceled. But is the "doer" gone? No, the "doer" still exists. A Jnani just does not drop dead after gaining Jnana. His mind and body still function. He teaches, writes, sings, dances, rules kingdoms, engages in debates, can be seen meditating or contemplating, does politics, and like Krishna, can even engage in war. As the following quote shows,

"Not by non-performance of actions does man reach 'actionlessness"; nor by mere renunciation does he attain success (liberation). "– Bhagavad Gita 3.29

To illustrate the point that the Self exists as a non-doer in the most extreme situations, like war, Krishna, encouraging Arjuna to fight the war, says,

"He who takes the Self to be the slayer and he who thinks He is slain, neither of them knows. He slays not, nor is He slain. "– Bhagavad Gita 2.19

"Whatsoever knows Him to be Indestructible, Eternal, Unborn, and Inexhaustible, how can that man slay, O Partha, or cause others to be slain? "– Bhagavad Gita 2.21

"They have an end, it is said, these bodies of the embodied-Self. The Self is Eternal, Indestructible, Incomprehensible. Therefore fight. O Bharata "– Bhagavad Gita, Verse 2.18

It should be noted that these are sayings bringing out the ultimate nature of reality. Nowhere is Krishna just influencing Arjuna to fight through a psychological pep talk. The subject matter of these sayings is not the mind, but the Self, so one cannot make psychological statements about Self, which is beyond mind and beyond all phenomena.

Also, despite the above quotes from Gita, some people have associated Jnana with physical sannyasa/renunciation. This is optional. A Jnani may or may not be a sannyasi physically. But mentally, all Jnanis are sannyasis because they have not renounced merely actions; they have renounced the doer of all actions. So a Jnani does not bother about the kinds of action he does, whether he should physically renounce the world or continue with the world. Any such bother in his mind indicates that he takes himself to be the doer. All his actions are coming from his unexhausted prarabdha karma. However, all people under the spell of Maya – samsaris and yogis – want to see some special physical marks of a Jnani – clothes, poverty, tradition, scholarship, etc. A samsari/karmi seeks distinctions, and that is the root of his suffering. But the Jnani seeing Self everywhere does not see or seek distinctions. For him, everyone, every moment is nothing but Self.

"The knowers of Self, look with an equal vision on a brahmana endowed with learning and humility, a cow, an elephant, a dog, and an eater of dogs."– Bhagavad Gita 5.18

So while other people may see a Jnani as having something special, a Jnani knows that he has nothing special that others don't have. The only thing he has is the knowledge of that, which he and everyone already are.

A Yogi who is following Advaita, on the other hand, is one who sees distinctions, who does not have the equal vision of a Jnani but is striving to have that equal vision. He does not see Self everywhere, every moment, because he does not have direct knowledge of Self. A Yogi is yet to arrive at this knowledge. It does not mean that right now, he or everything is not Self. Just that a Yogi's mind under the spell of Maya does not have knowledge of already existing Self.

This Self Knowledge can appear only in a specially prepared mind. So a Yogi has to do some special practice of body control or mind control to convert the indirect Knowledge of Self into direct knowledge. So different forms of Yoga are prescribed in Advaita to control mind, body, and senses of a Yogi, like – Karma Yoga, Bhakti Yoga, Raja Yoga, and Jnana Yoga. In all these Yogas, there is an implicit notion of practice. What are all these practices intended for – to end all practice.

To get released from the notion of practice and doer and attain the vision of Self/Atma/Witness who is not the doer.

So, in essence, a Jnani is a person who "sees himself as Atma/Self/Witness and not as the doer." Till even the slightest notion of "doership" exists, a person has to keep practicing Yoga.

But all these Yogas are prescribed in Advaita to arrive at a Non-Dual vision. Not for those who are satisfied with Duality as the final reality. This is a very tricky area. Because Yoga is also taught by several Dualistic schools like Patanjali, Tantra, and Samkhya, some of these Yoga practices have crept into Advaita. The Yogas in Advaita are a preparatory stage for Jnana. They are not in any case meant to do anything more than that. So let us look at the difference between dualistic Yoga schools and Advaita because they compromise the non-dual vision of Jnana revealed by Advaita. Unfortunately, many Advaitins have unwittingly adopted these notions and even been teaching them.

Yoga of Dualistic Schools – Doership born out of Experience and Experiencer

Dualistic schools take this world of plurality as real. Since plurality is real, the world of experiences is real. Since experiences are real, the Experiencer is real.

A Yogi, afflicted by Maya or notion of being an experiencer and with "doership," would like to do something with what he is experiencing – feeling/thinking/doing. In summary, the Yogi takes himself as an experiencer first. He then has the feeling/bhavana of pain/pleasure of raag/dvesha tormenting him constantly. So he wants control over experience. All control implies doing – the desire to push certain objects and to acquire certain objects of experience. Till there is the body/mind/intellect, the three gunas are in sway. And these gunas are going to create sensations/thoughts/feelings/emotions – all kinds of experiences.

The Gita says,
"Sometimes the mode of goodness becomes prominent, defeating the modes of passion and ignorance, O son of Bharata. Sometimes the mode of passion defeats goodness and ignorance, and at other times ignorance defeats goodness and passion. "
Bhagavad Gita, Verse 14.10

Till the body/mind exists, these gunas are in sway: there is absolutely no doubt about it. Every form of Maya is made of Gunas. The Gunas can never be brought to rest. The only place of rest is the Self which is Trigunatitha – beyond the three Gunas.

Solutions of Dualistic Karmi/Dharmi/Yogi vs. Solution of the Jnani for the problem of the Experiencer

From the last quote of the Gita, one sees that the gunas are constantly recycling, never at peace, creating a troublesome experience for all people – the Karmis, Dharmis, and the Yogis. The natural impulse, conditioned by Maya, for Karmis and Yogis is to alter the experience. This very notion of trying to alter experience is the beginning of the "doership." The Experiencer gives rise to the doer.

The Karmi is the doer manipulating the gross objects of his experience to get pleasure

The Dharmi is the doer manipulating his thoughts of rajas, tamas and sattva to becoming predominantly sattvic.

The Yogi is the doer manipulating his mind or controlling his mind to remove all thoughts and reach Samadhi.

All three classes of people – Karmi/Dharmi/Yogi – share the same assumption. What is the premise? The assumption is that they are experiencers, experiencing a plural world and that this experience has to be either made pleasurable or brought to naught by the ending of mind: as in Samadhi. All of them have started with an illusion that the world is real, that the body/mind is real, that Experiencer and experiences are real. Once all of them are taken as real, the only option left is to make experience confirm some notion of peace and pleasure, halt the recycling of gunas, or make them predominantly sattvic.

What do all these classes of people get as a result of their efforts?

The Bhagavad Gita says,
"Those situated in the mode of goodness gradually go upward (to the higher planets); those in the mode of passion live in the middle (on the earthly planets), and those in the mode of ignorance go down (to the hellish worlds). "– Bhagavad Gita 14.18
So the Karmis find themselves back in this world, in the cycle of birth and death. The Dharmis find themselves going to the higher worlds.
What about dualistic Yogis? The highest result in it is the attainment of Samadhi. This Samadhi is attained by manonigraha or control of mind, which penultimately results in Nirvikalpa Samadhis. If they go further, finally, manonasha/ destruction of afflictive binding emotional states of mind. Why is this their solution? It is so because, as experiencers, they have taken the world to be real and the mind to be their problem, and they shall not rest till it ends in manonasha.
How is the Jnani different from them?
The Bhagavad Gita says,
"When the seer does not see an agent other than the gunas and when he knows himself as beyond the gunas, he gains my nature. "
"Crossing these three gunas, that are the cause of the body, the embodied one, released from birth, death, old age and sorrow, gains immortality. "– Bhagavad Gita 14.19 and 14.20

A Yogi who has proceeded through the path of Yoga to attain Jnana, under the guidance of a teacher who has Self Knowledge, undertakes Yoga only to get Jnana. His teacher would have helped him negate all the gunas superimposed on his Self, gradually, through different teaching methodologies ranging from Karma Yoga to Raja Yoga to Jnana Yoga. For such a prepared mind, attainment of Jnana finally happens when he knows that he is not the gunas but their Witness/Self.

So the Jnani solves the problem of experience by understanding that he is not the three gunas. In his essential nature as Atma/Self/Witness, he is beyond both the experience and the Experiencer. So he is not interested, not at all bothered, not at all concerned about changing anything in his experience. He knows that he is their Witness and that as Witness he is untouched by the three gunas. There is never any contact of the Self/Atma/Witness with the gunas, so he does not bother changing them, controlling them or manipulating them. This is the Asparsha Yoga/Contactless Yoga of Gaudapda.

The Bahagavad Gita quote 14.20 shows that the "embodied one" is released from all suffering and attains immortality. This is the Jnani who is the Jivanmukta – one who has acquired the knowledge that being beyond the gunas; he is not the doer, but the gunas who are the doer.

As already stated previously in this Chapter, not being a doer does not mean he is seen doing nothing. He is seen doing but the Jnani knows that he is doing nothing: it is the gunas which are doing. Only when one does not have this firm and direct knowledge does one fiddle and medddle with gunas to make them sattvic, etc. A jnani being Self just witnesses them doing their work.

"Just as a well-lighted fire reduces wood to ashes, so too, Arjuna! the fire of (Self) knowledge reduces all actions (results of actions) to ashes. "– Bhagavad Gita 4.37

Questioning Death

When I was a young kid, I sometimes used to ask philosophical questions. I could ask the only person I had access to, my father, my first teacher. When I was perhaps five years old, I asked him, "What is the truth of life?" And I remember his answer as vividly as my question. He answered, "Death." Since he was a rationalist, he did not consider keeping a child away from facts, no matter how unpleasant they are. I forgot that answer through my years of schooling. All modern educational system is very efficient in making our engines of an industrial society. In these education factories, you never learn life; you only learn technology. However, I psychologically escaped the brutal regime of schooling and college, and from the depths of my Consciousness, recovered the question that had occupied my child's mind: the question of death.

There is a fascinating story in one of the Hindu religious scriptures called Kathopanishad: the story concerns a teenage boy who went to Yama, lord of death, to answer a question he did not have an answer to.

The gist of the story is that Nachiketa's father, a Brahmin in ancient India, was performing a sacrifice to give away all his wealth. Nachiketa was watching this ritual with the unblemished, innocent eyes of a teenager of the old days. He observed that his father was only giving away all his old, disabled cows as wealth. Seeing the hypocrisy and wanting to prevent his father from acting this way, he asks him a trick question, "Father, who have you decided to give me away to." He was trying to point to his father that just like he is his real possession, he should give away real wealth, as an act of sacrifice, rather than indulging in his subterfuge of giving disabled cows.

His father did not pay heed to him, like we all grown-ups do, considering such innocent questions asked by children as an absence of worldly wisdom. And, as all children whose upbringing in an atmosphere of strict authority do, Nachiketa pestered his father by repeating the same question three times. Finally, out of sheer irritation, his father, who was involved in the most serious sacrifice of giving away his wealth, scoffed at him, "Nachiketa, I give you to the God of Death."

So Nachiketa, not the one to disobey his father, treks to the abode of God of Death, Yama. There he asks Yama about the question to which he had never got a straight answer from anyone, "What lies beyond death for man, some say that he exists and some say that he does not?" Yama does not answer him straight. First, he dissuades him, saying that the answer is so complicated that even the gods are confused about it; that he can ask for anything else, any boon from him. But Nachiketa remains firm; he says, "I understand that the question is so difficult that even gods are confused. Thus I have come to thee. You are the only one who can give me this answer. I have searched elsewhere, and I could find no one who could give me an answer that satisfies my curiosity."

Yama, however, was not an easy teacher. He first tests Nachiketa's resolve by successively offering him greater and greater worldly pleasures. Nachiketa keeps rejecting each of these offers by saying, "What shall I do with these earthly treasures, as each one of them, no matter how wide and how great.

Ultimately, they are going to end in death. I want to find that, which is "undecaying" and immortal, so I have approached you, God of Death, who puts an end to every form."

And the story proceeds. Yama, overcome by Nachiketa's steadfast desire to find the answer to his question, instructs him on the nature of Self – Atman-Brahman, the immortal essence of man: which is never born and never dies. Nachiketa, having received the answer, meditates on Brahman and reaches liberation – immortality, freedom from the cycle of life and death. All existentialist philosophers of the west probably kept themselves ignorant of this philosophy. Otherwise, they would not have gone through the existential pangs of emptiness and meaningless of life posed by the question of death.

I loved this story the first time I came across it. I had not read it in the Kathopanishad when I first heard it. I did not even know what Upanishads were by that time. I listened to the story orally, sometime around my early 20's, narrated by some person in a group discussion. I don't know whether the person did not convey the whole story or whether I missed the end. Still, for many years, till I came to reading the Upanishads, I knew the story only, except the last part where Yama gives Nachiketa the knowledge of immortal Self and Nachiketa realizes it. The story resonated deeply with me: it had so many parallels. While in my second year in college, I was struck by a question, "What is the purpose of life because everything we achieve is annihilated by death?" This question was almost a paraphrase of Nachiketa's question, "What lies for man after death?" In college, I had determined that finding out the answer to this question would be my life. Like Nachiketa, I resolved that nothing whatsoever would come in the way of my quest to get an answer to this question. And, thankfully, since I had not heard of Yama's answer as part of the story, I was insulated from the answer. I say, insulated, because getting the answer would have killed my self-inquiry: And it did so, for some time.

For the next twenty-five years, every move of my life was just about seeking an answer to this question. The question itself kept changing form, breaking down into simpler, though wider forms of inquiry. I was no ascetic, having retreated from the world to contemplate on that question. How could I? Let alone contemplate, I did not even know how to approach the question. There was just this question raging and burning in my mind. Like fire, it seemed to do nothing but paralyze me, take away meaning from every single thing form of activity I had done and wanted to do in the future. At that time, I had just come into a relationship with my would-be wife, . Even that relationship was something that I stopped feeling. I would sit beside her for hours with this hopeless fire burning. Sometimes I would fear that I would become insane. I longed to get back to my everyday life with its simple, warm, fuzzy pleasures. But the question refused to go.

Coincidentally, since we are on the subject of stories, there is another story of Buddha – the enlightened one, which recounts how he got into self-inquiry. At the time of his birth – you know the myths, such people cannot have a normal birth – sages prophesied that he would leave the palace, kingship, kingdom in his quest to find the end of suffering for man. On hearing this prophecy, Buddha's father decided to imprison Buddha in the palace to never see any human suffering. But suffering has its valuable ways to find itself in the Garden of Eden. So one day, Buddha sneaked out with his charioteer friend, Channa, in disguise, to see life outside the palace from his own eyes. The story, as it goes, talks about Buddha seeing a very old man, a sick man, a dead man, and an ascetic in succession. Buddha was shocked, never having seen any such things in the charade created by his father in the palace. He queried Channa incredulously whether he would meet the same fate as these people, to which Channa silently responded, "Yes!" Buddha asked Channa what the ascetic was up to. Channa answered that he was a person who had renounced the world to understand and end suffering. Well, that was it for our Buddha. The carefully constructed world of his palace broke. If life will end in death, he did not see any point in carrying on with all that facade.

So, here again, we have the same ingredients cooking in the pot: suffering, death, and a resolve to go beyond death. The word "Katho" in the phrase Kathopanishad comes from the Sanskrit language, meaning distress. So Nachiketa, too, was asking Yama a question that was distressing him. In history, Buddha and Nachiketa realized something beyond death; like Buddha, like Nachiketa, I too decided to dedicate my life to finding an answer to man's mortality.

Death is not only for Nachiketa, a Hindu or Buddha, a Buddhist. Death is for every human being. It is a fact, undeniably. And yet, somehow, strangely, there seems to be a spell cast on all humans by some force that they live in absolute ignorance of this finality. Like the Buddha or Nachiketa, we all see death all around us. But somehow, there seems to be such immunity in our lives that, unlike Buddha and Nachiketa, we are never disturbed enough to question death. Are we all escaping this question? Is our whole life and living, the vast and complex society with all its organizations, systems, technologies, and entertainment, just a toy to keep you engaged? Is it a toy to absorb you so that you do not ask the most fundamental question about your life: death? Does society help you escape asking the question of death?

A few weeks back, a lovely, caring, silent, observant sixteen–year–old girl in our neighborhood committed suicide by hanging herself. She used to maintain a written diary. One of her last entries read, "If one has to die anyway, why should one live?" She did not find an answer like Nachiketa or Buddha. She may have used this question as a means to justify her escape from the suffering she was facing. But see the same pattern repeating – distress and death, suffering and death, or disturbance and death.

So, if we are not disturbed, we have made ourselves immune to it. And when we make ourselves immune to a fact, our entire structure of life is based on a falsity. For what would happen if we allowed the fact of death in our lives. Would we not question every single act that we do in our lives today? Would not every action that we do to acquire create the question, "What is the point of all this, all our striving and straining, our pride and hurt, all our attachments if all is going to end in death?"

Yes, I know your answer! Why bother about it? You know Julius Caesar in William Shakespeare's play answered, "Cowards die many times before their death, the brave but die only once." Okay, so we all are supposed to live bravely. Like Caesar, loot and conquer, make and break empires, make a place in the history of man, a history of conquest, might, power, and untold human suffering. And we praise these heroes, these brave heroes who spilled blood, made innumerable humans suffer for their acts of bravery.

Okay! Was Ceaser brave? Or was he in fear? Who is bold, a man who faces the fact of death while living or the one who escapes it, pushing it as some event in the future, turning a blind eye to it? Is it this fear which leads to the human behavior of conquest and brutality? And here I am not only talking of some dusty, ancient Roman times. Is our modern world any different? Has it faced and questioned death? Has loot, conquest, domination, and spilling human blood stopped? Nowadays, you don't even see the face of your killer; it is some world bank, some economic sanction, grinding poverty, poisoned air and water, global warming.

Is not bravery then living with the fact of death? What would such a life mean? Are you interested in this question? Or are you interested in the escapes, the brave life of Caesar? When you see the fact, face death while living, then your life would have a different significance. If every human being faced this fact rather than escaping it, we would have a different society; not the one built by the brave Caesar. Death comes to everyone, regardless of whatever nation, race, caste, class you belong to. It comes to the believer and the non-believer. It comes to the materialist and the spiritualist. It comes to the capitalist, socialist, and communist. The question of death is common to all forms, and this question is not a figment of thought, some theory which one can dispute. Oh yes, re-incarnation! Yes, sir, you may keep on re-incarnating and keep getting killed by the Caesars of the world or, like the Caesars, keep killing the rest of the people in the world. But, no matter how many times you re-incarnate, the question of death will stare at you, which you shall keep escaping; and we shall have the same hell on earth.

Yama, the God of Death instructs Nachiketa about his true Self, immortal – unborn and undying. Buddha found emptiness. Both found an answer to go beyond the puzzle of death. This is what self-inquiry leads to ultimately – freedom from birth and death!

Journal of an 18 Years Old Girl

Death: My Greatest Fear!

We all have to die one day. No one wants to die, and no one knows when and how they are going to die. It's a sudden phenomenon. It's the ultimate truth that we all have to die, and it's also true that there is no new life till there is no death. I have an extreme fear of death. I don't know how and when I will face death. 'Death is not by choice! Death is the end of every breath, every thought, feelings, everything. Everything will end in a splash of a second. It happens in a blink of our eyes." What will I feel when I'll count my last breath"? "Will I die with immense fear"? "Will I feel beyond fear"? What is going to happen? These questions will remain until I don't face death. Whenever we encounter something, we get to know what it is ultimately. At that moment, these questions transform into reality, or we can say we get the answers to these questions. Why do we feel sorrow when we hear something about death or that someone died? Why do we cry after someone's death when it's known that every single being to die?" Why death creates grief and fear"? 'Is it something like a curse, or is it something beyond our happiness'? I want to know: "what death is"?

My Response

"You have written this journal after hearing my lecture on Death?" So, if you have understood the ideas in-depth, you would have seen that all the characters in the Lecture who were concerned with death decided to devote their whole life to inquire into it.and they all realized that which is beyond death. The question is whether you, too, are willing to devote your entire life to reach the answer.

While the historical characters mentioned there – Nachiketa and Buddha – started with a similar quest of finding a way out of suffering and deathand they found that the cause of suffering is attachment to the world of eternally changing forms.

Buddha's Solution to the Fear of Death

Buddha found that there is "No-self" anywhere. The concept that there is an inherent self anywhere is ignorance. The body-mind-intellect are all like parts of a machine, but there is no self or soul to be found anywhere when one sees deeply. So when the illusion of self ceases, only this vast nature is a constant field of change and flow. Life is like a river of nature that is constantly flowing.

Shortly after Buddha got enlightened before he started teaching, he is said to have undergone the following reflection:

"Monks, the thought arose in me thus: "This truth which I have realized is profound, difficult to see, abstruse, calming, subtle, not attainable through mere sophisticated logic.
"But beings revel in attachment, take pleasure in attachment, and delight in attachment. For beings who thus revel, take pleasure, and delight in attachment, this is a complicated thing to see: that is, the law of conditionality, the principle of Dependent Origination. Moreover, this is challenging to see: the calming of all conditioning, the casting off of all clinging, the abandoning of desire, dispassion, cessation, Nibbana. If I were to give this teaching and my words were not under-

stood, that would make for weariness and difficulty."

This paragraph shows that attachment is the main cause of suffering. It also mentions the way out of suffering, which he calls Nibbana (Nirvana). The method to attain Nirvana, according to Buddha, is to understand how the world and suffering arises. He says Nirvana can be attained by understanding the law of Dependent Origination.

The Law of Dependent Origination

The Dependent Origination (DO) cycle is a description of life- or world-evolution. It shows the universe functioning according to the natural processes of growth and decline, ceaselessly unfolding at the dictates of cause and effect. So what is this Dependent Origination (DO)? It is twelve links of cause and effect.

With Ignorance as a condition, there are Volitional Impulses.
With Volitional Impulses as condition arises Consciousness.
With Consciousness as a condition arise Body and Mind.
With Body and Mind as condition, wake the Six Sense Bases
With the Six Sense Bases as condition arises Contact.
With Contact as a condition arises Feeling
With Feeling as condition arises Craving
With Craving as condition arises Clinging
With Clinging as condition arises Becoming
With Becoming as condition arises, birth
With birth as condition arises Aging and Death,
Sorrow, Lamentation, Pain, Grief, and Despair

Thus is the arising of this whole mass of suffering. So to end all suffering, one has to complete ignorance. But, according to Buddha, the contrived process of Craving and clinging, based on ignorance of that true nature of life. It causes the mistaken perception of and attachment to a self—'creating a self with which to clog up the flow of nature.' So existence is bound by ignorance, lived with clinging, in bondage, contradicting the law of nature, and lived with fear and suffering.

The Path to Nirvana – End of Cycle of Birth and Death

So Buddha's solution to going beyond fear of death is to remove the basic ignorance that there is an inherent self. The notion of self is nothing but attachment to some aspect of the ceaseless flow of nature and trying to make it permanent. The notion of self starts the whole process of cause and effect resulting in the ceaseless cycle of birth and death of body which leads to suffering. The Enlightened one according to Buddha is one who knows this principle of cause and effect called Dependent Origination.

The path to Nirvana with respect to DO can be said to be this:

With the complete abandoning of Ignorance, Volitional Impulses cease.
With the cessation of Volitional Impulses, Consciousness ceases
With the cessation of Consciousness, Body and Mind cease.
With the cessation of Body and Mind, the Six Sense Bases cease.
With the cessation of the Six Sense Bases, Contact ceases.
With the cessation of Contact, Feeling ceases.
With the cessation of Feeling, Craving ceases.
With the cessation of Craving, Clinging ceases.
With the cessation of Clinging, Becoming ceases.
With the cessation of Becoming, Birth ceases.
With the cessation of Birth, Aging and Death, Sorrow, Lamentation, Pain, Grief and Despair cease.

Nachiketa's Solution to the Fear of Death

Nachiketa, on the other hand, is a character in the Katha Upanishads, so he talks about finding the true Self that is beyond birth and death. According to Upanishads and Vedanta, our true Self is never born and it never dies. Our true Self is that which witnesses or is aware of all the changes that happen in our body/mind/intellect, without ever getting involved in these changes or without getting affected by them. How does one come to know about one's Eternal Self?

Two Paths of Preya (pleasure) and Shreya (ultimate happiness)

In the beginning of his instruction, Yama, the Lord of Death, instructs young Nachikaeta about two paths : The path of preya or pleasure and the path of shreya or goodness.

One thing is shreya (the good) and (quite) different is preya (the pleasant). Leading to different ends as they do, they both bind man. The good befalls him who accepts the good, but falls away from the goal who chooses the pleasant. (Katha Upanishad, 1st Mantra, Canto 2)

The term preya means that which is pleasant, immediately attractive; the term shreya means that which conduces to true welfare, which is ultimately beneficial. Talking about attachment with respect to these two paths, Yama, further says

Both shreya and preya approach man; the dhira (wise man), examining the two (well), discriminates between them. The wise man verily prefers shreya to preya; but the foolish man chooses preya through love of gain and attachment. (Katha Upanishad, 2nd Mantra, Canto 2)

So, from the beginning itself, it is made clear that there are two ways of living in the world. One way is to be attached to pleasures got through objects (preya) and the other is to the path of ultimate happiness (shreya). There is a choice which each one must make between these two paths.

This choice is necessary because one has to penetrate the illusion of the world as seen by the senses. Yama says that death is for those who think that the only reality is that which our senses show.

The truth of the hereafter does not shine before that child (childish person) who is inattentive, and befooled by the delusion of wealth. "This world (seen by the senses) is and there is no other"—thinking thus, he falls into my (death's) clutches again and again. (Katha Upanishad, 6th Mantra, Canto 2)

Role of Shrutis/Upanishads as a Means of Self Knowledge

Yama seems to be saying that the world as we see through our senses is a delusion. So there must be a way to penetrate this delusion and find the real. For Buddha, the ignorance could be penetrated by insight gained through reasoning and understanding the process of Dependent Origination. But in Vedanta, it is not reasoning that can give insight into the nature of reality. As Yama says,

This (Atman) can never be well comprehended if taught by an inferior person, even though variously pondered upon. Unless taught by another (who has realized his oneness with It), there is no way (to comprehend It). Subtler than the subtlest is It, and beyond tarka or logical reason. (Katha Upanishad, 8th Mantra, Canto 2)

I have covered the topic on "Why Shrutis are the Final Authority?" in one of my previous articles where I have given the reason why in Advaita Vedanta, reality can be understood only by the shrutis/Upanishads when taught by a teacher who is a realized being. And what reality do the shrutis finally reveal?

The discerning man (knows that he) is not born nor does he die; he has not come into being from anything; nor has anything come into being from him. This (Self of man) is unborn, eternal, everlasting, and ancient; It is not destroyed when the body is destroyed. (Katha Upanishad, 18th Mantra Canto 2)

The teachings of the Upanishads reveal that eternal Self which is the essence of everyone. The body that we take to be ourselves is nothing but a superimposition on this real Self just like a mirage seen in the desert. The body dying has no effect on the Self just as the presence or absence of mirage water has no effect on the desert sand.

If the killer thinks that he is killing, and the killed thinks that he is killed, both of them do not know that It (the Self) kills not nor is it killed. (Katha Upanishad, 19th Mantra Canto 2)

Journey to Self Knowledge

Like in the case of Buddha, the first aspect that was discussed with Nachiketa was attachment (path of preya). The path of goodness (shreya) would lead Nachiketa to the goal whence there is freedom from the cycle of birth and death.

But he who is possessed of right understanding, with manas (mind) held and ever pure, reaches that goal whence there is no birth (return to worldliness) again. (Katha Upanishad, 8th Mantra Canto 3)

Like Buddha gave the twelve links of Dependent Origination as a means to reach Liberation, Nachiketa was given a similar path. The state, which is to be attained (through the spiritual journey), is a journey which begins with the sense-organs which are gross, and proceeds through comparatively subtler and subtler aspects—that state is to be realized as the pratyagātman, the inner Self. In order to convey this truth, the Upanishad proceeds as follows.

The sense-objects are higher than the sense-organs; the manas (mind) is higher than the objects; the buddhi is higher than the manas; the mahān ātmā (great self) is higher than the buddhi.(Katha Upanishad, 10th Mantra, Canto 3)

The avyakta (undifferentiated nature) is higher than the mahat (mahān ātma); the Puruŝa (the infinite Self) is higher than the avyakta. There is nothing higher than the Puruŝa; that is the finale, that is the supreme goal. (Katha Upanishad, 11th Mantra, Canto 3)

Liberation/Moksha from the Jaws of Death

For the one who completes the journey from the senses to the final Self one is liberated from death.

By realizing that Ātman which is soundless, touchless, formless, imperishable, similarly without taste, eternal, without smell, beginningless and endless, (even) beyond the mahat, and immutable, one is liberated from the jaws of death.(Katha Upanishad, 15th Mantra, Canto 3)

Enlightenment through Words

For almost any individual, the word Enlightenment would conjure up an image of a person sitting in a meditative posture doing meditation. It is not without basis, as almost all systems or paths that promise Enlightenment to prescribe some form of yoga/action to 'attain' Enlightenment. For every dualistic system, action is a means of Enlightenment. But Advaita Vedanta stands apart from all these systems. It declares that Knowledge and not action is a means to liberation.

One of the meanings of the word Upanishads is "sitting down near," referring to the student sitting near the teacher while receiving spiritual Knowledge. So the picture here is not of a person meditating but of a seeker listening to the words from a teacher.

In this chapter, I will elaborate a bit about this unique method of Enlightenment in Shankara Advaita Vedanta and share a dialogue between me and my student in my NEEV Advaita Study Group who gets enlightened during the discussion.

What is Enlightenment in Advaita Vedanta

According to the true tradition of Gaudapada – Shankara Advaita Vedanta, Enlightenment is to have an intuitive knowledge of the ultimate non-dual reality called Brahman/Self, which is eternal and formless referred to as Sat-Chit-Ananda or eternal Existence-Consciousness-Bliss. It is to know oneself and the world as Brahman/Self beyond the perishable body/mind/intellect.

Why Knowledge and Not Action is a Means of Knowing Self/Brahman?

Brahman/Self is the ultimate and only reality as taught by the Upanishads/Srutis. For an extended discussion on Upanishads as Srutis, please see my Chapter "The Origin of Advaita". If Brahman is the only reality, and it is eternal and formless if this is what we all are, then how do we see this plural world? How do I see myself as an individual with a perishable body? Again, the srutis tell us that this plural world of phenomena, including our body/mind/intellect, is born out of a fundamental metaphysical error called avidya/ignorance. When we misperceive something, we project something else upon it. The stock example provided in Advaita is that of a snake mistaken on a coiled rope in the twilight. Because of ignorance/wrong Knowledge, we come to see a snake on the rope.

In the same way, we come to see a plural world of subjects and objects, a world of duality superimposed on Brahman like a snake on the rope. Thus, although we are eternal Existence-Consciousness-Bliss, a body and world are superimposed on the non-dual reality. Because we identify with our body and this world as accurate, we are subject to all its painful dualities of birth and death, pain and pleasure, right and wrong, and good and evil.

Just like no amount of beating the snake on the rope with a stick will free us from the fear and suffering produced by the snake, in the same way, no amount of action can free us from the ignorance we have about the true nature of reality. The only way we can get liberated from all fear is to shine a light on the object appearing as a snake and discern its true nature to be a rope rather than a snake. Ultimately, the Knowledge that it was a rope and not a snake frees us from fear and all suffering.

The other important aspect that stands out in this example to show that Knowledge and not action is a means of liberation from suffering is that throughout the incident of mistaking the rope as a snake, and finally, coming to know the rope as the rope, there was absolutely no change in the status of the rope: the rope remained a rope. There was no production of rope at any instant. The snake was not real. In the same way, Enlightenment in Advaita does not involve any action because nothing new needs to be created. Only the ignorance of the nature of reality has to be removed. Advaita is not about becoming a new kind of person or attaining a new type of experience or state.

It is not speaking of any transformation of any kind. Why? Because Brahman, the ultimate reality is already self-existent at all times. It is always the same and changeless because it is formless. There is no transformation ever happening in Brahman. All changes are happening in the plural world, which is a product of ignorance. So action is possible only in the pluralistic world, which is superimposed on Brahman through ignorance. How can there be any action potential in a non-dual, partless, formless reality? When we see a movie on the screen, all action is being perceived against the changeless, action-less background of the screen.

From the previous discussion, it is evident that no form of action can be the means to liberation in Advaita Vedanta because of the following

1. Action is a product of ignorance. It means that the actor and action arise only after ignorance has projected a plural word of subjects and objects on Brahman's formless, non-dual reality. Brahman as reality is a state before emerging of the actor

2. Action is used for the following purposes: creation, modification, attainment, and purification. Because of the eternally self-existent nature of non-dual Brahman, it neither needs to be created nor can it be modified, attained, or purified. So action is useless!

Shabda/Words of Sruti/Upanishads as the Only Means of Knowledge

To gain Knowledge, we require a means. For example, to know color, we need the eyes as the means. Now we shall discuss how the words of the Sruti/Upanishads, handled by a teacher, who is themselves a knower of Brahman, can be the only direct means of knowing Brahman and getting enlightened. It could either be the spoken word or the written word.

Six Means of Knowledge/Pramanas

"Pramana" means "valid means of knowledge." There are various means by which correct Knowledge is obtained. While the number of pramanas varies widely from system to system, many ancient and medieval Indian texts identify six pramanas as proper means of accurate Knowledge and to truths: Three central pramanas which are almost universally accepted, are perception (Sanskrit pratyakṣa), inference (anumāna), and "word," meaning the testimony of past or present reliable experts (Śabda); and more contentious ones are comparison and analogy (upamāna), postulation, derivation from circumstances (arthāpatti), and non-perception, negative/cognitive proof (anupalabdhi). Pratyakṣa (direct perception).

All these Pramana are used in day-to-day life. All that we see, hear, and perceive by senses are called "Pratyaksha." "The water exists because I can see it, and I can drink it" comes under Pratyaksha. "There is a smoke which I can see, so definitely there must be fire or factory somewhere"-comes under Anumana/Inference. "Similar to Cow, even Yaks provide milk" or "Unlike Tigers, Elephant has tusks"- these come under Upamana or Comparison. Similarly, statements like "John who went to the Himalayas says it is very Cold"-comes under Verbal Testimony.

No Scope of Any of the Pramanas Except Shabda/ Word of Sruti to Reveal Brahman

All the six pramanas can be grouped under two pramanas: pratyaksha (perception) and shabda (verbal testimony); because the pramanas of anumana (inference), upamana (comparison), arthapatti (postulation), and anuplabdhi (negative proof) are all based on the senses like pratyaksha (perception).

From our discussion about the nature of Brahman in the previous paragraph, it would have become apparent that Brahman cannot be an object of perception. As Shankara says,

"This principle is not within the scope of perception, as it does not have form or color or any other perceptible attribute. And it cannot be the object of inference or the other means of empirical Knowledge either, as it does not have any property to serve as an inferential sign or to provide any of the other prerequisites of an inference". (Bs. Bh.II.i.6)

So all means of Knowledge based on the senses are eliminated in one stroke as a means of knowing Brahman. Hence, we are left with only Shabda or verbal testimony as to the means. We are told that not the oral testimony of any individual but only that of Sruti can be considered to be the means to know the supersensible entity called Brahman. But why the Shruti?

This is because the Shrutis/Upanishads are not of human origin. I have discussed this topic in detail in the Chapter – The Origin of Advaita. It is an essential contention of both Advaita Vedanta and Purva-Mimamsa that the Vedas are eternal, uncreated, and authorless (apaurusheya). The claim for the infallibility of these texts follows directly from this contention. The Knowledge of the Absolute first manifests itself at the beginning of a world period. It is in the mind of Hiranyagarbha or Brahma, who has received the Veda from the supreme Lord. Hence, at the highest level, Veda is not just the "means" to attain The Highest Knowledge but "Is" the Highest Knowledge itself. Brahman is described as "Satya," "Jnana," and "Ananta." Brahman is "Knowledge itself," and hence, Brahman is the source of all Knowledge. It is in this sense that Vedas are described as "Apaurush-eya." The method, carried on continuously by a succession of Teachers beginning with Brahma, has even come down to certain Teachers of modern times.

The Claim of Authority of Srutis/Upanishads Rests on Universally Verifiable Experience

Because the Srutis/Upanishads in the hands of a qualified teacher are the only means of knowing Brahman, it does not mean that they reveal something utterly unknown to human experience. Brahman being our own essential nature, is not entirely unknown. Thus, as Shankara says in his Brahmasutra Bhashya introduction,

"The Self is not absolutely beyond apprehension, because it is apprehended as the content of the concept 'I,' and because the Self, opposed to the non-Self, is well known in the world as an immediately perceived (i.e., self-revealing) entity."

"Besides, the existence of Brahman is well known from the fact of Its being the Self of all; for everyone feels that his Self exists, and he never feels, 'I do not exist. Had there been no general recognition of the existence of Self, everyone would have felt, 'I do not exist. And that Self is Brahman." (Bs. Bh. 2.3.7)

The problem is that even though Self is known, it is

known in a general way with its superimposition. We cognize the shape of the snake as the shape of the rope, so the rope is not entirely unknown even when we perceive a snake on it. Similarly, the two quotes above show that we already know the Self as existence and consciousness, i.e., a self-revealed entity. Even when there is the error of supposing the body, senses, and organs to be the Self, this self-luminous principle remains the inmost principle of all, superior to all through being immediately self-evident. For we have the Upanishadic text,

'That which is immediately evident is the Absolute, that is the Self, interior to all" (Brhad.III.iv.1).

Since Brahman is a Self-revealing entity, the work of the srutis is not to reveal Brahman but to remove the ignorance that superimposes a plural universe on Brahman. So as Shankara says,

"If you object that, if the Absolute is not an object of Knowledge, it cannot be known through the Veda, we reply that this is not so. For the aim of the Veda here is to put an end to distinctions imagined through ignorance. The Veda does not aim to expound the Absolute as if it were an object characterizable as this or that. What, then, does it do? It does eliminate distinctions such as knower, Knowledge, and known, which ere imagined through ignorance. And it does so by teaching that the Absolute, because it is the innermost Self, is not an object of Knowledge." (Bs. Bh. 1.i.4)

Ultimately the work of the srutis is to negate all that is not Brahman. When all superimpositions on Brahman are negated, the luminosity of Brahman is revealed. The work of any means of Knowledge is to indicate its object. So as Shankara says,

"In the inquiry into the nature of Brahman, it is not merely Srutis, etc., alone that is the valid means of Knowledge, as is the case in the inquiry into the nature of Dharma (religious duty). But also Srutis etc. and direct intuition and the like are here the valid means according to the applicability. For Knowledge of Brahman has to culminate in intuition, and relates to an existent entity." (Bs. Bh. 1-1-2).

The Srutis do not exercise any authority where their evidence is contradicted by other means of Knowledge like perception, inference, etc. This goes on to show that Srutis are not rejecting science. On the contrary, they support science and reveal that reality is beyond the realm of scientific understanding. As Shankara says,

"Nor are the Srutis supposed to have authority in matters which are contradicted by other means of knowledge, as for instance if they said, 'Fire is cold and wets things.' If, however, a passage is ascertained to have the meaning given by the Srutis, then the evidence of the other means of Knowledge must be held to be fallacious.

For instance, the ignorant think of fire-fly as fire, or of the sky as a blue surface; these are perceptions no doubt, but when the evidence of the other means of Knowledge regarding them has been definitely known to be true, the perceptions of the ignorant, although they are definite experiences, prove to be fallacious. Therefore, the authority of the Vedas being inviolable, a Vedic passage must be taken exactly in the sense that it is tested to bear and not according to the ingenuity of the human mind. The sun does not cease to reveal objects because of the ingenuity of the human mind; similarly, the Vedic passages cannot be made to give up their meaning. Therefore, it is proved that work does not lead to liberation. Hence, the present section is introduced to show that the results of work are within the pale of relative existence." (Br. Bh. 3.iii.1)

So just like the results of science are open to verification and validation to anyone who is willing to follow the procedure of study and experiment, in the same way, the ultimate reality of Brahman is verifiable and open to validation by anyone who undertakes the study of teachings of srutis under a qualified teacher.

The Process of Enlightenment in Advaita Vedanta

Three practices of Jnana Yoga of Advaita Vedanta are shravana (listening/reading), manana (reflection/reasoning/dialogue), and nidhidhyasana (contemplation). A seeker comes to Jnana Yoga only after gaining qualifications of Viveka (discrimination between real and unreal), vairagya (dispassion), shad sampatti (six virtues for mind control), and mumukshutva (intense desire for liberation). These characteristics are developed by any of the traditional yogas: Karma Yoga, Bhakti Yoga, or Raja Yoga. I follow the unique psycho-philosophical teachings of J Krishnamurti. A person with an intellectual bent of mind can start with Jnana Yoga from the spiritual journey. Once these qualifications are adequately developed, the teacher, who is himself a knower of Brahman unfolds the teachings to the student, who diligently follows the three processes of shravana, mañana, and nidhidhyasana. A very qualified student will get liberation by just shravana, the middle grade one through shravana and manana, and the grade beneath that has to do all three practices.

When the student is listening to the words of the teacher, then they are a knower, for name's sake. The very knower is told, "You are Brahman." That means the knower has to give up the status, 'I am a knower.' That knower, who has identified with the body-mind-sense complex, himself is dissolved in the wake of Knowledge. As Shankara says,

"For the Self is not anything brought in to anyone as 'something new, for it is self-established and self-manifest from the start. The Self does not depend on any means of Knowledge to be known since the means of Knowledge depend on their existence and power to operate on it. 'They belong to it and are only brought into play to establish objects of knowledge which (unlike the Self) are not yet established." (Bs. Bh. II.iii.7)

In all other pramāṇa operations, the knower continues to be the subject related to the object known. This is the difference between the śabda-pramāṇa revealing the fact 'I am Brahman' and all other pramāṇas. In the operation of all the other means of Knowledge like perception, inference, presumption, etc., the knower retains himself and enjoys the pramāṇa-phala, the result of operating the pramāṇa. Here the knower sits relaxed, exposed to the teaching, which resolves the knower as Brahman finally. Therefore, this pramāṇa is a different thing altogether. It has to be handled. That is why śraddhā becomes important here. You must have the buddhi, 'I am letting the pramāṇa operate upon me.' Just as you allow a surgeon to operate upon you because you have śraddhā in him, so too you require śraddhā to allow this pramāṇa to operate upon you.

Ātmā is already self-evident, and it is alupta-dṛk, a seer that never ceases. It never even winks. It is always a witness. But it is a witness only with reference to whatever is seen. By itself, it is in the form of consciousness. This self-evident ātmā is Brahman. That is the teaching. Because of this teaching, a vṛtti takes place in the mind, which destroys ignorance and itself goes away. That vṛtti, 'I am Brahman/Self/Eternal Witness', is called ātmaikya-bodha or aparokṣa-jñāna. Sometimes the word anubhūti or anubhava also is used for Knowledge, but these words also indicate the immediate recognition of the Self as the result of the teaching. With this knowledge, one gains freedom. After this, nothing needs to be done. For we see in the following quotes from Shankara

"In worldly experience, we find that color manifests as soon as there is contact between the visual organ and light. In the same way, Ignorance of the Absolute disappears. the moment that direct Knowledge of it arises." (Brhad. Bh.I.iv.10)

"All experience, whether secular or based on Vedic teaching, comes to an end in the case of the man of steady wisdom, in whom metaphysical discrimination has arisen. For his ignorance has come to an end, end that experience was based on ignorance. For when there is Knowledge, Ignorance dis-appears. It is like the abolition of the darkness of night when the sun rises." (Bh.G.Bh.II.69)

"Immediately Knowledge of the Self has been obtained; it puts an end to ignorance. No process occupying time is admitted here. (Bs. .Bh.IV.i.2)"

Prarabdha Karma After Self Realization

There are two standpoints to explain this. First, from the Absolute perspective of Awareness, there was never any birth of anybody. Second, from the empirical viewpoint, Advaita explains the appearance of a body according to the theory of Prarabdha Karma. In this chapter I am going to discuss a particular stage of a seekers journey where he has attained direct Self Knowledge and become a jnani. But further work remains where the seeker has to let the Self Knowledge burn all his vasanas/karmic tendencies. For this, Advaita uses the model of Prarabdha Karma. As already mentioned, from the standpoint of the Absolute, no karma exists, so all the teachings on Prarabdha Karma are only provisional teachings helpful for a seeker to finally attain absolute self realization. The Jivanmukta is a person who has attained absolute self realization. He has endded with his vasanas and the concept of karma. In this chapter, however, I am concentrating on the phase of a seeker's journey where he/she is dissolving Prarabdha Karma till the very concept of Karma dissolves.

The present body/mind/intellect has come to existence based on acts done in previous lives. Prarabdha Karma is that portion of Karma that has started bearing fruit in the present life. It gives birth to the current body, the circumstances in which it is born, the situations the body has to face to exhaust this Karma, and ultimately, the time when the body will die. While Self Knowledge puts an end to two other kinds of Karma called sanchita karma and agami Karma, it does not end prarabdha karma. The momentum of prarabdha karma is supposed to continue even after a person has gained knowledge of the ultimate Reality. Only when all the prarabdha karma is exhausted, the body dies.

Three points that one needs to pay attention to in the above paras are
The exhaustion of Prarabdha Karma is about both the good and evil works.

Prarabdha Karma is more potent than knowledge and will work itself out no matter what. The only thing left is the BMI (Body/Mind/Intellect) to experience the results.

If no Prarabdha Karma remained to be exhausted, there would be no teacher to teach Self Knowledge.

The Jnani as Self is not affected by any form of Karma. The Prarabdha Karma only affects the BMI of the Jnani.

Shankara on Action After Self Realization

For Shankara, as I have mentioned on several occasions, Advaita is to do with the lifestyle of a monk. In his book

Upadeshasahasri, right in the opening verses itself, he says his preference clearly:

Verse 1: "We shall now explain a method of teaching the means" to liberation for the benefit of those aspirants after release who are desirous (of this teaching) and are possessed of faith (in it).

Verse 2. That means liberation, viz. Knowledge should be explained repeatedly until it is firmly grasped for a pure Brahmana disciple who is indifferent to everything transitory and achievable through specific means. Who has given up the desire a son, for wealth and for this world and the next," who has adopted the life of a wandering monk and is endowed with control over the mind and senses, with compassion? As well as with the qualities of a disciple well known in the scriptures, and who has approached the teacher in the pre-scribed manner, and been examined in respect of his caste, profession, conduct, learning, and parentage.

This effectively shuts out the possibility of liberation for householders. But both the Upanishads and the Bhagavad Gita do not concur with Shankara that liberation is a province only for the monks. Regarding Gita, In Upanishads, there is mention of several self-realized householders like Yajnvalkya, Ushati Chakrayana, and King Janaka in Brhadaranyaka Upanishad, Satyakama Jabala of Chandogya Upanishad, etc. Several post-Shankara Advaita kinds of literature like Panchadasi and Ashtavakra Gita also do not make Advaita realization solely the province of monks.

Continuing with Shankara: even if a householder gets self-knowledge, according to him, he ultimately renounces all actions. Shankara, however, provisionally grants a life of active outward action in rare circumstances. We see his views in the following quote from Bhagavad Gita:

"However, one who is a perceiver of 'inaction' etc. is free from actions owing to the very fact of his seeing 'inaction' etc. He is a monk who acts merely to maintain the body. Being so, he does not engage in actions, although he might have done so before the dawn of discrimination. He again, having been engaged in actions under the influence of past tendencies. Later on, he becomes endowed with the fullest self-knowledge. He surely renounces (all) actions and their accessories as he does not find any purpose in activity. For some reason, if it becomes impossible to renounce actions, and he, for the sake of preventing people from going astray, even remains engaged as before in actions—without attachment to those actions and their results because of the absence of any selfish purpose—, still he surely does nothing at all! His actions surely become 'inaction' because of having been burnt away by the fire of wisdom." (Shankara's Commentary on Verse Bh. Gita verse 4.19)

Considering the quote above, we cannot thus find fault in Shankara's philosophy of Prarabdha Karma despite his monastic predilection. Because his last lines in the above quote accept, perhaps with a noticeable reluctance, that actions do not compromise the knowledge of a self-realized being in any way: all his actions are burnt in the fire of self-knowledge. And only unselfish actions remain as we see in Bhagavad Gita "Verse 3.25: Bharata! Therefore, just as the unwise, attached to the results, perform an action, so too would the wise perform the action without attachment. Desirous of doing that which is for the protection of the people."

The fact is that a realized being does nothing at all. This inaction in action and non-action, which is a fact for the Jnani/Self Realized Being, is a source of great perplexity to ordinary people who see such a man was performing all actions yet claiming to do nothing at all. But Shankara had no doubts about it at all. How could he? He was a Jivanmukta and an active teacher and writer of Advaita, traveling the length and breadth of the country.

Self Realized Being: Inaction in Action and Action in Inaction

Before we plunge headlong into discussing prarabdha Karma for a self-realized being/Jnani as discussed in texts other than Shankara, we must understand his special status mentioned above. Even though he seems to be acting, he knows himself to be the Self/Witness/Awareness, who is not the thinker/doer/experience, but the mere Witness of all their acts. All actions are performed by the three Gunas, which make up Maya – sattva, rajas, and tamas, while as Self, the Jnani is trigunatitha: beyond the three Gunas. An analogy here exists with various physiological functions of the body, like the beating of the heart and the digesting of food, which proceeds on their own accord: without any effort or active intervention or action from our side. We witness them. For a Jnani, the same goes for the mental functions of thinking, decision-making, and experiencing. All are happening on their own while he is their mere, untouched Witness.

Therefore, the difference between an ignorant man and the man of Self-knowledge lies not in the actions they perform but in the consciousness with which they perform their actions. In the case of a man of Self Knowledge, this difference in consciousness is not easily perceived by ordinary people and may pass entirely unrecognized by them. Therefore, although the two persons outwardly appear to be the same, they are poles apart.

Panchadasi on Prarabdha Karma

Having understood the special status of the Jnani/Jivanmukta, and his elusive status as an actor and a non-doer, even though he is seen having a body/mind/intellect. We are in a better position to look at the experiential aspects of Prarabdha Karma mentioned in texts that accord with Shankara's view of Prarabdha. I empathize with these because my own experiences corroborate the experiences shared in these texts.

Amongst all the texts, there is a work by Swami Vidyaranya written just over half a century before called Panchadasi, which has got the most detailed description of Prarabdha Karma and its experiences for a Jnani that I have come across. It has devoted over 50 verses on this topic exploring it through multiple lenses and sustained by reasoning. In the following sections, I will quote and explore these verses giving examples from my personal life.

A Jnani is Not Necessarily a Renunciate or a Monk

Unlike Shankara and in tandem with Bhagavad, Gita Panchadasi does not restrict Self Realization to monks and renunciates. Like Gita, Panchadasi opens out its discussion on Prarabdha Karma with the example of King Janaka. We have:
Verse 7.130. (Doubt): How then the ancient knowers like Janaka administered kingdoms? (Reply): They were able because of their conviction about the Truth. If you have that, then, by all means, engage yourself in logic or agriculture or do whatever you like.

It has an encouraging tone towards work post Self Realization, recommending fields as diverse as absolutely physical agriculture to completely mental activities like learning the art and science of logic. After my Self Realization, I did carpentry for a couple of years and then switched to writing and teaching Advaita. Coincidentally I too love philosophy and logic. I guess most Jnana Yogis do.

To an onlooker, all the work done by a Jnani/ may seem to be driven by some aim or purpose. For a Jnani will appear to do all work with utter seriousness and even strive for perfection. But from within, he is absolutely actionless. He is nothing but the Witness of the vasanas that are exhausting themselves in the form of work. While others derive and create a self-identity through work, a Jnani/Jivanmukta does not. He sees it as the play of the gunas. Thus, Panchadasi says:

"Verse 7.131. Once he is convinced of the unreality of the world, a knower, with mind undisturbed, allows his fructifying Karma to wear out and engages himself in worldly affairs accordingly. "

A Newly Initiated Jnani Can Suffer Temporary Lapses in Self Knowledge Due to Force of Prarabdha Karma But Recovers From It

This is something that Shankara, too, has discussed in his commentaries that a Jnani, mainly who has newly acquired Self Knowledge, can suffer occasional lapses from his knowledge due to the force of the fructifying Karma. A good teacher helps the student stabilize in Self Knowledge after he has attained it. Thus, we can see that all this is a long and sustained process. Panchadasi brings this about through many vivid examples and comforts the Jnani that such lapses are only temporary. One can come back to Self Knowledge by mere remembrance of it. In the ending verses, it gives an interesting twist to the famous story of the 'Tenth Man', employed by Advaitins to teach students how knowledge and not any form of action can help you know who you truly are and liberate you from the sense of all limitations of birth and death.

Verse 7.244. After a man has realized the nature of the

rope, the trembling caused by the erroneous idea of the snake disappears gradually only and the idea of the snake still sometimes haunts him when he sees a rope in darkness.

Verse 7.245. Similarly the fructifying Karma does not end abruptly but dies down slowly. In the course of the enjoyment of its fruits, the knower is occasionally visited by such thoughts as 'I am a mortal'.

Verse 7.246. Lapses like this do not nullify the realization of Truth. Jivanmukti (liberation in life) is not a vow, but the establishment of the soul in the knowledge of Brahman.

Verse 7.247. In the example already cited, the tenth man, who may have been crying and beating his head in sorrow, stops lamenting on realizing that the tenth is not dead; but the wounds caused by beating his head take a month gradually to heal.

Verse 7.248. On realizing that the tenth is alive, he rejoices and forgets the pain of his wounds. In the same way liberation in life makes one forget any misery resulting from the fructifying Karma.

Verse 7.249. As it is not a vow and a break does not matter, one should reflect on the Truth again and again to remove the delusion whenever it recurs, just as a man who takes mercury to cure a certain disease eats again and again during the day to satisfy the hunger caused by the mercury.

"Verse 7.250. As the tenth man cures his wounds by applying medicine, so the knower wears out the fructifying Karma by enjoyment and is ultimately liberated. "

Self Knowledge is Not Opposed to Fructifying Experiences of Prarabdha Karma

After illustrating how the Prarabdha Karma can cause temporary loss of knowledge for a Jnani who has newly gained Self Knowledge. The discussion shifts to how Prarabdha Karma acts even for a seasoned Jnani, anticipating objections by people as to how a Jnani. Who is the epitome of knowledge can still be subject to the force of Prarabdha Karma in terms of experiencing pain and pleasure? The Panchadasi presents us with an array of examples and logic. Ultimately it also shows how Self Knowledge does not necessarily mean the destruction of the phenomenal world as it is not opposed to its appearance. Self Knowledge only indicates that the world is real, only like a dream or a mirage. A Jnani experiences pain and pleasure produced by Prarabdha

Karma, knowing them to be only as real as a dream.

Verse 7.175. The function of knowledge is to show the illusory nature of the world, and the function of fructifying Karma is to yield pleasure and pain to the Jiva.

Verse 7.176. Knowledge and fructifying Karma are not opposed to one another since they refer to different objects. The sight of a magical performance gives amusement to a spectator in spite of his knowledge of its unreality.

Verse 7.177. The fructification of Karma would be considered to be opposed to the knowledge of Truth if it gave rise to the idea of the Reality of the transitory world. Still, mere enjoyment does not mean that the enjoyed thing is real.

Verse 7.178. Through the imaginary objects seen in a dream, there is the experience of joy and sorrow to no small extent; therefore, you can infer that through the objects of the waking state also there can be the same experience (without making them real).

Verse 7.179. If the knowledge of Truth would obliterate the enjoyable world, then it would be a destroyer of the fructifying Karma. But it only teaches its unreality and does not cause its disappearance.

Verse 7.180. People know a magical show to be unreal, but this knowledge does not involve the destruction of the show. So it is possible to know the unreality of external objects without causing their disappearance or the cessation of enjoyment from them.

A Jnani Has No Choice to Avert His Actions Born of Prarabdha Karma

A Jnani is neither attached to virtuous actions nor is he attached to any vice. As a non-doer, his actions are just a product of Prarabdha Karma. Nothing can stop the Prarabdha Karma from fructifying and give the designated experiences. Let's examine the following verses from Panchadasi.

It starts the discussion in the form of a dialogue with a deliberate introduction of a doubt as to how a Jnani, who is said to be a person who knows the falsity of all objects, can be subjected to the vagaries Prarabdha Karma. It then goes into detail into various ways in which Prarabdha Karma can be expended.

Verse 7.151. (Doubt): When discrimination is ever awake regarding the defects of the objects of enjoyment, how can the desire for pleasure be forced upon him by his fructifying Karma?

Verse 7.152. (Reply): There is no inconsistency here, for the fructifying Karma expends itself in various ways. There are three kinds of fructifying Karma' producing enjoyment with desire', 'in the absence of desire' and 'through the desire of another.

The following verses show that even the knowledge of the consequences of particular actions is not enough to stop the Prarabdha Karma from acting. It is not that the Jnani is not aware of the results of their acts, but the Prarabdha Karma has an unstoppable force. Experientially I have felt driven to do specific actions after Self Realization, and the power behind these acts was extraordinary. A Jnani is a person who has done Buddhi Yoga, a highly philosophical affair, so it is incredibly foolish to assume that the Jnani/Jivanmukta is unaware of the consequences of their actions. As the succeeding verses show, even the Lord cannot stop the inexorable law of Karma, citing examples of Yudhisthra, Rama and Nala followed by a dialogue between Krishna and Arjuna culled from Bhagavad Gita.

Verse 7.153. The sick attached to harmful food, the thieves, and those who have illicit relationships with the wives of a king know well the consequence likely to follow their actions, but despite this, they are driven to do them by their fructifying Karma.

Verse 7.154. Even Ishvara cannot stop such desires. So Sri Krishna said to Arjuna in the Gita:

Verse 7.155. 'Even wise men follow the dictates of their nature. Their innate tendencies prompt beings; what can restriction do ?' (Reference to *Bhagavad Gita Verse 3.33)*

Verse 7.156. If it were possible to avert the consequences of fructifying Karma, Nala, Rama and Yudhisthira would not have suffered the miseries they were subjected to.

Verse 7.157. Ishvara Himself ordains that the fructifying Karma should be inexorable. So the fact that He is unable to prevent such Karma from fructifying is not inconsistent with His omnipotence.

Verse 7.158. Listen to the questions and answers between Arjuna and Sri Krishna from which we know that a man has to experience his fructifying Karma though he may have no desire to experience it.

Verse 7.159. 'O Krishna, prompted by what does a man

sin against his will as if some force compels him to do so ?'

Verse 7.160. 'It is desire and (its brood) anger, born of the quality of Rajas. It is insatiable, the great source of all sins; know it to be your enemy.'

Verse 7.161. 'O Arjuna, your own Karma, produced by your own nature, compels you to do things, even though you may not want to do them.

Verse 7.168. That which is not destined to happen due to our past Karma will not happen; that which is to happen must happen. Such knowledge is a sure antidote to the poison of anxiety; it removes the delusion of grief.

Finally, we can round off this discussion on the inevitability of Prarabdha Karma to commit him to act irrespective of virtue and vice by the following quote of Panchadasi

Verse 7.132. Do not fear irregularity when the wise engage themselves in actions according to their Karma. Even if it happens, let it be; who can prevent the Karma?

Even the Virtuous Actions Done by a Jnani/Jivan-mukta Are Part of His Prarabdha Karma

Since the Jnani is a non-doer, he is beyond both acts of virtue and vice. Thus, he does not claim to be a doer of any virtuous acts and takes their credit. He is therefore not a social worker, even if he does any social work. He knows that all these acts are nothing but his Prarabdha Karma taking its course. The Jnani, however, is not subject to further Karma because of his actions propelled by exhausting Prarabdha Karma. He does not get attached to his virtuous deeds and derives pleasure out of them. The ajnani will get connected to the joy born out of righteous acts and will long to have more joy in the future. To bring out this aspect, we have the following verses in Panchadasi

Verse 7.162. When a man is neither willing nor unwilling to do a thing but does it for the feelings of others and experiences pleasure and pain, it is the result of 'fructifying Karma through the desire of others.

Verse 7.163. (Doubt): Does it not contradict the text at the beginning of this chapter which describes the enlightened man as desireless? (Reply): The text does not mean that desires are absent in the enlightened man, but that desires arising in him spontaneously without his will produce no pleasure or pain in him, just as the roasted grain has no potency.

Verse 7.164. Though looking the same, the roasted grain

cannot germinate; similarly, the desires of the knower, well aware of the unreality of objects of desire, cannot produce merit and demerit.

Verse 7.165. Though it does not germinate, the roasted grain can be used as food. In the same way, the desires of the knower yield him only a little experience but cannot lead to varieties of enjoyment producing sorrow or abiding habits.

Verse 7.167. 'Let not my enjoyment be cut short, let it go on increasing, let not obstacles stop it, I am blessed because of it' – such is the nature of that delusion.

A Jnani too Undergoes Psychological Suffering But With A Difference Due to Prarabdha Karma.

People have the feeling that a Self Realized being has gone beyond all fear and suffering. But this is not true. All Jnanis have to undergo physical and psychological suffering caused by fructifying prarabdha karma. The Panchadasi says this categorically,

"Verse 7.133. In the experience of their fructifying Karma the enlightened and the unenlightened alike have no choice. Still, the knower is patient and undisturbed, whereas an ignorant man is impatient and suffers pain and grief. "

As I have mentioned in the subheading, there is no choice for the Jnani to face fructifying both pleasurable and painful prarabdha karma, just that the Jnani is better equipped to deal with it. As already hinted in the previous verse, a Jnani has different knowledge. He knows that all experiences are impermanent objects arising and falling in Awareness, while he as Awareness is their unchanged Witness. So even when the experience is taking place, he has the detachment from it, which is not visible to others. He has an absolute still center, which is untouched by all the play of vasanas and gunas. He knows that this play is going to end as his vasanas exhaust. Thus, Panchadasi says in the following verses,

"Verse 7.134. Two travelers on a journey may be equally fatigued, but the one who knows that his destination is not far off goes on quicker with patience, whereas the ignorant one feels discouraged and stays on longer on the way."

'Verse 7.166. The fructifying Karma spends its force when its effects are experienced; it is only when, through ignorance, one believes its effects to be real that they cause lasting sorrow. "

"Verse 7.169. Both the illumined and the deluded suffer from their fructifying Karma; the deluded are subject to misery, the wise are not. As the deluded are full of desires, of useless unreal things, their sorrow is great. "

"Verse 7.171. The wise man is convinced that worldly desires are like dream objects or magical creations. He knows further that the nature of the world is incomprehensible and that its objects are momentary. How can he then be attached to them ?"

"Verse 7.174. This world of duality is like a magical creation, with its cause incomprehensible. What matters it to the wise man who does not forget this if the past actions produce their results in him ?"

A Jnani Also Enjoys and Gains Pleasure from Objects in Moderation Due to Prarabdha Karma

Just as a Jnani is not immune to suffering due to fructifying Karma, he is neither immune to getting pleasure from objects. Giving an interesting analogy of a crow with a double vision, the Panchadasi has the following verses.

Verse 11.128. The sage, looking now at the bliss of Brahman and now at such worldly objects as are not opposed to it, is like a crow that turns its eye from one side to another.

Verse 11.129. The crow has only a single vision that alternates between the right and left eyes. Similarly, the vision of the knower of Truth alternates between the two types of bliss (of Brahman and the world).

Verse 11.130. Enjoying the bliss of Brahman taught in the scriptures, and the worldly bliss unopposed to it, the knower of Truth knows them both in the same way as one who knows two languages.

However, these verses do not mean to show that the Jnani is interested in pleasures like the ordinary person. For it says,

Verse 11.17. The infinite Self alone is bliss; there is no bliss in the finite realm of the triad (knower, known, and knowing). This Sanatkumara told the grieving Narada.

The Jnani is quite aware of the above. Thus even though he is compelled towards deriving pleasure from objects due to his fructifying Karma, he is very cognizant that the source of all bliss is nothing but Self. This is brought out in the following verses of Panchadasi

Verse 11.122. A woman devoted to a paramour, though engaged in household duties, with all the time be dwelling in mind on the pleasures with him.

Verse 11.123. Similarly, the wise one who has found peace in the supreme Reality will be ever enjoying within the bliss of Brahman even when engaged in worldly matters.

The bliss of Brahman being spoken about is the reflection of Brahman in a sattvic mind. Depending upon the vasanas of a Jnani, it takes time for a mind to attain the state of sattva, which can reflect the bliss of Brahman, after achieving Self Knowledge. Thus, the Panchadasi says,

Verse 11.124. Wisdom consists of subjugating the desires for sense-pleasure, even when the passions are strong, and engaging the mind in meditation on Brahman with the desire to enjoy bliss.

Even as Jnani is enjoying sense pleasures, his remembrance of Self is intact. If the vasanas are very strong, he has to detach and focus exclusively on the recollection of Self. At other times, this remembrance of Self comes automatically to the mind of a Jnani, and it acts as a purger of all thoughts of objects. The set of verses (7.146 – 7.150) which I quote in the paragraph below from Panchadasi bring out this aspect of remembrance of Self in experiential and philosophical terms quite beautifully. They show the kind of reasoning that goes in the mind of a Jnani, which he silently Witnesses. Before we get to these verses, I would like to quote some verses which talk about the social life of a Jnani.

Verse 7.143. If a wise man is compelled to enjoy the fruits of desires by the force of his fructifying Karma, he does so with indifference and great reluctance like a man who is impressed for labor.

Verse 7.144. The wise, having spiritual faith if forced by their fructifying Karma to live a family life, maintaining many relations, always sorrowfully think 'Ah, the bonds of Karma are not yet torn off.'

Verse 7.145. This sorrow is not due to the world's afflictions but a dislike for it, for the worldly afflictions are caused by an erroneous conviction about its Reality.

To me, the above two verses, while getting the general drift of a Jnani's mind rightly, appear a bit of a stretch. A Jnani indeed has a natural preference for solitude, but it would be incorrect to say that a Jnani does not prefer any company or have sexual desires. Yajnavalkya, the great Jnani in Brhadaranyaka Upanishad had two wives. The sexual desires last as long as the Prarabdha Karma deems it that way. Whether the Jnani acts on them or not, and in what manner, is also the province of Prarabdha Karma. So there are certain 'worldly afflictions like sex, which, if Prarabdha Karma favors, a Jnani certainly do not dislike, even though he 'knows' their unreality, and he certainly does not feel like 'impressed for labor' when acting on them. However, a Jnani can say that he is not blinded by these desires and pursues them indiscriminately. The following verses from Panchadasi, in my view, show quite accurately the kind of moderation to sense pleasures that comes naturally to any Jnani. The opening verse sets the tone of the arguments related to moderation of sense pleasures which the later verses follow.

Verse 7.146. A man endowed with discrimination sees the defects of enjoyment and is satisfied even with little, whereas he is subject to illusion is not satisfied even with endless enjoyments.

Verse 7.147. 'The desires are never quelled by enjoyment but increase more like the flame of a fire fed on clarified butter.'

Verse 7.148. But when the impermanence of pleasure is known, the gratification of desires may bring the idea of 'enough of it.' It is like a thief, who, having been knowingly employed in service, does not behave like a thief but as a friend.

Verse 7.149. A man who has conquered his mind is satisfied with even a little enjoyment of pleasure. He knows well that pleasures are impermanent and are followed by grief. To him, even a little pleasure is more than enough.

Verse 7.150. A king who has been freed from prison is content with sovereignty over a village, whereas when he had neither been imprisoned nor conquered, he did not attach much value even to a kingdom.

The previous paragraphs deal with the experiential aspects of Prarabdha Karma as discussed exclusively in Panchadasi text. However, there are other post-Shankara texts in Advaita literature like Ashtavakara Gita and Avdhuta Gita that also support and give some experiential descriptions of Prarabdha Karma. I did not include them as Panchadasi has already stated what is found in these texts – in different words – so quoting these texts would only add to philosophical redundancy.

The Liberated Being : Beyond all Acts – Good & Bad

History, culture, and mythology all create a prototype of an enlightened being or a Liberated Person. These prototypes inform the ordinary person about the kind of greatness of person or personality that a liberated person is. The characters of enlightened beings are worshipped as Gods or saviors or beings with superhuman powers. However, the highest truth, which only Advaita Vedanta elucidates through the Vedas, is more straightforward.

You are the truth you are seeking.

The truth is deceptively simple. I say so because our minds are geared to look outside and be attracted by forms. This creates a split between you and the world outside. The liberated being, who in Advaita is called a Jnani, has gone beyond such a split and acquired a non-dual vision. What is that vision, and who is a Jnani? How does he act? I explore these questions in this article.

The Jnani – Liberated Being

The Jiva/individual soul, as a thinker/doer/experiencer, is tossed in the dualities of samsara – pain and pleasure, good and bad, right and wrong, ignorance and enlightenment. As a Jiva, he is always trying to "become": become good, become better, become knowledgeable, become detached, become enlightened.

However, with the rise of Jnana/Self Knowledge, his perception shifts from duality to non-duality instantaneously. To understand and appreciate what I mean by this, a person unfamiliar with Advaita would have to read the Chapter – Self Inquiry and Insight Into One's True Nature. But, as this chapter notes, it takes years and years of sadhana/preparation before this insight happens.

Knowing his essential nature to be Self, the Jiva becomes a Jnani freed from all notions of duality. This freedom and

perfection are instantaneous with the rise of direct Knowledge. Freed from the idea of being a thinker/doer/experi-
encer, the Jnani is freed not only from all notions of becoming
but also from all works, including the notion of good works
and evil works.

After that, there is nothing left for the Jnani to attain
or lose, in any way, no matter what acts are seen to be
performed by him. So while others may judge his actions in
terms of duality – such as good and evil, he knows that he
does nothing as an actionless Self. So the body of the Jnani
carries on till his prarabdha karma exhausts, and it finally
drops.

This is an accurate account of the rise of Jnana and
the status of a Jnani. But many people find themselves in
disagreement with many facts stated in this account. I am
writing this article to dispel their doubts, quoting passages
from Chapter 4 – Results of Knowledge (Jnana Phala),
Brahma Sutra Bhashya of Shankaracharya (Translation by
Swami Gambhirananda), addressing all erroneous notions.

A.) No further acts or practices by a Jnani are required
to stabilize in Jnana
"On the realization of that (Brahman), (there occur) non-
attachment and destruction (respectively) of the succeeding
and earlier sins."– Bs.Bh – Verse IV.i.13

The commentary from Shankara to this verse reads,

"When That, viz Brahman, becomes realized, then come
the non-attachment of subsequent sins and the destruction of the earlier ones. Why? "Because it is so declared (in
the scriptures). Thus it is declared in the course of dealing
with the Knowledge of Brahman that a future sin might be
expected to arise in the usual way does not arise in the case
of a man of Knowledge: "As water does not stick to a lotus
leaf, even so, sin does not contaminate a man possessed of
knowledge" (Ch IV.xiv.3). So also, the past fluffy tip of a reed
placed in fire burns away completely. Similarly, all sins are
burnt away (Ch V.xxiv.3). Here occurs another declaration
about the destruction of the result of work: "When the Self
which is both high and low is realized, the knot of the heart

gets untied, all doubts become solved, and all one's actions become dissipated" (Mu.II.ii.8)

The commentary on this verse ends with the lines,

"It is also unreasonable that the result of Knowledge (which is immediate) should be mediate (as the opponent's theory implies). Hence the conclusion is that sin becomes dissipated when Brahman is known as"– Bs.Bh – IV.i.13

We can note the following points from this quote

1.) The destruction of all sins of the past AS WELL AS NON-ATTACHMENT OF FUTURE SINS.

2.) No future sin can arise in a man of Knowledge like it may happen in the case of an ordinary man

3.) All actions become dissipated

4.) The results of Knowledge is immediate

All these go to show that by the mere dint of direct Knowledge, a Jnani is freed from all actions, the result of all actions of the past and the result of all actions he shall do in the future. Not only this, all his actions become dissipated. So after attainment of direct Knowledge, there is no practice of any kind to become more stabilized in Jnana or to attain bliss or to renounce the world. Direct Knowledge is the seal for the past, present, and future. We shall see this clearly in the quote of the following paragraph

B.) The rise of Jnana is instantaneous: not a gradual process in time due to certain practices or actions

The action does not lead to Jnana. Activities are considered to be only indirect means of Knowledge. How? By purifying the mind and making it ready. Ready for what? Ready for Jnana (akhandakara vritti) to arise. The arising of this Jnana is not the result of any action whatsoever. Firstly, action is not opposed to ignorance. Secondly, all activities happen in space and time, so they can only produce finite results. No action can result in infinite Brahman/Self. The Brahmasutra Bhashya shows this by two points.

"The knower of Brahman has this realization: "As opposed to the entity known before to possessed of agentship and experience by its very nature, I am Brahman which is by nature devoid of agentship and experienceship in all three periods of time. Even earlier, I was never an agent and experiencer, nor am I at present, nor shall I be so in future". From such a point of view alone can liberation be justified."– Bs.Bh – IV.i.13

"I am Brahman, which is by nature devoid of agentship and experienceship in all three periods of time. Even earlier, I was never an agent and experiencer, nor am I at present, nor shall I be so in future". This clearly shows that no action produces Jnana. The doer never becomes Jnani. Only Knowledge, when it arises, frees one from the ignorance that one was ever a doer, is a doer, or will ever be a doer. The Jnani is one who knows that he was not a doer in all three periods of time."

The Bhashya clarifies what I had written in the earlier paragraph: No action/s can result in timeless Brahman because all actions result only in finite results. It says,

"Besides, liberation, unlike the results of work, cannot be produced by a concurrence of place, time, and causation, since that would make it impermanent."– Bs.Bh – IV.i.13

3.) The Jnani is not a "doer" of good works/bad works and neither attached to good works/bad works

As such, the Jnani is not the doer of any works. We have seen this already through my earlier quotes. But for the Jivas operating in Maya, the notion of duality is nigh impossible to eliminate. They almost always conflate a Jnani with a doer of good works, thereby relating Jnana to certain acts. While the Jnanis may appear to be 'good people or seem to be doing good works, to some or great extent, it is because they could not have come to Jnana without having a sattvic mind and tremendous vairagya. However, the Jnani has no intent or attachment to do either good works or bad works.

1.) A Jnani knows himself as Self/non-doer, while the gunas do the action.

2.) A Jnani sees all acts as Self, so he does not have the vision of duality. Though people may classify his acts in dual terms, he is neither attached to good or evil actions.

The following quote from Bhramasutra Bhashya shows that the Jnani has given up the notion of doership of all actions. He is not choosing in any way to do good works or becoming a doer of good works.

"To the man of knowledge occur the non-attachment and destruction "of the other as well," of virtue also, as of sin itself. Why? ....In the Upanishadic texts like, "He conquers both of them" (Br. IV.iv.22), the destruction of virtue, just as much as of vice, is declared since the destruction of action consequent on the realization of the Self that is not an agent occurs equally in the cases of virtuous and vicious acts, and since Upanishads speaks of destruction all works without any exception in "and all one's actions become dissipated" (Mu. II.ii.8). Even where the single word vice is used, the word virtue is also to be understood because its result is inferior to Knowledge. Moreover, in the Upanishad itself occurs the word vice to convey the idea of virtue as well. Thus in the sentence, "Day and night cannot reach this barrage (which is Self)" (Ch. VIII.iv.1), virtue is introduced along with vice; then it is said, "All sins desist from It (the Self)," thereby using the word sin (vice) to indicate virtue as well without any distinction. Bs.Bh – IV.i.14

4.) The Jnani does not cease to act after the dawn of Knowledge

Some people associate Jnani with physical actionlessness with arising of Jnana. This implies that a Jnani 'becomes' someone other than what he was. But arising of Jnana, as we have seen earlier, is not the result of any action or becoming. As already quoted above, the ONLY WAY in which liberation can be justified is, "I am Brahman, which is by nature devoid of agentship and experienceship in all three periods of time. Even earlier, I was never an agent and experiencer, nor am I at present, nor shall I be so in future" So Jnana is not associated with any change whatsoever in his actions except the shift in identity from being a doer to being a non-doer/Self.

Some people give the logic that since Self is actionless, the Jnani being Self, cannot do, or ceases to perform, all actions; or that the Jnani, getting Knowledge of Self, drops down dead. However, this is not the view shared by Brahmasutra Bhashya. The verse I am quoting below clearly says that even though the Jnani is a knower of his essential nature as Self, the actions of the body/mind/intellect continue because of prarabdha karma.

"But only those past (virtues and vices) get destroyed which have not begun to bear fruit, for death is set as the limit of waiting for liberation."– Bs.Bh – Verse IV.i.15

Commenting on this verse in his Bhashya, Shankaracharya writes,

"After the acquisition of knowledge, those virtues and vices that have not begun to yield their fruits and that were accumulated in earlier lives or even in this life before the dawn of knowledge are alone destroyed, but not so are those destroyed whose results have already been partially enjoyed and by which has begun this present life in which the knowledge of Brahman arises."
Bs.Bh – IV.i.15

And finally, to seal all doubts on two issues
1.) Whether the body acts after Self Knowledge
2.) Whether the Jnani 'performs' only 'good acts' and not 'bad acts.'

I am quoting the final words of Shankaracharya in Brahmasutra Bhashya,

"As for the Knowledge of Self as the non-performer of any act, that destroys the results of works by first sublating false ignorance, even when sublated, continues for a while owing to past tendencies like the continuance of vision of two moons. Furthermore, no difference of opinion is possible here as to whether the body is retained (after Knowledge) for some time or not by knowers of Brahman. For when somebody feels in his heart that he has realized Brahman and yet holds the body, how can this be denied by somebody else? This very fact is elaborated in the Upanishads and the Smritis and in the course of determining the characteristics of "the man of steady wisdom" (sthitaprajna – Gita, II.54). Hence the conclusion is that only those virtues and vices are washed away by Knowledge which has not begun to bear fruit."– Bs.Bh – IV.i.15

The Ego

Question.

A child who gets praised since the beginning develops an ego. How can he reduce it to create a balance?

What is the meaning of "reduction of ego"? Can there be anything called reduction? Is there a universal scale or chart which rates ego by some quantifiable data? Perhaps we have a standard in our mind which judges something as more self-centered and something as less.

Is the saint having less ego than a criminal? Both have fear, desire, the want for social approval. Does a social activist or an environmentalist have less ego than a capitalist? Is an environmentalist or social activist free from fear, desire, hurt, and anger? Society may give more respect to a saint, social activist, or environmentalist, but all have the basic move-ments of ego – attachment, fear, desire, hurt, and anger.

If I have understood this as a parent, we will not train our children to become someone, not teach/them to any pattern of society. The psychological way of "becoming" had anchored the ego in the early stage of development.

Since we are all conditioned in childhood by our parents, school, society, and institutions to a pattern of psychological becoming, we follow all these patterns unconsciously. So it's not we living our ways out; instead, it is the patterns living us out.

When we talk of the reduction of ego, we shall fall into another pattern. If I am a capitalist pursuing naked success and power through wealth, I will become a social worker or an environmentalist, thinking it's a more noble work. But as I have noted before, if one examines all of them closely, each one has the ego that operates. Environmentalists and social workers fight each other, too, with their ideas of what will solve the situation. Both are also hungry for public rec-ognition and acclaim.

Moreover, no amount of system changes are going to solve the situation. The environmental and social problems are related to the greed of man. Until we address this, the problem will keep coming back in different forms.

If I am genuinely interested in the question of self or ego, we would be interested in ending it, not reducing it, which does not mean controlling our desires. On the contrary, it implies a desire for freedom, of living a life free of all conflict. Controlling desire, like a saint again, brings us to conflict. The act of following a teacher or spiritual path, or the following anyone, brings us into a conflict between what one is and what one should be. Thus it is only about control.

If one is genuinely interested in ending the conflict, one begins with understanding the roots of battle without the aid of any paths or methods. One sees that one conflicts because of various desires one has. Looking further, one realizes that these desires are conditioning imposed on oneself during childhood. There is social conditioning, and of course, biological conditioning too, which we shall put aside for the moment.

My upbringing since childhood conditioned me that I am nothing and a nobody if I am not successful. I feel small and lonely if I do not fit in the crowd, fit into society. I feel inferior in front of my peers who have big houses and cars. So I examine this whole notion of competition, success, and measurement. I see that society measures me through specific standards like money, knowledge, power, and ethics. I begin to know that these standards governed me, which I have never questioned. I never asked whether I should live up to these standards. I have just been mechanically following them. Questioning them would mean that I am no longer part of this vicious society. I am also going to lose my friends with whom I seek pleasure, security, and warmth. Questioning them would mean that I may lose my carefully erected social standing and status.

In effect, questioning would mean that I become psychologically alone. I am no longer attached to people and society for deriving any comfort, security, or pleasure. It does not mean becoming an ascetic. It means that one is not living one's life conforming to social standards but living life based on one's inquiry into self. Such a person is a lot more sensitive than a person imitating and working to society mechanically. One does not accept any authority of any kind, outwardly and inwardly. Again, this is a bit tricky. I am not talking of becoming a revolutionary, a person revolting against some system to bring about another system: like a communist trying to change a capitalist society. Whether one is a capitalist or communist, both bow to their fears inside. I am talking of freedom from the authority of fear inside the mind.

And I think there is nothing more urgent than this for any human being.

Puzzle of the Upanishads

From ignorance, lead me to truth;
From darkness, lead me to light;
From death, lead me to immortality
Om peace, peace, peace
~ Brihadaranyaka Upanishad (1.3.28)

The words of the introductory verse are from the patron of the yajña (Vedic ritual sacrifice), who recites them as the priest sings the Introductory Praise of the Sāman. As the author of this section of the Bṛhādaraṇyaka Upaniṣad points out, the unreal is death, and the real is immortality, even as darkness is death and light is immortality. In other words, the patron is saying, "Make me immortal." (1.3.28)

This was also the verse that used to be constantly in my mind at the end stages of my inquiry. In my Chapter "Questioning Death" I had discussed how the question of death played the most important role in my journey of self-inquiry. I have interwoven it with the role deaths plays in the story of Nachiketa in the Katha Upanishad and that of Buddha.

That the question of death would form a part of one's self-inquiry is inevitable. No matter what is one's philosophy, one has to contend with death if one has to know the truth of life. About three thousand years back, the concern with immortality – going beyond death – became a profound preoccupation with the people of the Vedic age. The Upanishads – the concluding portion of the Vedas – are engaged solely in the quest for that principle that lies beyond the pale of death.

Therefore, for any inquirer into truth, it would be a case of great exception that they have not had a brush with the Upanishads. "From every sentence, deeply original and sublime thoughts arise, and a high and holy and earnest spirit pervades the whole. There is no study so beneficial and elevating in the whole world as that of the Upanishads.

It has been the solace of my life, and it will be the solace of my death. They are the product of the highest wisdom... "said the German Philosopher Arthur Schopenhauer. That the Upanishads were his solace is acceptable but did Schopenhauer or can any casual reader of the Upanishads unlock the real knowledge of the Upanishads? The thrust of this article is to show that even though the Upanishads hold the promise to lead one to immortality, they are a puzzle.

A Short History of the Upanishads: From Rituals to Knowledge

The quest for immortality, a central theme of the Upaniṣads, is something new, something not found in the earlier Vedic literature. Indeed, between the earliest portions of the Vedas, the verses of the Ṛg Veda, and the Upaniṣads, which constitute the latest portions of the Vedas, separated by perhaps a thousand years, a dramatic change in worldview occurs. But we also find important continuities.

The thinkers of the Upaniṣads, like the Vedic thinkers before them, were concerned with finding the connecting threads that hold everything together. For Vedic thinkers, whose central concern was with ritual efficacy, it was imperative to know the connections between the human world, the ritual world, and the cosmic world in which the divine powers operated. Only with this knowledge was it possible to follow the patterns of connectedness between these three realms, and only by following these patterns could the rituals achieve their purpose of benefiting the people on whose behalf the offerings were being made. In the Upaniṣads, it was also important to know the connections between things, but now the connection that must be known in order to achieve immortality was the connection between the person and the ultimate ontological reality of the universe. As the various aspects of the person came to be connected to the ultimate Self (Ātman) and the various aspects of the cosmos came to be identified with an underlying reality called Brahman, the powerful knowledge that could liberate one from the cycle of re-death, that could achieve immortality, in the Upaniṣads was, in the final analysis, the connection between Ātman and Brahman.

Departing from the ritualistic traditions of the earlier Vedic age, the Upaniṣadic sages were engaged in a radical rethinking of the nature of self and reality that was destined to deeply influence the course of religion philosophy and life in India and beyond. Radical and profound, their discoveries were shared only with qualified learners, thereby creating a body of secret knowledge. According to the Chāndogya Upaniṣad, even Indra, king of the Gods, had to live with his teacher for 101 years, practicing self-discipline, before Prajāpati thought him prepared to receive the highest knowledge about the self.

The earliest collections of these esoteric teachings, the Bṛhadāraṇyaka, Chāndogya, Aitareya, Taittirīya, Kena, Kaŭha, Kausītākī, Praśna, Muṇḍaka, Maāṇḍūkya, Svetāśvatara, and Īśa Upaniṣads, were probably composed between 800 and 500 B.C.E. and have been commented on by most major Indian thinkers. Most are parts of Āraṇyakas and belong to Brāhmaṇas appended to the Vedas, thus revealing the textual continuity of the Vedic tradition. [1]

Central Doctrine of the Upanishads

The central Upaniṣadic concern to attain immortality requires answers to three questions: What am I, in the very depths of my being? What is the ultimate basis of all existence? And What is the relation between my deepest self and the ultimate reality?

What sets the Upaniṣads apart from the earlier scriptures is their emphasis on knowledge as a means of liberation. The rituals of yajña come to be regarded as taking a person only as far as the realm of the ancestors. Meditative knowledge is necessary to go beyond that, to achieve immortality. But the movement from ritual to knowledge as the way of salvation is by a gradual transformation of yajña into meditative wisdom through internalization. The Bṛhadāraṃyaka Upaniṣad (part of the Śatapatha Brāhmaṇa, which belongs to the Yajur Veda) shows how ritual is transformed into meditative knowledge. It begins with a description of the great horse sacrifice, which it then proceeds to interpret as being really an internal meditative act through which the whole world (not just a horse) is sacrificed. By this sacrificial act of renouncing the world, the individual achieves spiritual autonomy (rather than earthly sovereignty).[2]

The Bewildering Maze of Words in the Upanishads

"However, an examination of the contents of the Upanisads themselves will show that they were never confined to profound philosophical doctrines. On the contrary, all sorts of miscellaneous ideas, injunctions, incantations, theological interpretations, conversations, traditions, and so forth, regarded at the time are secret principles or secret teachings, were assembled and set down without any sequence. Consequently, even the sections that bear on philosophical thought may only include that as one of the secret teachings. And since the parts that do specially expound, philosophical thinking in clear and distinct terms is mostly of conversations and dialogues between master and disciple, father and child, husband and wife, etc. Or else records of debates held in public places, various and diverse philosophical thoughts are expounded in them. Still, neither is there any record of the speculations of one philosopher nor is there any collection of the opinion of philosophers belonging to a definite philosophical school founded by one person. On the contrary, these sections are no more than mere extracts from the various secret beliefs which many orthodox Brahmins, living for several centuries after the appearance of Sakyamuni, had advocated or adopted; the dates of these thinkers, moreover, differ significantly from one another, and there are not a few cases in which the name of the advocate of a particular doctrine has not been clearly recorded.

No philosophical school had yet been set up in such circumstances, nor had any fixed doctrine been established. "The Philosophy of the Upanisads" is a title like "philosophy before Socrates" or "the system of Old Testament ideas." One can see common tendencies, characteristics, and historical significances, but nothing like a "system" of Upanishadic philosophy is possible at all. If one tries to discover a "system," one can occasionally find some systematic explanations in individual conversations or particular passages out of the Upanishadic corpus. However, these frequent explanations are incredibly brief and were never put together in a complex detailed form. Accordingly, the "systems" in the schools of Indian philosophy or later centuries and those of modern Western philosophy are considerably different." [3]

Different Things Regarded as The Absolute in the Upanishads

"The Upanishads superficially read it to teach something about Brahman or Atman, about the universe and the individual soul.

Thus the Upanisads emphasize knowledge and cognition of the Absolute in particular, but what is this Absolute to be cognized? On this point, the explanations in the various passages of the Upanisads are by no means in accord. In addition to the creator Prajapati, other things related to rituals have already been set up as fundamental principles in the development of the world in Brahmana literature. In the Upanisads, still, others have been assumed as the basic principle. Chief' among them are the following :

1. Natural objects such as wind, water, ether, etc. (Although these are frequently regarded as the world principle in the Vedic Samhita, they are no more than merely mentioned in the Upanisads.

2. Vital force (prana). This was widely regarded in Vedic literature in general as the individual subject or the essential life-force of each existence, but also at the same time identical with the supreme principle of the myriad realities (A History of Early Vedanta by Hajime Nakamura, Vol. III, Part VI, commentary note on 1.6 of the Mandikya Karikas.)

3. Consciousness (vijnana). This word means individual cognition but is sometimes proposed as a metaphysical principle, which should be called pure spirit or absolute spirit. (ibid, Part 11, Chap. I, Sect, 2.)

4. Purusa (the primal man) This word initially meant "man" or "human being.", in the final period of the Rig-Veda, it was being taken as the fundamental principle which evolves the universe. Again, it also used it in the sense of "the basic substance of the person" and "the spiritual sell." More importance is given to "purusa" as a philosophical concept. the less was its significance, though, that was never altogether extinguished. (ibid, Part II, Chap. I, Sect. 5, item 2)

5. Being (sat) This is very important in the metaphysics of Uddalaka Aruni.(Chand. Up. VI.2.2.).

6. Non-being (asat).(RV. X, 72, 23; X, 129, 45 Tait. Up. I, 7 Chand. Up.111, 19, 1)

7. That which is neither being nor non-being.(Purusasukta (RV.X.129). This hymn also came to be regarded later as an

independent Upanisad.)

8. The Unevolved (avyakyta). (Brhad. Up. 1.4.7.)

9. The Inner Ruler (antaryamin). So-called because it exists latently within the myriad beings and controls them. (Ibid. 111, 7.)

10. The Indestructible (aksara). (Ibid. III, 8.)

11. Presiding Deity. It is imperative in the Upanisads Isa, Svetasvatara, etc.

12. Brahman. "Brahman" meant initially been the hymns, sacrificial addresses, and chants of the Vedas and, further, the mystical power latent in them, but it finally was taken among the Brahmins. They respected the Vedic rituals as the usual term for the fundamental principle of the world. "The word in time lost its original meaning in the Vedanta school to become a technical term used only for the Absolute itself.

13. Atman, The word "Atman" originally meant "Breath." Still, it was also employed derivatively in the sense of "vital force," "body," and further became a word meaning "one's self. As a philosophical concept, it had the technical meaning "one's ego," "one's self, and further, "soul."

Thus, each of these principles connotates as the world principle, the Absolute, in the respective passages of the Upanishads. It asserts that this evolved and brought about the phenomenal formation and perhaps also maintains and controls the entire world. Because these principles are concepts formally differing from one another, their mutual relations become a problem. But later, in the Vedanta school, they form a central concern of discussion. At any rate, one can say that to assume a unique fundamental principle and to explain the manifold and diverse aspects of the phenomenal world as based upon that principle. is one of the common characteristics of the thought of the Upanisads" [4]

Confusions Evinced by Modern Scholars

Considering the preceding paragraph, it is no surprise, therefore, that many a modern scholar has dipped into the profound wisdom of the Upanishads, nay, given their life to decoding the puzzle of the Upanishads through their scholarship and reading, and come up with the following verdict:

(1) "A system of the Upanishads, strictly speaking, does not exist. For these treatises are not the work of a single genius, but the total philosophical product of an entire

epoch." [P.Deussen, The Philosophy of the Upanishads, Publisher: T & T Clark. p. 51]

(2)"There is little spiritual in all this'; 'this empty intellectual conception, void of spirituality, is the highest form that the Indian mind is capable of ." Gough, quoted by [S.Radhakrishnan, Indian Philosophy. Vol. 1, 139]

(3) "If anything is evident even on a cursory review of the 'Upanishads -and the impression so created is only strengthened by a more careful investigation – it is that they do not constitute a systematic whole." [G.Thibaut, Vedanta Sutras. Intro. ciii]

"If we understand by philosophy a philosophical system coherent in all its parts, free from all contradictions and allowing room for all the different statements made in all the chief Upanishads, a philosophy of the Upanishads cannot even be spoken of." [Ibid, p.cxiv]

(4) "For gaining an insight into the early growth of Indian philosophic thought, this period (the Upanishadic period) is, in fact, the most valuable; though of systematized philosophy, in our sense of the word, it contains, as yet, little or nothing." [Max-Muller, Six Systems of Indian Philosophy by Max-Muller, Publisher: Longmans Green & Co., p.6]

"With us, a philosophy always means something systematic, while what we find here (in the Upanishads) are philosophic rhapsodies rather than consecutive treatises." [Ibid, p.182]

(5) "The Upanishads had no set theory of philosophy or dogmatic scheme of theology to propound; they hint at the truth in life, but not as yet in science or philosophy. So numerous are their suggestions of truth, so various are their 'guesses at God, that almost anybody may seek in them what he wants and find what he seeks. Every school of dogmatics may congratulate itself on finding its doctrine. In the sayings of the Upanishads." [S. Radhakrishnan, Indian Philosophy, p. 140]

(6) " This enhances the difficulty of assuring oneself that any interpretation by the fact that there are germs of diverse and incoherent thoughts scattered over the Upanishads." [Dasgupta, History of Indian Philosophy Vol. I. p. 41-42]

"Under these circumstances, it is necessary that a modern interpreter of the Upanishads should turn a deaf ear to the absolute claims of these exponents. And look upon the Upanishads not as a systematic treatise but as a repository of diverse currents of thought – the melting pot in which all later philosophic ideas were still in a state of fusion." [ibid, p. 42]

The Wrestlings of Ancient Teachers

"The apparent maze of various narratives, epigrams, symbolic expressions, metaphors, and similes, might have been a source of trouble even for the inquirers who came some centuries after creating the Upanishads by compiling in the various Vedic sub-schools. When later, they had to be revered and worshiped as an authoritative sacred canon of divine revelation. The thinkers of later centuries revered the Upanisads were under pressure to resolve the contradictions among somehow the various ideas. If theory "A" contradicts theory "B," it is impossible to admit both simultaneously. Truth must be only one. From among the approaches in the Upanisads, one must first pick out the actual teaching, which we can accept." [5]

"Yet, even if one determined the fundamental theory in this way, further problems remain. If one were to make any of the various doctrines of the Upanisads the correct approach or the accurate idea, how ought he to regard the other theories that contradict it? Since the Upanisads are given absolute authority as sacred canon in the orthodox Brahmanic teaching, it could not be allowed that some views were true and others false, for all the theories expounded in them have to be true. Again, why expounded that many different and diverse teachings in the Upanishad canon? 'The resolution and elucidation of such difficult questions became the second task of the scholars of later centuries who revered the Upanisads. And they came to be chiefly engaged in the uniting interpretation of the Upanisads." [6]

"They compiled the Vedanta Sutras: to demonstrate a unifying interpretation of the Upanishads. "However, since the meanings of Upanishadic utterances are ambiguous, there came to be several Vedanta philosophies, corresponding to differing interpretations of the essential genius of the texts that inspired them. Despite an evident similarity in terminology derived from their common allegiance to the same basic literature, these Vedanta philosophical systems vary substantially among themselves, and there is a polite but clear rivalry among them as to which system 'really.'"[7]

The Problem With Using Reason As a Means to Decode the Truth of the Upanishads

Numerous commentaries embody the conflicting inter-pretations of the several Bhashyakaras of Vedanta whose followers are extant to this day. For any scholar skilled in exegetics might bring out any other system of his own with-out impunity out of these utterances of the ancient sages. If only he could adduce consistently compelling reasons to show that his approach is consistent. And no one can rule out the legitimacy of the ingress of any system or systems in the future. Each of them rests its structure on the foun-dation of consistency and personal intuition and experience through spiritual discipline.

So clearly, the human mind cannot conclude that there is a single all-encompassing truth mentioned in the Upanishads.

Conclusion

Does this mean that the Upanishads don't have any central doctrine? Like most modern scholars and the many ancient ones, are we to believe that there is simply no single Absolute Reality that the Upanishads speak about. Do we resign to the dictates of reason and exclaim that "It is an issue that, like the case, may well be insoluble." [8]

Or do we have a clue in someone of utterances in the Upanishads like this one:

'This idea cannot be reached by mere reasoning. This idea, Oh dearest, leads to sound knowledge, only if taught by another; (Katha Upanishad 2.9)

I shall take this up for another article in the future.

Notes

[1] – The excerpts under this heading are from " The Indian Way: An Introduction to the Philosophies and Reli-gions of India," Chapter 4, by John M. Koller

[2] – ibid

[3] – All paragraphs under this section are from "A His-tory of Early Vedanta Philosophy – Hajime Nakamura," pages 109 & 110

[4] – ibid, pages 104-106

[5] – ibid, page 110

[6] – ibid, page 111

[7] – Karl H. Potter, Encyclopedia of Indian Philosophies,

Vol. 3 "Advaita Vedanta Upto Shankara And His Pupils," page 4

[8] – ibid

Fear

We all face conflict in our lives and relationships. The root of all conflicts is fear. One could say that the source is fear and desire, but one can easily see that fear is the opposite of desire. When we try to hold on to something we desire, it creates fear. Fear exists at different levels of our being. Since it is a primal emotion hard wired into our physical, emotional, and intellectual being, understanding fear and freedom from it is an enormously complex journey. There are various paths to facing and ending fear. In this article, after giving a brief introduction on the three broad ways of facing fear, I present a dialogue between me and a student of my Facebook Psycho-Philosophy Inquiry group, which I run, to teach self-inquiry based on the teachings of J Krishnamurti (JK).

The method followed by JK is that of choiceless Awareness of 'what is. According to his teachings, no amount of thinking and analysis can fundamentally solve the question of fear. All such attempts made by thought to solve anxiety are partial and breed further conflict because thought, the very object that we use for the psychological study, is the basis of fear. We cannot use the same instrument which causes the problem to solve the problem. So if thought cannot solve the problem, what can? According to JK, the answer is choiceless Awareness of thought from moment to moment is the only way to discover the entire tree of fear. We can see this in the discussion below, which starts after Simi, a student in the group, posts her journal. Her journal on how Awareness of thought is different from problem-solving seeds the dialogue on what is choiceless Awareness of 'what is, and how we can uncover all the layers of fears through it.

Three Broad Paths for Facing Fear

There are various paths, schools, and religions that talk about freedom from fear. Each has its methodology and consequently its vocabulary to solve the problem of anxiety.

However, there are

Theistic paths: These posit a benevolent creator surren-
dered to or appealed to solve all the fears and problems.
They can be called paths of devotion or the path of the heart.
For example, Dvaita Vedanta, Tantra, Christianity, Islam, etc.

Atheist paths: are those which do not start with any belief
in a Creator or God or a supernatural force whom we can
appeal to or surrender to solve our problems. Instead, they
proceed through processes of mental observation, deconstruction, and intellectual inquiry. These are called paths of
knowledge and mind/intellect. For example, Advaita Vedanta,
Jainism, Buddhism, and Sankhya.

Theist cum Atheist paths: There are still other paths that
use both the means. The theistic path is an entry point into
inquiry. And this is later sublated by an atheist form of a
deconstructive knowledge-based question or vice versa. For
example, Yoga, Tantra, Vishisthadvaita, etc.

My Path for Facing Fear

I am a follower of Advaita, that too Shankara's and
Gaudapada's radical Advaita, where, even in practice, God is
treated as a conditional concept to be negated. As an entry
into Advaita, I do not follow the more traditional paths of
Karma, Bhakti, and Raja Yoga, but the teachings of J Krishnamurti (JK), which are pretty akin to Sankhya school; which,
too, has no place for God in its system. I thought this preface
was necessary before proceeding further so that people can
appreciate that there are various ways to tackle fear, and
what I am sharing is the path that I followed.

However, at the cost of sounding vain or elitist, I say that
one cannot wholly solve the fear problem until any trace of
duality remains. It's only in the ultimate knowledge of a non-
dual reality as taught in Advaita or similar non-dual paths
that fear can end. As the Upanishad says,
"By mind alone could this (Brahman) be obtained (realized); then there is no difference here at all. He who sees
any difference here, goes from death to death." (Katha Up.
II.iv.11)

The dialogue I am presenting here does not take one to
the root of fear, which, according to Advaita, is ignorance

about reality's true non-dual, formless nature. However, choiceless Awareness of 'what is is a process through which one gets ready or qualified to enter the teachings of Jnana Yoga/Knowledge Yoga of Advaita and continues even after Sef Realization (but automatically). However, I should hasten to add that this is entirely my application of Krishnamurti's teachings. On the other hand, JK considered his teachings complete, not requiring additional instructions to complement his own. Moreover, he quite ferociously guarded any intrusions or representations of his teachings.

In my application of JK's teachings, I do not make a single alteration to what he taught. On the contrary, I love his teachings and am indebted to them for helping me in my spiritual journey.

Simi's Journal: Awareness and Problem Solving

Today as I woke up, I got fresh, and I saw it was raining outside, so I couldn't go to the terrace. So I did my meditation downstairs. I started watching my thoughts. So now I can watch them as they are, without modifying.

After meditating and having breakfast, I prepared for making the marketing phone calls. While doing phone calls, I was getting a kind of feeling, I don't know what it was, but I was aware of it.

Then today, I read the chapter "awareness." In this, I learned how eagerly we try to find solutions to our problems. We don't try to understand the problem; instead, we see an answer to it. The key is not separate from the problem; it is in the issue. The search for the solution is to avoid the problem. It is effortless to conclude, but understanding the situation is very difficult. To understand the problem, one must be free from the desire for an answer. Also, must establish the right relationship with the issue for understanding it deeply. How can there be the right relationship with the problem when we are only concerned with getting rid of it, that is, finding a solution to it. The approach to the problem is more important than the problem. Therefore, I also learned that Awareness is not the outcome of practice. It is the understanding of the full content. Awareness is the silent and choiceless observation of "what is."

Dialogue on Choiceless Awareness of Fear

Anurag: So, Simi, you have kept asking, what is choiceless Awareness of 'what is. If you remember, I told you I could not define it in positive terms.[1] You cannot define what it is, but you can tell what it is not. In this journal, you are talking of another way of 'what it is not. It is not a means for problem-solving. We do problem-solving for technical things like repairing a gadget or doing some maths or planning a journey. In all these situations, we use our past knowledge or try to experiment and create new knowledge. But psychological problems cannot be solved by past psychological knowledge. Past psychological knowledge is the reason for our problems. So when we see that no thinking can solve psychological problems, how do we 'solve' the problem?

The first thing to understand is what you have written – the solution is not away from the problem. It is in the problem itself. Only in looking at the complex web of the problem will it end ultimately. You don't try to think and come up with some solution. You keep watching the problem over several days, months, years. It depends upon the depth of the problem. The problem keeps revealing newer and newer facets and fears.

The difficulty in staying with a problem is that we resist any movement that is giving us pain or not giving us pleasure. There is an unconscious built-in body mechanism that wants to avoid looking at painful and fearful feelings. So problem-solving, as K rightly mentions and which you have written, is not any problem-solving. It is a means to escape the pain of looking at the problem. To escape the pain, we take up partial solutions, which create further problems. It's like escaping coronavirus. We wear masks, and then these masks pollute the environment. (just taking a technical example for simplicity). So the only way of solving a problem is not by finding a solution to the problem but by ending the pain. How does the crisis end? It ends on its own when we watch it through and through. Krishnamurti also used to say, "If we have a problem A, and we want to solve it, we create another problem B. So instead of creating two problems now – A and B, stay with A.'

Simi: Yes, sir, I was continuously asking what is choiceless Awareness, but after you explained and read this chapter. I found that I have an urge to find the answer to this question. And I also got to know that Awareness is, staying with this question, not seeing the answer. So, I was not looking into the question, instead of trying to find the answer.

Anurag: Simi, your real question is not what is "choiceless Awareness of what is. Your real question is something else. You are trying to use choiceless Awareness as a solution to solve that problem. That is why you are trying to find what is choiceless Awareness. You want to use it as a tool to take you to some state.

Most of the time, what we are wanting is a state of experience of some kind – peace, bliss, beauty, or ecstasy. The desire for experience is tremendous. To reach such an experience, we think Choiceless Awareness is away from a means or a tool is when you are no longer Choicelessly Aware.

Simi: Maybe, sir, it is what you are saying; I will look into it. But how will I know that I'm using it as a tool?

Anurag: Simi, why are you interested in asking what is choiceless Awareness of what is?

Simi: I want to be choicelessly aware.

Anurag: Why do you want to be choicelessly aware?

Simi: I want to know every thought, feeling, desire, and fear which I have.

Anurag: So how do you know fear?

Simi: Sir, I know about fear when I feel uncomfortable and have a sense of danger or insecurity.

Anurag: And then what do you do?

Simi: Then I try to look into it, why I fear, and the reason behind it.

Anurag: Yes. So you try to think about it. Analyse-it. Find a reason for it. Right?

Simi: Yes, sir, I try to find out.

Anurag: Great. Now, what will happen if you don't try to find out the reason?

Simi: Then I will be with the fear, just doing nothing but being with it.

Anurag: What do you mean 'being with it'?

Simi: It will be there, and I will be aware of it too, but not trying to find the reason for it.

Anurag: So this is what is called choiceless Awareness of 'what is.'

Simi: Not trying to find a reason for the cause of the

feeling.

Anurag: Yes. When you try to find the cause, you have gone into thinking rather than being aware of 'what is' from moment to moment.

Simi: So here I was stuck thinking about the cause rather than being aware.

Anurag: Absolutely. Now, do you understand? You are not looking at the problem. You were trying to solve the problem.

Simi: Yes, sir, I was trying to solve the problem. When the crisis comes, without understanding, what the problem is, I try to find the answer.

Simi: And this happens in a few moments and unconsciously.

Anurag: Good. What will you do from now on?

Simi: So from now I won't try to find the answer for it. I will stay with it, try to understand it, but also at the same time not finding the cause for it.

Anurag: What do you mean by staying with fear and understanding it? Don't tell me, "I will not try to find a solution." Instead, please tell me what will happen when you stay with fear.

Simi: When I will stay with the fear, it will reveal itself. I will get to know about it more deeply.

Anurag: How?

Simi: I don't know, sir.

Anurag: Good. It's good to say, "I don't know."

Anurag: What will happen to a feeling of fear if you are not trying to end it with some thought-out solution? Will it move, stay fixed, or drop down that instant?

Simi: It will move, sir.

Anurag: But let's say that while watching it move, you reach some conclusion. Then what will happen?

Simi: Then the reason for the fear will come on its own.

Anurag: Ha! Ha! Ha! See, see the tendency of the mind, Simi. It is so hell-bent on finding the reason for fear. Carefully read what I have stated. While watching, you have reached a CONCLUSION.

Anurag: Is concluding the ending of fear?

Simi: Yes, sir, it is the ending of it.

Anurag: Not at all Simi. The conclusion was nothing but thought-the cunningness of mind trying to find some solution to escape the pain of facing fear.

Anurag: The fear did not end. You ended it with your thought conclusion.

Simi: But then it has not ended; it will be just my conclusion.

Anurag: Yes, but that is what I am saying. You said that concluding is the ending of fear. Didn't you?

Simi: Yes

Anurag: Good! So now, how do you watch fear completely?

Simi: Without reaching any conclusions.

Anurag: Yes, Simi. When you are watching something, the watching happens from moment to moment only till you not reach any conclusion at any moment. The moment you conclude, the watching stops, and you have gone into a cycle of thinking. Do you see this?

Simi: Yes, sir, I can see this.

Anurag: So how do you understand what is choiceless Awareness of 'what is?

Simi: Yes, sir, watching from moment to moment, without reaching any conclusion.

Anurag: Great. So do you end to fear, or does fear ends itself?

Simi: Fear ends itself when seen as it is.

Anurag: Yes. So I hope it is clear to you that any attempt to end fear by thinking (modifying, distracting, finding a cause for it, or finding a solution for it) is the movement of fear itself. So thought cannot end anxiety because thought and thinking are fear themselves.

Simi: That means we don't have to do anything, neither making conclusions, just watching its movements.

Anurag: Absolutely, Simi!

Simi: Yes, sir, now it is clear.

Anurag: Great! Now do it and see It will be an explosion.

Simi: Yes, sir, I will do

Simi: And thank you, sir, for helping me come out from this confusion. This dialogue helped me a lot.

Anurag: Thanks, Simi. This should be a gamechanger for you

Simi: Yes, sir

Anurag: Also, Simi, you have now gained some understanding of the power of dialogue. It would be best to do this often with me to understand subtler and subtler aspects of mind.

Simi: Yes, sir, I got to know some of it. And now onwards, I will be having a dialogue with you.

Anurag: Simi, there is an entire tree of fear. When you

begin watching it, your mind will move into different dimensions. Your spiritual growth will begin.

Anurag: There are small fears like twigs and branches, and then they shall lead you gradually to the trunk and then to the root of all fear.

Simi: Yes, sir, I want to know the root of all fear.

Anurag: That cannot happen through thinking, Simi. It can only happen when you understand that no thought can take you to the root, except choiceless Awareness of 'what is' from moment to moment.

Simi: Yes, before that, I must start with the choiceless Awareness.

Anurag: There is no starting and ending of choiceless Awareness, Simi. It is new all the time.

Simi: So, sir, how can we be aware of "what is"?

Anurag: There is no "how" Simi. The only answer is don't judge, don't control, and don't modify. Because if you do these, the 'what is converted to an idea which you cling to. 'what is' can never become a formulaic kind of activity. It is always new, always revealing.

Simi: One must-see "what is" as it is, according to its flow.

Anurag: Yes, Simi. 'What is is not a state of mind. It is about seeing how the mind flows from moment to moment. There is no practice in that state. It can never be old. Every time you start, it is new. JK calls it living and dying from moment to moment.

Simi: Yes, sir, I have a question here, how one becomes aware from moment to moment?

Anurag: I have given you the answer. It is not in the form of a positive method. A positive approach is only a formula, a practice. So one cannot say how it is to be done. One can only speak about it in terms of what does not need to be done.

Simi: Ok, sir.

Love

Traditional Advaita talks about the emotional and psychological preparation one must cultivate for self-inquiry in terms of Sadhana Chathusthaya, the four qualities to get to the insight of Self/Brahman/Awareness in Advaita. The four qualities are:

Viveka/discriminative capacity

Vairagya/detachment from objects

Shat Sampatti – Wealth of six virtues: control of mind, control of senses, the endurance of opposites, cutting down on all inessential work of life, faith in the teachings, and the teacher (not a blind one: what we say, 'faith pending confirmation') and focus on the goal.

Mumukshutva/Intense Desire for Enlightenment

For those who want to come to that level, the journey stretches hundreds of miles after Viveka. This is the journey of Love in which all the knots of the heart have to get untied. It is a long process of shattering where the mind/Viveka ultimately exhausts itself and the mind ends, or as Krishnamurti says – in tandem with the highest seers – the mind enters the heart.

"Verse 4.85: What else remains for him to be desired when he has attained to the state of the Brāhmaṇa—a state of complete omniscience, non-duality and a state which is without beginning, end or middle?"

Gaudapada, Mandukya Karika

"Verse 4.86: This (i.e., the realization of Brahman) is the humility natural to the Brāhmaṇas. Their tranquillity (of mind) is also declared to be spontaneous (by men of discrimination). They are said to have attained to the state of sense-control (not through any artificial method as it comes quite natural to them. He who thus realizes Brahman which is all-peace, himself becomes peaceful and tranquil."

The verses above, especially the last one, bear out the fact that the teachings of Krishnamurti has its precedent in the teachings of the ancients as old as Gaudapada.

NEEV Centre for Self Inquiry

We have closed down NEEV Vidyalaya permanently as this academic session came to an end. In its place, we are go establishing NEEV Centre for Self Inquiry89 – a space for a library, dialogues, and retreats for individuals genuinely interested in finding truth freedom And love through self inquiry

NEEV initially worked with slums, farmers, women, and children, providing them with health, livelihood and education through different projects.

After some years, we realized that we are just treating the symptoms of the problems. Our efforts were akin to bandaging wounds and sores of society. As we dressed some, new sores would develop. So we shifted our attention from bandaging wounds to finding the process which creates these in the first place.

Almost all people who think beyond personal advancement, seem to get quite contented with bandaging wounds. There is a reason for this. These people draw a lot of respect from society for the mere fact that they are thinking beyond personal gain. However, a closer look would reveal that people who bandage wounds are still working for personal gains, albeit not strictly in economic terms. Such people thrive on respect and approval lauded to them by society. A subtle self-identity of being saviors, martyrs, do-gooders, and reformers is created. And because such people thrive on the plaudits bestowed on them by society, they shall never question society. Social workers and society form a symbiotic relationship. Community creates wounds, the social worker heals them without asking, and the society lauds the social worker in return. Both thrive, doing their well-rehearsed roles, and human misery continues unabated.

We got our share of plaudits from society but did not want to bask in them. Discontentment seethed and made us go beyond addressing symptoms to searching the roots of diseases in society. Our study of feudalism, capitalism, socialism, globalization, nationalism, class conflicts, caste divisions, and religious antagonisms began with this. Suddenly, the lenses through which we viewed the world changed. Even more fundamentally, we realized that we were viewing the world through lenses, through layers of unquestioned conditioning gathered through education, society, religion, and science. The study was revealing and, at the same time, deeply upsetting. The Newtonian world with definite laws and orders and unquestioned stability disintegrated into the chaos of the quantum world under the changed lenses.

The same world appeared differently under different lenses. There was a crumbling of social values; societies sacred and pious were revealed to be carefully designed ploys of capitalism, feudalism, or religions to subjugate and control humans and society. We discovered that we were enslaved to different isms without knowing that they ever existed. The capacity of these isms to exert influence on our lives and society can be judged by the fact that we do not even see them operating.

With the discovery of all these "isms" and lenses, it became imperative for us to find a solution to these problems. It wasn't about running health camps and giving livelihoods and wiping tears. It was about finding a solution to the vast forces of capitalism, consumerism, and nationalism because these diseases caused symptoms like poverty, environmental degradation, and terrorism. It was not about sharing sob stories of human misery and eliciting society's pity to help the needy. It was about illuminating society about how isms trapped it. It was about disturbing society rather than healing wounds. Thus began our search for a systemic solution to these problems.

After carefully studying various solutions like communism, socialism, environmentalism, we settled for two solutions that we thought would address these problems fundamentally. The first was social entrepreneurship, and the second was education. With the zeal of discoverers and pioneers, we went about trying these solutions on the ground. This was when we started encountering the hard crust of human reality, squalor, dirt, and greed behind the veneer of respectable society. Cold intellectual analysis of capitalism, consumerism, etc., melted into a molten living reality, making its effect felt in all our relationships. Suddenly strongly held polarities that stood firmly opposed to each other seemed to dance in the play of opposites. Rich and poor, developed and undeveloped, right and wrong, good and bad, friends and foes, heroes and villains, saints and criminals all started losing their boundaries and seemed to fade into each other seamlessly.

Our own solutions started to come under the lens of inquiry. Suddenly, paradoxes started rearing their heads. Were our own solutions part of the problems? Was education solving the problems or creating them? Are the ideas we create, for instance, in social entrepreneurship part of the solution or responsible for creating the problems? At the deeper levels, I discovered that reality is paradoxical. The hard dualities that operate in the Newtonian world vanish. Light can be studied as a wave or a particle. Subatomic realms are more space than matter. The limits to scientific thought are reached as the observer is seen to be the observed in the quantum realm.

The study of the world and its problems finally brought us to something one least suspects – our self. This is an oversimplification of sorts as I have to condense a journey of twenty years in a few thousand words. I was doing self-inquiry all along. It was an inner inquiry probing the nature of my mind and thought which started way back in my college days in 1998. What really happened through all our work in NEEV was that finally, the inner inquiry fused with the outer inquiry about the world. The wave that went out was the wave that came in. There was a realization that one's self is the world. The consciousness of an individual was the consciousness of the whole of humankind. And what needed transformation was consciousness. For this world is the content of human consciousness. The observer is the observed. We are the world. The root of all problems in the world is that we are caught in a dualistic consciousness. The ancients called it Maya, which means we are caught in an illusion of reality.

There can be a transformation in the world only if there is a transformation in the consciousness of every individual: no systems, no isms, no reformations, no schools. And no science/technology can alleviate human suffering because all of these have the same underlying root – a dualistic consciousness of Maya that fragments the world into parts, which divides people into individual selves and veils the nature of reality. Any movement born from this consciousness is dualistic, partial, and divisive. Whether it is education, social work, governance, or even spirituality – it does not matter. As long as they spring from the consciousness of duality, there is bound to be conflict and suffering.

Having seen this as clear as daylight, it only made sense that we close down NEEV Vidyalaya and devote all our remaining lives to transforming consciousness through self-inquiry. So we are converting NEEV Vidyalaya to a center that shall house a library and video room for subjects related to self-inquiry. It shall also be a place where people interested in self-inquiry can come for a silent retreat to have dialogues with me on self-inquiry.

Appendix

As all beings are naturally conditioned to attend and be incessantly preoccupied with objects, the non-dual self-inquiry also follows the natural bent of mind in examining things, proceeding from gross ones and subsequently moving to subtler ones. In the beginning stage, i.e., Psycho-Philosophical Inquiry, we saw that the inquiry was about understanding the reason for conflict and suffering due to the gross external world. At this level, the duality of thinker and thought was too subtle to be questioned. As the student moves deeper into meditative inquiry, the domain shifts from the gross world to the subtler world objects of the mind, where the duality of thinker and thought is questioned and negated. Post this, the inquiry stage is set to shift from understanding experiences to understanding the very structure of knowledge. There are three primary insights one gains in this inquiry,

- **All objects are impermanent**
- **An illusory Thinker-Doer-Experiencer tries to manage these impermanent objects continuously**
- **The Thinker-Doer-Experiencer as the cause of suffering**

CPSIA information can be obtained
at www.ICGtesting.com
Printed in the USA
LVHW010338070722
722844LV00009B/582